John Elliott Cairnes

Political Essays

John Elliott Cairnes

Political Essays

ISBN/EAN: 9783337078485

Printed in Europe, USA, Canada, Australia, Japan

Cover: Foto ©Suzi / pixelio.de

More available books at **www.hansebooks.com**

...IRNES, M.A.,

Emeritus Professor of Political Economy in University College, London.

London:
MACMILLAN AND CO.
1873.

[*The Right of Translation and Reproduction is reserved.*]

A FEW words of explanation and apology are needed for the following Essays. With the exception of that entitled "Fragments on Ireland," and the second of the Essays on Irish University education, all have been in print before. Some of them were suggested by occurrences of the day, and, the occasion of their publication being passed, there might seem to be no reason for their reappearance now. In reply to this objection, should it be urged, I can only express my belief that, though the subject may in some instances be occasional, the treatment will be found not to be so. For example, the Essay on Army Reform was suggested by the Franco-German war of 1870-71, and the first few pages are devoted to an examination of the state of our military defences as they stood at that time; but this is merely an introduction to a general discussion of the relative advantages and disadvantages of national and standing armies—a subject, the interest in which, though it is not what it was two years ago, assuredly has not died out, and may at any moment recover its former intensity. Similarly, with regard to the first Essay on Irish University education. Though called forth by the educational crisis of 1865-6, the principles discussed are applicable to the general question of university reform, and have a direct bearing on the present position of the Irish University question.

The "Fragments on Ireland" have not, except in a few passages, appeared before in print, though written so far back as 1866. They were intended to form parts of a small volume on the industrial condition of Ireland, of which the practical aim was to lead up to a discussion of the Land question, then pressing for solution. The work was interrupted by ill-health, and meanwhile the Irish Land question was taken up by the Liberal party in the House of Commons, and received, by the passing of the Irish Land Act of 1870, at least a provisional settlement. The original purpose of the work was thus in a great measure accomplished; but the preliminary discussions comprised such subjects as the crisis of 1847, considered in connection with its historical causes; the emigration, its character and significance; and an examination of the new forms into which industrial life in Ireland was shaping itself under the powerful influences developed by recent events. These subjects appear to me to possess an interest apart from the particular purpose for which their examination had been undertaken: indeed there are few questions which can arise in the course of legislation for Ireland—even if we could consider the Irish Land problem as definitively settled—which do not require for their intelligent discussion a constant reference to the crises through which the country has recently passed, as well as a correct apprehension of the nature and direction of the economical forces now shaping its industrial career. I have, therefore, thought it well, as a contribution towards the elucidation of these subjects, to include in the present volume such fragments of the work commenced in 1866 as I found suitable for this purpose.

I am here anxious to make my warm acknowledgments to my friend Professor Nesbitt, for the invaluable assistance he has given me in preparing both this and the preceding volume for the press. I have had the advantage, not only of his constant and vigilant criticism of my arguments, but also of his ungrudging services in correcting the proofs throughout.

I have also to thank the proprietors of the several periodicals, in which the Essays now reprinted originally appeared, for their courtesy in permitting the republication.

J. E. CAIRNES.

KIDBROOK PARK ROAD,
BLACKHEATH, S.E.
March 1873.

CONTENTS.

ESSAY	PAGE
I. Colonization and Colonial Government	1
II. The Revolution in America	59
III. International Law	109
IV. Fragments on Ireland :—	
1. The Agricultural Revolution—Protection and Free Trade	127
2. The Emigration	141
3. The Irish Cottier	151
4. Irish Landlordism	167
V. Our Defences: A National or a Standing Army?	199
VI. Thoughts on University Reform *à-propos* of the Irish Educational Crisis of 1865-6	256
Note	314
VII. The Present Position of the Irish University Question—1873	323

POLITICAL ESSAYS.

I.

COLONIZATION AND COLONIAL GOVERNMENT.*

I PROPOSE to invite your attention this evening to the subject of colonization and colonies. I have selected this subject because it seems to me to offer, at the present time, some aspects of more than usual interest. It is no exaggeration, I think, to say that this country —indeed that the world—has arrived at a critical epoch in colonial affairs. In the progress of colonizing enterprise, we have reached, or almost reached, a point at which further progress in the same pursuit must become impossible, for the sufficient reason that the field for its exercise will soon cease to exist. The earth, indeed, is still very far from being full; but glance over the map of the world, and outside tropical regions say where the country is to be found which has not already been occupied and settled by man—in which, at least, the germ of political society has not been planted. I think you will find that

* A Lecture delivered before the Dublin Young Men's Christian Association, 26th October, 1864.

North-Western America is now about the only considerable space of which this description can, with approximate truth, be given, and already the work of colonization is busy there : "A region," says Mr. Merivale, in the last edition of his important work, "of no small interest to observers of our times, as affording the last open field for European emigration. The remainder of the extra-tropical world is now filled up [occupied ?]. No other site is left for the foundation of future empires. Its occupiers will be the latest adventurers in that vast work of European colonization which began scarcely four centuries ago. The duty left for future time will be only to fill up the outlines already traced in days of more romantic adventure."*

But again, from a political point of view also, we have arrived at a critical stage in colonial history. You are probably aware that within the present year the British colony of Canada has taken a step which is virtually an act of sovereignty. It has undertaken, of its own motion, without consultation with the mother country, to reform, in the most radical and sweeping fashion, its political system, and, not content with this, it makes overtures to all the other American colonies to enter with it into a single grand federation —a federation the mere magnitude of which, should the plan, as seems probable, take effect, must, one would think, effectually unfit the new state for the position of even nominal dependence.† Indeed, as

---

* "Colonization and the Colonies." By Herman Merivale, A.M., Professor of Political Economy. New Edition, 1861, p. 116.

† " British North America will become the fourth maritime power in the world. England, France, and the United States will alone have a marine superior to ours. Isolated from one another, we could claim

regards this point, the promoters of the scheme—though they have quite recently somewhat changed their language *—have made no secret of their aspirations. "Whether the day for its accomplishment has yet arrived," said Mr. Brown, the minister who originated and has taken the most prominent part in bringing forward this grand scheme—"whether the day for its accomplishment has yet arrived is a fit subject of inquiry; but, assuredly, no Canadian has a claim to the name of statesman who has not looked forward to the day when all the British portion of this continent shall be gathered into one. . . . We must look forward to the day when the whole of British America shall stand together, and, in close alliance and heartiest sympathy with Great Britain, be prepared to assume the full duties and responsibilities of a great and powerful nation." Such are the plans now formally promulgated, and such is the language now publicly uttered by the leading men of Canada. The tone adopted towards Great Britain is indeed respectful, and even cordial. There is no formal defiance of her authority: there is only the quiet assumption that she will, as a matter of course, acquiesce in the nullity of her own supremacy. And Great Britain does acquiesce. From no British statesman of the least mark, from no political party here of the slightest weight, has any sign proceeded

only a very low place among nations; but bring us together, and there is no country, save England, to which we owe birth—save the United States, whose power is derived from the same parent source as our own—save France, from whom many of those here present have sprung, can take rank before us."—COLONEL GREY at the Montreal dinner.

* See post, pp. 49, 50.

of opposition, or even of protest, against the impending revolution.

It seems, then, that, both as regards the external conditions of colonization and the political principles on which colonies are ruled, we have reached a critical stage in colonial history; and it has therefore occurred to me that a brief retrospect of the past course of colonial enterprise and government might, at the present time, possess some interest for this Society. Such a retrospect can, of course, only be—if for no other reason, because of the limitations in point of time which an address of this kind imposes—of the most imperfect and summary kind: still I venture to hope it may not prove altogether uninstructive. When a great and pregnant change is approaching, there is an advantage in reverting our gaze from the present and future to the past, and in tracing the causes, many of them perhaps scarcely perceived at the time, which have at a distance prepared and led up to the catastrophe. The crisis, thus regarded, shapes itself before our mental eye in its true proportions. We can appreciate its meaning and drift, and are enabled to estimate at something like their real value the importance of the issues it involves.

And here, to mark in some degree the limits within which I propose to confine myself in this address, it may be well if I state at the outset the sense in which I use the word "colony." I take the definition given by Sir G. C. Lewis:—"A colony properly denotes a body of persons belonging to one country and political community, who, having abandoned that country and community, form a new and separate society, independent or dependent, in some district which is wholly or nearly uninhabited, or from which they expel the ancient inhabitants."*

You will observe that, according to this definition, wholesale migrations of entire peoples—such as took place on a great scale on the breaking up of the Roman Empire—do not constitute colonization; for here it is not a body of people belonging to a political community who abandon their original country, it is the community itself. Again, the definition excludes from the category of colonies such dependencies as British India, where the bulk of the inhabitants have never migrated from any given political community, but are a composite body, made up partly of the aboriginal people, and partly of immigrants who have reached the country at various times and from various quarters, the English forming quite an inconsiderable fraction of the whole. For the same reason, all mere military stations, such as Malta and Gibraltar, must be excluded from the category of colonies proper. On the other hand, the definition does not exclude cases which some people might regard as inconsistent with the idea of a colony. The body of persons who migrate and form the new society may be either "independent or dependent." In modern times, indeed, the idea of political dependency has come to be very generally associated with the conception of a colony; but it is no necessary part of that conception; nor was the word so understood in ancient times. All the more celebrated colonies, for example,

* "Essay on the Government of Dependencies." By G. C. Lewis, Esq., 1841, p 170.

of the Greeks and Phœnicians, the two greatest colonizing nations of antiquity, were, in a political sense, absolutely independent of the mother state. In short, if you desire to form a true idea of a colony, you have only to follow the fortunes of a swarm of bees. The swarm leaves its parent hive—the original community; it coheres in a distinct society; it settles in a new locality, either previously unoccupied, or from which it has expelled the former inhabitants: what may be the nature of its further connection with the mother hive it is not necessary to consider: whatever this be, the swarm is not the less a true image of a colony proper. Such were the colonies founded by the Greeks and Phœnicians in ancient times on the islands and along the shores of the Mediterranean and Euxine Seas; such, in modern times, were those founded by Spain, France, and England in the New World; and such are those which we are even now building up in Australia and New Zealand.

Having thus determined the proper sense of the word "colony," we now proceed with our review, taking as its starting-point what may be regarded as the opening of modern colonization, the discovery of America. That supreme event had no sooner happened than the leading nations of Europe—Spain, Portugal, France, England, the Dutch Republic—hastened to the scene of action, eager to assert, each for itself, a right to a place in the greatest field ever thrown open to human energy and ambition. The numerous enterprises which followed are among the most striking and picturesque episodes in history, and are, doubtless, familiar to most of those whom I address, associated as they are with the well-known names of Cortes, Pizarro, Cabot, Drake, Raleigh, Gilbert, and in later times, with those of the Pilgrim Fathers, William Penn, and others. The movement, begun in the sixteenth century and continued till the present time, has now, as I have just remarked, all but completed its work of scattering the seeds of political society over the habitable globe.

The career of modern colonization has thus extended over nearly four centuries. We shall find it convenient to divide this term into three periods—the first extending from the conquest of the New World down to the American War of Independence; the second, from the date of that event to the year 1830; and the third, from the year 1830 to the present time.

Contemplating the first of these periods—that which extends from the conquest of the New World down to the American War of Independence—we are struck with the predominance of the purely commercial, or perhaps it would be more correct to say, the purely monetary spirit of its colonization; a feature which distinguishes it alike from the present age, and from the age of Grecian and Roman colonization which had preceded it. The spirit of that epoch is, I say, distinct from that of the present age; for, although, doubtless, commerce has not been absent from the aims of colonizing adventurers in recent times, and although, in the event, colonial enterprise has powerfully promoted commercial expansion, still if we look to the motives of the actual emigrants—still more, if we look to the legislation of Parliament

—we shall find that commerce has occupied, in connection with recent schemes of colonization, quite a secondary place. The true character of that movement, as I shall hereafter show, has been industrial and social—its chief aim being to provide an outlet for the surplus population and capital of the old country—a motive which, by a singular coincidence, it shares with the earliest historical colonization—that of Phœnicia and Greece. As for the colonization of Rome, it was, as is well known, essentially military and imperial; the colonies of Rome having little of the character of industrial and trading settlements, and being, in truth, mainly garrisons planted in the countries which she had conquered.

What, then, distinguishes the colonization of the first period of modern colonial history, is the intensely commercial, or, rather, as I have phrased it, monetary spirit in which it was conceived.* The impulse under which the discovery of the New World took place may typify for us the motives under the influence of which its subsequent colonization, for at all events two centuries, was carried on. That impulse had its source in an intense thirst for the precious metals; for, as you will remember, the voyage of Columbus was undertaken in the hope of finding a passage by a western route to the East Indies—then supposed to be of all the world the region richest in gold and silver. The desire for metallic wealth, strong at all times, seems at

---

* It ought to be observed that there are to this statement some notable exceptions, more particularly in English colonization. With New Englanders, for example, it was always a boast that "they were originally a plantation religious, not a plantation of trade."

this particular epoch to have been exceptionally powerful. Not only did it inspire the adventure which resulted in the great discovery; it was among the principal causes which hurried across the Atlantic the eager emigrant crowd who peopled the western world when it was found. And when at length settlements were established, and the business of colonial legislation began, we find the same passion governing with no less powerful sway the councils of statesmen and princes.

The passion for the precious metals was thus, at this period of the world, for whatever reason, driven to excess; and, as sometimes happens, the prevailing crave was exalted into a dogma. It was proclaimed on high authority, that all wealth, properly so called, consisted in gold and silver. The doctrine found a favourable audience; it was accepted; and for some two centuries held its ground—held its ground, not as the tenet of a sect, or as the belief of a particular people, but as a truth, adopted in good faith, and systematically acted on by all the leading nations of Europe.

Wealth was thus held to consist in the precious metals; and wealth was power. It followed that the great object of statesmanship should be to increase in the statesman's country the stock of gold and silver. Colonial policy was moulded under the influence of this view. Colonies were valued, not for their social advantages, as opening a new career to a superabundant population at home—indeed superabundance of population was, according to the notions of that time, a good to be coveted, not an evil to be avoided,

—not for the economic gain of supplying our wants at cheapened cost, not even for the imperial reason, as extending the range of national power,—but simply and solely as they could be made the means of increasing the nation's supply of gold and silver.*

Let me here endeavour to convey, in as few words as I can, a general idea of the nature of the expedients by which it was attempted to give effect to this view. They would naturally vary according to circumstances. Where the colonies were themselves productive of the precious metals, the legislator would go direct to his object; on the one hand encouraging mining pursuits, on the other excluding foreign nations wholly from the colonial trade. In this way, while he developed the "wealth" of the colonies to the utmost, he, at the same time, secured to the mother country its entire appropriation. Where this was not the case—where the colonies did not yield gold or silver—a more circuitous course would be necessary. Foreign trade would not here be proscribed (for it was only through foreign trade that colonies, which did not themselves contain the precious metals, could perform the function required of them): it would be "regulated"—exportation would be encouraged, importation controlled, so as on the whole to make debtors of foreign nations, and leave a "balance" of gold and silver, which might be directed to the home country.

But it will be well to observe somewhat more in

---

* "The maintenance of the monopoly has hitherto been the principal, or, more properly, the sole end and purpose of the dominion which Great Britain assumes over her colonies."—*Wealth of Nations*, p. 277 (M'Culloch's Edition).

detail the actual working of the system. And to this end we may take the cases of Spain and England. For the purpose of reaping the promise of the accepted creed, the position of Spain was the most favourable which it is possible to conceive. The portion of the New World which fell to her lot was rich in the precious metals beyond former experience. It was also an advantage of her position, regarded from the same point of view, that her government was despotic, as thus no constitutional obstacle could stand in the way of her statesmen to hinder them from giving the fullest effect to their policy. They availed themselves of this liberty to the utmost. All intercourse of foreigners with the colonial subjects of Spain was interdicted under capital penalties.* The intercolonial trade was placed under the severest restrictions. Not only was the industry of the colonies excluded from many branches of manufacture carried on in the mother country, but even the culture of the vine and the olive was prohibited under severe penalties ; and in this way capital and industry were, from lack of other channels, forced into mining pursuits. Lastly, by a regulation, which, for its mischievous absurdity, has, I think, scarcely a parallel even in the history of commercial legislation, the whole colonial trade, the better to bring it under the eye of the Spanish Government, was required to pass through a single port in Old Spain. And what was the result of this throughgoing application of the principles of the commercial system to

---

* Subsequently commuted to imprisonment for life. "They even shunned the inspection of strangers," says Robertson, "and endeavoured to keep them from their coasts."

conditions so singularly favourable for the experiment ? It is written in the early arrest of all healthy progress in the Spanish colonies, and in the rapid decline, so long as the system was persisted in, of the trade and power of Spain. "Sixty years after the discovery of the New World," says Robertson, "the number of Spaniards in all its provinces is computed not to have exceeded fifteen thousand." More than two hundred years afterwards—that is to say, about the middle of the eighteenth century, "when," according to the same authority, "the exclusive trade to America from Seville was at its height," the freight of the two united squadrons of "galleons" and "flotas," as they were called—the sole medium by which the legal traffic of Spain with her colonies could be carried on—the freight, I say, of these united squadrons did not exceed 27,500 tons—less than a twentieth part of what England now sends to the single port of Melbourne—scarcely more than the burden of a single vessel, the *Great Eastern*, now in the mercantile marine of England.

This was the extent of the legal trade of Spain with her colonies when the old colonial policy had reached its height: it by no means, however, represented the whole of her colonial trade. By much the most important portion was carried on by the smuggler. "The contraband trade of the Spanish colonies," says Mr. Merivale, "became in the early part of the last century [some fifty years previous to the culminating period of the exclusive system just referred to] the most regular and organized system of that kind which the world has ever witnessed. The English led the way in it. . . . The Dutch, French, and other nations seized on their share of the spoil. Jamaica and St. Domingo became complete entrepôts for smuggled commodities, whence they were transported with ease to the continent. . . . Buenos Ayres rose from an insignificant station to a considerable city, merely from being the centre of the contraband traffic between Europe and Peru. The Spaniards guarded their coasts with an expensive maritime force, while they resorted in the interior to the strange measure of making smuggling an offence cognizable by the Inquisition. But all such efforts were fruitless to check the force and violence of the ordinary trade. The flotas and galleons sank to insignificance; and their owners were glad to make these licensed squadrons serve for introducing the contraband commodities of other nations."*

Such was the culmination of the commercial system in the instance of a nation, fitted above all others, by extraordinary privileges of position, for realizing in an eminent degree the benefits which that system promised, and which stopped at no interference with the industrial freedom of its subjects, however extravagant or however violent, which seemed calculated to give to it practical effect.

Let us now turn to England, not less a stickler than Spain for exclusive principles in commercial policy, but differing from Spain in this respect, that she did not command the same advantages for their practical enforcement.

For, in the first place, there was this capital circum-

* " Colonization and the Colonies," pp. 15, 16.

stance distinguishing the colonies of England from those of Spain : the English colonies were destitute alike of gold and silver mines. England, therefore, could only hope to accomplish the great end at which all colonial legislation then aimed—the augmentation of her stock of the precious metals—by indirect methods. The expedients which she actually adopted for this purpose may be summed up under the four following heads :—

First: She reserved to herself the monopoly of all those colonial staples which served as raw material for her manufactures. By this means she expected, in cheapening the cost of her manufactures, to undersell foreigners, to extend her exports, and thus to draw to herself gold and silver through the balance of trade.

Secondly : She excluded from the colonial markets all foreign manufactures and other products which came into competition with her own.

Thirdly: She prohibited the colonists from engaging in any manufacture which was carried on in the parent-state : according to an oft-quoted remark of Lord Chatham, the colonists had no right to make so much as a nail for a horse-shoe.

On the other hand, in compensation for these restrictions on the commercial liberty of the colonists, the mother country was content to impose some fetters on herself, giving to the colonists the monopoly of her markets as against foreigners for such commodities as she in her wisdom permitted them to produce. By this means it was expected that mother country and colony would play into each other's hands, reciprocally support each other, and, at the expense of the foreigner, draw boundless wealth to themselves through the balance of trade.*

Such was the general scope of the English colonial system. The restrictions it embodied were indeed sufficiently vexatious and mischievous: nevertheless, if we look to the substance rather than to the form—to the practical effect rather than to the theoretic purpose of her regulations, we shall be disposed to say that the colonies of England enjoyed, at all events by comparison, a very goodly amount of commercial freedom. No attempt, for example, was made by Great Britain to exclude her colonies from the trade with foreign nations: it was only sought to "regulate" that trade; nor did she forbid her colonies from trading freely with one another. Further, the absurd expedient adopted by Spain of requiring her whole colonial trade to pass through a single port, had no counterpart in the colonial system of England, which at least left open the trade, under whatever restrictions, to all British subjects upon equal terms. Besides, not a few of those restrictions, which looked harsh on paper, were found in practice to be sufficiently harmless, often prescribing to the colonists a course which would have been equally adopted without any such command. Of this character were the laws directed against colonial manufactures—laws which, of course, the colonists never thought of violating while they had more profitable means of employing their capital in other pursuits. "Such prohibitions," says Adam Smith, "without cramping their industry, or restraining it from any employment to which it would have

* "Wealth of Nations," Book IV. chap. vii. Part 3.

gone of its own accord, are only impertinent badges of slavery, imposed upon them without any sufficient reason by the groundless jealousy of the merchants and manufacturers of the mother country."*

But between the colonization of Spain and that of England there was a difference deeper and more radical than gold and silver mines, or any mere commercial legislation—powerful as no doubt these causes were—could bring to pass; a difference, which did far more than any incidents to which I have yet referred, to produce that broad contrast in the subsequent colonial careers of the two countries, which is one of the most striking facts in the history of that time.

The government of Spain was a highly despotic and centralized system: the government of England was popular and free, and gave scope to local institutions; and these characteristic attributes of their respective governments were transferred, in even an exaggerated form, to the possessions of the two countries in the New World. The colonial government of Spain stands out a singular and portentous phenomenon in history. At its head the Royal Council of the Indies, an autocratic body in which the king presides, having its seat at Seville in Old Spain, exercises supreme control in the last resort over every department of colonial administration. Under the Royal Council come the Viceroys of Mexico and Peru, governing through a strongly organized bureaucracy, nominated by themselves and composed exclusively of natives of the mother state—" within their own pre-

* "Wealth of Nations," p. 261.

cincts," says Robertson, "as despotic as the monarch of Spain himself." The government thus constituted, the Feudal System and the Romish Church take their place side by side in the full maturity of their mediæval pretensions: the Feudal System, with its narrow maxims, its strict entails, its various anti-commercial and anti-industrial incidents; the Church, served by a hierarchy of numerous orders, the great majority of whom are, by a preposterous policy, consigned to spend their time in religious houses, consuming in celibacy and idleness the wealth of a country which calls aloud on all sides for population and the hand of labour. By a curious—I imagine a unique—act of condescension, the Church in the American possessions of Spain acknowledged the supremacy of the civil power;* but not the less is she impelled by her old instincts, and acts her old part. In fine, to complete the picture, the Inquisition is seen to rise, scowling with ill-omened aspect from its gloomy portals over the nascent civilization of the New World.†

And now contrast with this the broad features of popular liberty disclosed in the early charters of the English colonies—meagre, but unambiguous, witnesses of the genius which there presided. The first Charter of Massachusetts "gave power for ever to the freemen of the company to elect annually from their own number a Governor, Deputy-Governor, and eighteen Assistants, on the last Wednesday of Easter Term; and to make laws and ordinances—not repugnant to the laws of England—for their own benefit,

* Robertson's "History of America," vol. iv. pp. 45, 46.
† Ibid., book viii.

and the government of persons inhabiting the territory."* The Connecticut Charter is drawn up upon the same model; its framer being charged to comprise in it "liberties and privileges not inferior or short to what is granted to the people of Massachusetts." † In the southern colonies, though the form of government is different, the spirit which animates it is the same. Thus Lord Baltimore, the founder of Maryland, is authorized "by and with the advice, assent, and approbation of the freemen of Maryland, or the greater part of them, or their delegates and deputies, to enact any laws whatever, appertaining either unto the public state of the said province or unto the private utility of particular persons;"‡ and so of the others. In not a few of those early charters, indeed, representative government is not expressly mentioned; but, as Mr. Merivale points out, only because this was "assumed by the colonists as a matter of right." In these cases, "houses of representatives" used—to borrow the quaint language of a historian of the time—to "break out" in the colonies on their settlement; § the doings of which houses, although without warrant of any written constitution, were, as a matter of course, recognized by the government at home. Political powers of the most extensive kind— often without any limit whatever, other than those implied limits which the fact of allegiance involved— were thus freely conferred on the early English

---

* Palfrey's "New England," vol. i. p. 291.
† Ibid., vol. ii. p. 573.
‡ "The Art of Colonization." By Edward Gibbon Wakefield, p. 229.
§ As, for example, in the settlement of Providence. See Palfrey's "New England," vol. i. pp. 423 25.

colonists. Nor did they remain unexercised. Whether "breaking out," or established by formal authority, the colonial assemblies from the first assumed to themselves, in all that related to their internal interests, the most complete powers of government.

That this was so is indeed obvious on the most cursory reading of the colonial history of these times. The most striking fact connected with the early English colonies is the extraordinary variety of political institutions which prevailed in them. Take, for example, the subject of religion—a subject with reference to which it was a grand object of the governments of England at this time to enforce uniformity. In the colonies there are as many religions predominant as there are religious denominations amongst the colonists. Thus, in the New England colonies, we find Puritanism in the ascendant; in Virginia and Carolina, the Church of England is established by law; in Pennsylvania, Quakerism prevails; while for Roman Catholics, Maryland is the land of promise. Whatever in effect was the religious belief prevailing in a colony, that was reflected in its legislative assembly, and embodied in its laws. And as it was with religion, so it was with all other matters connected with the colony's internal concerns; for example, with the laws of inheritance, and with what has been made the subject of so much discussion in late times— the disposal of its waste lands, and the mode of dealing with native tribes. In the regulation of their external commerce, indeed, the colonies, as will be gathered from what I have already said, were content to submit to the central government; but in all else they were their own masters. Like the Corcyræans of old, they could boast that they relinquished their country, " in order to be equal in right with those who remain, not to be their slaves."

It was these things, still more than the discrepancies in the commercial codes of the two countries, which brought out the broad contrasts between English and Spanish colonization. From the first, the Spanish colonists fell under the blight of an all-pervading despotism; while the colonists of England, whom the tyranny of Charles and Laud never reached, masters of their persons and property, thought and spoke, laboured and traded, under the inspiring consciousness of liberty. Hence it happened that, while the colonies of Spain, albeit embracing the richest portions of the New World—rich with the products of the tropics, as well as with that on which she set more store, the precious metals—languished in the midst of their marvellous resources, and never prevented, or even for a moment retarded, her decline, the colonies of England, almost from their first establishment, steadily progressed,—the most important of them exhibiting, at the close of their dependent career, an example of rapid and brilliant progress such as the world had not hitherto witnessed, and finally, on their severance from the mother country, taking rank among nations almost at once as a first-class power.

So far, then, as to the first period of colonial history which I proposed to examine. Henceforward I shall confine myself exclusively to the examples of colonization and colonial policy furnished by Great

Britain. I have taken the American War of Independence as an epoch; because, while it terminates the political connection of Great Britain with her most celebrated colonies, it also marks a change of vital moment in her colonial policy. Up to that time, the colonies of England, though controlled in their external commerce, yet as regarded their internal affairs—in all that related to their most intimate concerns—were emphatically self-governing. Thenceforward, until quite recent times, the government of her colonies was carried on in England through the Colonial Office, a department of State conducting its affairs through an organization analogous to that employed by the Royal Council of the Indies. A centralized bureaucracy thus took the place, in English colonial affairs, of the municipal system of the earlier period. It will be worth while to consider here what the causes were which led to this remarkable change.

In the first place, then, the War of Independence, and its unlooked-for issue, produced in England a feeling of profound mortification—an exacerbation of temper, which naturally lent itself to arbitrary measures. England—so the case was put by her statesmen—had conceded to her North American colonies almost complete self-government. Under her liberal treatment and fostering care, those colonies had grown in population and wealth with unexampled rapidity—had in a century and a half attained to the stature of a nation. And what was the result? What was the return made to England for this liberal treatment? That the moment these dependencies were invited to contribute towards a revenue, from the expenditure of which they had profited scarcely less than the mother country herself—a revenue which had more than once been spent in wars waged for their defence, and which had resulted in their aggrandizement,—that moment these favoured dependencies repudiated the just demand, rebelled against their indulgent protector, and asserted their independence. It was thus that the question of colonial government presented itself to the mortified spirit of Englishmen after the loss of a colonial empire, on the retention of which, it was at that time very generally thought, England's rank in the scale of nations depended. It was, then, not unnatural, that the resolve should be taken to tighten the bond of dependence in the case of such colonies as still remained; nor were other events wanting about this time to strengthen this disposition.

The French Revolution was then on the point of breaking out. The catastrophe no sooner came than a violent reaction in English political opinion set in—a reaction which has left deep traces on the political history of that time. The Liberal party, as favourers of the French Revolution, were stricken with hopeless unpopularity. The Tories, led by Pitt, now scared from his liberal creed, were carried to power by immense majorities. The whole thought and passion of the nation were exhausted in antagonism to France and French principles, and whatever in any way favoured popular right was looked on as infected with the fatal taint. Colonial Government could not but follow the general tendency. In the colonies, as elsewhere, liberal institutions fell under discredit, and the rights of the colonists receded before the pretensions of the central power.

But there was one cause more potent for this result than all the rest. It was about this time that England founded her first convict colony. The practice of transporting criminals to remote dependencies—a practice not unknown to antiquity—had indeed been adopted by Great Britain, in common with other European countries, in the times anterior to the American revolution; but it was then confined within narrow limits. In Maryland, for example, which in those times was one of the principal receptacles of this class of emigrants, the proportion of convicts to the whole population did not, in the middle of the last century, exceed 2 per cent.* The practice, however, did exist. Now, by the result of the revolutionary struggle, this outlet for the criminals of England was suddenly cut off; and this at a time when, no doubt in consequence of the same event, the prisons of England were extraordinarily full. A pressing practical problem was thus presented to the statesmen of England—a problem which, much as it has since been discussed, cannot yet be said to be fully solved—how is England to dispose of her criminals? In an evil hour the idea suggested itself of establishing a penal settlement. The connection of the two events is sufficiently indicated by their chronological sequence. The Peace of Paris, by which the independence of the United States was recognized, was signed in 1782. The first penal colony of England was founded in New South Wales in 1788. Ere

* "Colonization and Colonies," p. 350, note.

many years had passed, there was witnessed, for the first time in history, the unedifying spectacle of a community in which the bulk of the population were felons serving out the period of their punishment. From that time until quite recent years, the practice of penal colonization became a settled portion of the policy of Great Britain.

Now, I need not tell you that this use of colonization was quite incompatible with the idea of colonial self-government. Colonies in which the majority of the inhabitants were felons of the deepest dye clearly could not be trusted with political rights. And the precedent established in those cases, as will be readily understood, quickly reacted upon the general system of our colonial government.* The establishment of the Colonial Office, which took place in 1794, may be regarded as the external symbol of the change.†

The practice of penal colonization, concurring with the other influences I have mentioned, thus definitively determined the course of English colonial policy in the direction of centralization and absolutism; and this

* "It is a remarkable fact, that until we began to colonize with convicts towards the end of the last century, the imperial power of England never, I believe, in a single instance, attempted to rule locally from a distance a body of its subjects who had gone forth from England and planted a colony."—WAKEFIELD'S *Art of Colonization*, p. 228.

† Previous to this time the business connected with the colonies, which was almost exclusively commercial, had been assigned first to a Board, and afterwards to a permanent Committee of Privy Council, which had the management of "Trade and Plantations." For a short interval, indeed, during the American struggle—from 1768 to 1782—a Secretary of State for the American Department existed: it was the office of this functionary which Burke's Bill abolished. See Lewis's "Government of Dependencies," pp. 160-62.

was about the least serious of the evils which that system entailed. It brought colonization itself into disrepute. It corrupted the whole tone of English thought on the subject. It may be doubted if even yet we have fully recovered from its effects.

The plan of penal colonization, it is true, presents certain obvious advantages of an economic kind: let us, by all means, recognize them. It secures to the colony an ample supply of that of which colonies have most need—labour; it secures to it also, besides this cheap means of production—cheap to the colony, but very far from cheap to the taxpayers of the mother country, who bear the expense of transporting and guarding these promising emigrants—it secures, I say, to the colony, in addition to this cheap means of production, a market for its products in the large government expenditure which the military and police establishments, indispensable to such settlements, always entail. It confers these advantages, and by this means it galvanizes into a precocious prosperity the settlements which are the victims of the loathsome patronage. But what an idea must our statesmen have had of the art of colonization—of what Bacon calls "the heroic work" of building up new nations—when they turned for the materials of the structure to the hulk and gaol! "Imagine," said Dr. Hind, "the case of a household most carefully made up of picked specimens from all the idle, mischievous, and notoriously bad characters in the country! Surely the man who should be mad or wicked enough to bring together this monstrous family, and to keep up its numbers and character by continual fresh supplies, would be scouted from the society he so outraged—would be denounced as the author of a diabolical nuisance to his neighbourhood and his country, and would be proclaimed infamous for setting at nought all morality and decency. What is it better, that, instead of a household, it is a whole people we have so brought together, and are so keeping up?—that it is the wide society of the whole world, and not of a single country, against which the nuisance is committed?"

But the evils of convict settlement did not end here. We know that the existence of slavery in a country is able, by its vile associations, to degrade honest industry, and make men ashamed of useful occupations: in like manner, the practice of convict settlement brought discredit upon the whole art and business of colonization. That "heroic work" became associated in men's minds with ideas of infamy and crime. This aspect of the case is brought out, not less strongly than quaintly, by Charles Lamb, in a letter addressed to a friend in the "Hades of Thieves"—the upperworld *alias* for New South Wales. He thus describes, in his grotesquest vein, the conditions of a society in which, not in theory but in fact, *la propriété est le vol*. "I see," he says, "Diogenes prying among you with his perpetual fruitless lantern. What must you be willing to give by this time for the sight of an honest man! You must have almost forgotten how *we* look. And tell me what your Sydneyites do? Are they th—v—ng all the day long? Merciful heaven! what property can stand against such depredations! The kangaroos—your aborigines—do they keep their primitive simplicity un-Europe-tainted, with those little short fore-puds, looking like a lesson framed by nature to the pickpocket. Marry, for diving into fobs, they are lamely provided *à priori;* but if the hue-and-cry were once up, they would show as fair a pair of hind-shifters as the expertest locomotor in the colony. We hear the most improbable tales at this distance. Pray, is it true that the young Spartans among you are born with six fingers, which spoils their scanning? It must look very odd, but use reconciles. For their scansion it is less to be regretted; for, if they take it into their heads to be poets, it is odds but they turn out, the greatest part of them, vile plagiarists. Is there any difference to see between the son of a th—f and the grandson? or where does the taint stop? Do you bleach in three or four generations? I have many questions to put, but two Delphic voyages can be made in shorter time than it will take to satisfy my scruples. Do you grow your own hemp? What is your staple trade?—exclusive of the national profession, I mean. Your locksmiths, I take it, are some of your great capitalists."

Now observe the effect of this state of opinion on colonization. In early times the best families in England did not disdain to bear a part in colonizing enterprises. Sir Humphry Gilbert, Sir Walter Raleigh, Lord Baltimore, William Penn—a courtier as well as a Quaker—were all identified with the cause of colonization. Cromwell, Hampden, Pym, Vane, were eager to try their fortunes in the colonies.* The watchword

---

* "Settled history has made another mistake in leading us to suppose that the Puritan emigrants belonged chiefly, like the Cameronians in Scotland, to the humbler classes at home: most of the leaders, on

of the most enterprising spirits in those days was, "Westward Ho!" In the present day colonization has again acquired something of its ancient prestige; and if our aristocracy do not now emigrate with the same eagerness as in the Elizabethan and Carolan times, our middle classes at least—the sons of our landed gentry, our trading and professional classes—show no reluctance to embrace a colonial career. But in the half century which followed the American war of independence, respectability in every form shrank from colonization as from assured disgrace. Was it strange? The founders of our colonies during this period were no longer the Raleighs, and Baltimores, and Pilgrim Fathers of the early times, nor yet the Wakefields and Torrenses, and Godleys of a later day, but escaped convicts, expirees, and ticket-of-leave men, the reckless and profligate in every rank of life, or paupers "shovelled out" on the colonies by the overburthened parishes of England.

Such was the depth of degradation to which the practice of colonization had sunk in this, the second, certainly the most inglorious period of its history. It may be briefly characterized as the period of convict settlement, pauper emigration, and Colonial Office supremacy.

The American war of independence served to mark for us the termination of the first period of our colonial history. That which I shall take as our next landmark is an event as obscure as the former is famous;

the contrary, were of the gentry class, being persons of old family, the best education, and considerable property."—*The Art of Colonization*, p. 160.

and yet, unconspicuous as it is, it is no less than the other the forerunner of momentous changes in our colonial history. This event is the formation of the Colonization Society. It was established in 1830, "an unknown and feeble body," says Mr. Wakefield, "composed chiefly of very young men, some of whose names, however, have long ceased to be obscure, while others are among the most celebrated of the day." The Society, as such, had indeed a brief existence; but its principles took root; its members long continued to act together; and recruits of the highest promise quickly joined them. Foremost among such recruits was one whose name, in this place naturally recurs to us; but in no place could the name of Whately be omitted from the story of colonial reform without ignoring one of its most important pages. In 1832 appeared his "Thoughts on Secondary Punishments," a work in which, with that vigorous logic and homely satire in which he was so great a master, he exposed and denounced—going at once to the root of colonial evils—the convict system. "It was a wicked and unblessed thing," he used to say, adopting the language of Bacon, "to take the scum of people and wicked and condemned men to be the people with whom you plant." This was to plant the land with "nettle-seed." The defenders of transportation pleaded that it conferred a double benefit—at once a relief to the mother country and a boon to the colony. Whately replied that it was doubly cursed, demoralizing mother country and colony together—the former by accustoming her to meet temporary exigencies by a recourse to radically vicious expedients—expedients which, opening to criminals an almost assured road to prosperity, involve a permanent encouragement to crime ; and the latter, by corrupting its national life at the source. In the wide range of that great man's intellectual activity there is surely no topic on which his remarkable powers have been exerted with more signal success, or been productive of greater or more lasting utility.

Colonization had, as I have said, at this time reached the nadir of its decline. The colonial reformers proposed to rescue it from its degradation, and re-establish it in the grandeur of its true proportions before the English people. Since the subject had last seriously attracted the attention of political thinkers, Political Economy had taken rank among the sciences. The most eminent of those who took part in the new movement—Wakefield, Torrens, Charles Buller, Sir William Molesworth, Whately—had mastered the knowledge, and approached the subject of colonization with all the advantage which this acquisition conferred. For the first time something like a sound and complete theory of colonization was put forth— sound at least, I do not hesitate to say, in its essentials. The theory has now little more than an historic value : still the large space which it for many years filled in colonial politics, and the great practical results which have flowed from it, will perhaps justify an attempt to state briefly its leading principles.

The fundamental cause and the justification of colonization are to be found in the laws of population and capital. In old countries population and capital tend to become redundant. Of this there is abounding proof. The redundancy of capital in old countries is evinced by many obvious circumstances—for example, by the difficulty of employing it advantageously, by the low rate of profit which it brings, by its constant exportation for investment to other lands. The redundancy of population is even a more patent fact. ` Which of us has not painful experience that "all the gates are thronged with suitors," that "all the markets overflow"? As to the facts, therefore, there can be no doubt. The cause has been traced by Political Economy to the limited quantity and capacity of that agent from which ultimately the elements of subsistence and the materials of wealth are drawn—the land of the country. Now, in new countries the conditions of production are exactly reversed. Fertile land exists there in abundance, while capital and labour are scarce. Seen in this light, the true remedy for our evils at once appears. It is, that what is in excess in each should be brought to supplement what is deficient in each; in a word—that we should colonize. "When I ask you," said Charles Buller, in that great speech which gave an earnest of future statesmanship which the gifted orator was never destined to fulfil, "when I ask you to colonize, what do I ask you to do, but to carry the superfluity of one part of our country to repair the deficiency of the other—to cultivate the desert by applying to it the means that lie idle at home; in one simple word, to convey the plough to the field, the workman to his work, the hungry to his food."

But at this point I fancy I hear the familiar ring of a well-known objection:—What! encourage the bone and sinew and industrial enterprise and accumulated wealth of the country to leave it! Well, I will meet the objéction frankly. I would by all means encourage the bone and sinew and industrial enterprise and accumulated wealth of old countries to leave them for the purpose of colonization; and I would do so in order to increase in those very countries, bone and sinew and industrial enterprise and accumulated wealth. If 'you think this paradoxical,* I will ask you to consider a familiar case. The United States are colonies of England, founded by the exportation thither, some two centuries ago, of those elements of material prosperity which I have named. Do you think that England is now the poorer for that exportation? Suppose this argument against exporting bone and sinew had prevailed in the seventeenth century, and that the British American Colonies had never been planted, do you think that the England of our day would support, in consequence, a larger population in greater affluence? It is surely unnecessary to remind you that the colonies of England—I mean the countries planted and peopled by England, whether now politically connected with her or not—are as necessary to the support of her people as the soil on which they tread. It is an obvious fact that England, from her own

---

* The paradox, still so mysterious to many people, was propounded and solved by Franklin a century ago. "There are supposed," he said, "to be now upwards of one million souls in North America; ... and yet, perhaps there is not one the fewer in Britain, but rather the more; on account," he adds, "of the employment the colonies afford to manufacturers at home;" on account, we should now prefer to say, of the cheapened subsistence with which they supply them.

soil, is physically incapable of giving subsistence to the human beings who now cover her surface; and that if she has been rendered capable of supporting her present immense population, and supporting them in such comfort as they enjoy, this is due principally to the fact that she has for centuries been a colonizing country. She has sent abroad her sturdy and enterprising sons to countries abounding in all that she has needed; and the descendants of those emigrants are now at once the most constant customers for her products, and the surest caterers for her wants. She has parted with her bone and muscle and industrial enterprise and accumulated wealth, and the result is, she has multiplied indefinitely all these elements of her greatness. Colonization thus confers a double benefit: it relieves the old country from the pressure of its superabundant population, and gives a field for its unemployed capital; while, at the same time, by opening up new lands and placing their resources at her disposal, it widens indefinitely the limits which restrain her future growth.

Well, this point having been made good—a basis for their activity having been found in the nature of the case—the colonial reformers had next to deal with the practical question, How is colonization to be carried on? By what means are men and capital to be transferred from one end of the globe to the other—men, that is, of the right quality, in the right proportions, keeping in view always the great ultimate end—the founding of a new nation? The solution of this problem propounded by the reformers was as follows:—First, they maintained that the lands of a new colony, instead of being granted away gratuitously with lavish profusion, as had been the almost universal practice of the English governments up to that time, should be sold, and sold at a substantial and a uniform price.* Secondly, they insisted that the proceeds of the land sales should be employed as an emigration fund to assist the poorer classes in emigrating. Thirdly, they urged that this assistance should be given with discrimination; that is to say, that the emigrants should be selected—the conditions of age, sex, health, respectability, &c., being taken account of—with a view to the needs of new colonies. And, fourthly, they contended for the principle of colonial self-government. Thus, to recapitulate—the sale of wild land at a uniform price, the application of the proceeds to assist emigration, the selection of the emigrants, and self-government for the colonies—these may be taken as the cardinal points in the reformers' charter. They did not, indeed, comprise the whole programme of the reformers—at least of the more sanguine of the group, in whose fervid imaginations the art of colonization grew rapidly into a wonderfully elaborate and complete system. For these visionaries—as I think I may now venture to call them—the ideal of an English colony was England herself, in little, transferred to the other side of the globe—an epitome, perfect in all its parts, of the society from which it issued—England, with its

---

* The reader who desires to inform himself on the doctrine, once so warmly debated, of a "sufficient price" for colonial land, is referred to akefield's "Art of Colonization," Letters xlvii.—lii.; and, on the other hand, to Merivale's "Colonization and the Colonies," Lectures xiv.—xvi.; also to Mill's "Principles of Political Economy," book i. chap. viii.

capitalists and labourers, its hierarchy of ranks, its hereditary aristocracy, its landed gentry, and, of course, its Established Church *—transferred complete, as by the enchanter's stroke, to the pastoral wilds of Australia! The idea was a taking, perhaps a noble one; unfortunately it has not proved practical. The progeny is, in fact, turning out something very different from the parent's image. In place of feudal subordination there is democracy; in place of a high electoral qualification, manhood suffrage; in place of primogeniture, equal division of property; in place of State churches, voluntary religious associations. In fact, the ducklings are rapidly taking the water; but if they are, it is scarcely, methinks, for us to act the idle part of the nursing hen moralizing from the brink.†

* This was, I believe, the original idea, which however in the end developed into something more reasonable as well as more liberal—"that of established churches." "As a colonizing body," says Mr. Wakefield, "composed, like the legislature, of people differing in creed, we determined to assist all denominations of settlers alike, with respect to religious provisions. We have assisted Roman Catholics according to their numbers, and the Church of Scotland on the same principle." He adds the following creditable anecdote. "Among the first emigrants to New Zealand were some Jews, who asked us, 'with bated breath and whispering humbleness,' if a priest authorized to kill animals for meat according to Jewish custom, could have accommodation in the ships. We treated the inquiry as a request, and granted it with alacrity, taking care besides that every arrangement should be made to satisfy their religious scruples. The Jews of England have since done the New Zealand Company's settlements more than one service."—*Art of Colonization*, pp. 56, 57.

† "And even supposing this aristocratic reverie capable of being accomplished, what interest have the English people in its accomplishment? Why should they desire to plant among the communities of the New World a hostile outpost of feudalism and privilege, the source of division, jealousy, and war? What reason have they to fear the sight of great commonwealths based on free reverence for equal laws

But leaving these refinements of political speculation, respecting which opinions will naturally differ, the four positions which I have stated furnished at least a sound basis for practical work. Sustained as these positions have since been by fuller discussion, as well as by the severer test of actual experiment, they may now be taken as the admitted and approved groundwork of the colonizing art.*

and prospering without lords or dependants? Why should they look with jealous malignity on the mighty development of the Anglo-Saxon race, emancipated from Norman bonds, over a continent which its energy and patience have made its own? Why should they desire to thwart the manifest designs of Providence, which has willed that a new order of things should commence with the peopling of the New World? . . . .

"By the issue of their enterprise, victorious though chequered, victorious though now wrapped in storm, man has undoubtedly been taught that he may not only exist, but prosper, without many things which it would be heresy and treason to think unnecessary to his existence here. It is a change, and a great change; one to be regarded neither with childish exultation nor with childish fear, but with manly reverence and solicitude, as the opening of a new page in the book of Providence, full of mighty import to mankind. But what, in the course of time, has not changed, except that essence of religion and morality for which all the rest was made? The grandest forms of history have waxed old and passed away. The English aristocracy has been grand and beneficent in its hour, but why should it think that it is the expiring effort of creative power, and the last birth of time? We bear, and may long bear, from motives higher perhaps than the public good, the endless decrepitude of feudalism here; but why are we bound, or how can we hope, to propagate it in a free world?"—*The Empire*, by GOLDWIN SMITH, pp. 142-145.

* "Let us divest it" [the modern scheme of systematic colonization], says Mr. Merivale, "of the too exact form in which it has been presented by some of its supporters; let us dismiss all idea of a precise proportion between land labour and capital, an exclusive employment of the land fund on emigration, and of a 'mathematically' sufficient price; let us consider its principles as confined to the sale of land at as high prices as can reasonably be obtained, and the strict devotion of the proceeds to a few essential purposes, among which the supply of labour holds the principal place; let us consider it, moreover, as chiefly applicable to colonies raising large quantities of exportable produce, and perhaps also to other colonies, so distant from the mother country, that the stream of

The colonial reformers of 1830, I have said, propounded a theory: they were, however, very far from being mere theorists: their aims were essentially practical; and they were eager to proceed from speculation to action.

Among their first converts was Lord Howick, the present Earl Grey, who early in 1832, before he had been a year in office, took the first great step in the right direction, by promulgating regulations whereby, in the principal colonies of England, the sale of waste land was substituted for the irregular practice of gratuitous grants; and whereby further, in two important colonies—New South Wales and Van Diemen's Land—the purchase-money thus obtained was directed to be used as a fund for assisting emigration. This was the first victory of the reformers; the second occurred some four years later. It consisted in the appointment—made while Earl, then Lord John, Russell held the seals of the Colonial Office—of the Land and Emigration Commissioners, as a machinery for superintending and generally promoting emigration.

These were important achievements; but the reformers naturally desired some fairer field for the trial of their principles than settlements already saturated with the dregs of a convict emigration. They

emigration needs to be artificially directed to them; let us, I say, subject the theory to all the qualifications I have suggested, although not all of them with equal confidence, and we cannot then fail of being struck with its simplicity, its facility of adaptation, its high practical utility. Never was there a more remarkable instance of the success of a principle against all manner of misapprehension—against the fear of innovation—against corrupt interests—against the inert resistance which all novelty is sure to encounter."—*Colonization and the Colonies*, pp. 427, 428.

aspired to be themselves the founders of colonies. The site which they selected for their first experiment was South Australia. In 1836, the Act of Parliament was passed by which that model colony * was founded.

From this point the new principles steadily gained ground. In 1837, the New Zealand Association, with Mr., afterwards Sir Francis Baring at its head, was formed for the purpose of colonizing New Zealand in conformity with the new doctrines. After a prolonged controversy with more than one government, it at length succeeded, in 1846, in obtaining from Parliament charters for the settlement of Wellington, Nelson, and New Plymouth. Within a few years Canterbury and Otago were added to the achievements of the Association in the same region. Meantime the principles of the reformers respecting the disposal of the public land and the transmission of emigrants, modified, it is true, to meet the views of successive Colonial Secretaries, were adopted for all the Australian colonies. Thus rapidly were the fortunes of English

---

* I say "model" colony ; for, although it is true that the Wakefield School were far from satisfied with the degree of recognition obtained for their views in the original constitution, it is beyond question that it embodied the most important of their characteristic doctrines : on the whole, too, and notwithstanding the first breakdown, they have no reason to be dissatisfied with the result of the experiment. " Notwithstanding," says Mr. Wakefield ("Art of Colonization," p. 50), "this grievous mistake, and the numerous mistakes into which the Commissioners fell, the plan worked even better than its authors now expected. A fine colony of people was sent out ; and, for the first time, the disposal of waste land, and the emigration of shipfuls of labourers to the other side of the world, was managed with something like system and care." And see Merivale's " Colonization," &c., New Edition, Lecture xvi. and Appendix.

colonization retrieved. In 1830, the colonies were spoken of in leading reviews as "unfit abodes for any but convicts, paupers, and desperate and needy persons." Before five years had passed, the best minds in England had identified themselves with the cause of colonization; within twenty years a whole group of new colonies were founded, which are now amongst the most interesting and promising which own allegiance to the British Crown. The Colonization Society had done its work.*

It had, perhaps, done more than its work—more, at least, than many of those who took part in its early deliberations had consciously aimed at. Among the numerous reforms comprised in the programme of the colonial reformers, self-government for the colonies occupied a principal place. In this, too, the reformers have succeeded — succeeded beyond their hopes — succeeded, it may yet prove, beyond their wishes.

During that period in which the colonies were ruled through the Colonial Office—that is to say, from 1794 down to quite recent times—there was maintained in many of the colonies a make-believe of self-govern-

---

* "Like most projects based on theory," says Mr. Merivale, "however far-sighted and comprehensive, the so-called South Australian, or Wakefield scheme of colonization took in practice a different course from what its inventors anticipated, and its results were in many respects curiously divergent from those with a view to which it was constructed. But it would be a great error to infer on that account that it was unsuccessful; on the contrary, there are in history very few instances to be found in which a system, devised in the closet by studious men, and put in execution in a new and distant world, which those men had never seen, has produced such extensive and beneficial results. . . . . It is not too much to say," he adds, "that the success of our Australian colonies is in a very great measure attributable to their lessons."—*Colonization and the Colonies.* New Edition, 1861, p. 470.

ment. The colonies, many of them at least, received so-called "constitutions." These constitutions, however, notwithstanding that they in general comprised a representative assembly, in fact signified extremely little. The representative assemblies had no substantial functions. The real powers of government lay in an Executive Council—a council of which the members, nominated directly or indirectly by the Colonial Minister, and holding office during his pleasure, were entirely independent of the representative bodies, and might, and frequently did, set them at defiance, and govern in direct opposition to their views. This was the state of things which prevailed in the so-called "representative colonies" of England down to 1846. But in that year a change took place: the reformers were strong enough to carry a measure, by which representative government in Canada was converted from a sham into a reality. The principle, once made good, was rapidly extended; and I believe, at the present time, the Cape of Good Hope is the only considerable English colony in which responsible government, in the fullest sense of the word, does not prevail.*

The mode in which this pregnant change was effected is deserving of attention, as illustrating the vast consequences which, in political affairs, sometimes depend upon apparently trivial circumstances. Formerly, on the nomination of members to the Executive Council, the appointment was made "during pleasure"—the pleasure, that is to say, of the Colonial

---

* "Colonization and the Colonies." Appendix to Lecture xxii. [Responsible government has since been conceded to the Cape.]

Office; the practical effect being that the members held office during life. But from the time that the new measure came into force, the words "during pleasure" were omitted; and instead, the members were appointed on the understanding that they should hold their posts only so long as they retained the confidence of the colonial assemblies. The change, almost infinitesimal in appearance, amounted in its consequences to a revolution; for it at once brought the executive into subordination to the legislature. Power and patronage passed in a moment from the Colonial Office to the colonial assemblies. The Council might still be appointed by the Home Government; but it could only exercise its powers in conformity with the views of the local body. In this way, after the lapse of a century, has Great Britain come round in her colonial policy to the point from which she started. In early times self-government used, as we saw, to "break out" in the English colonies—the natural outcome where two or three Englishmen met together to build up society in a new land; and now, after much groping amongst other systems, the country has returned to its primitive faith. Reason and experience have set their seal on what was at first prompted by the instincts of free men.

And now, availing ourselves of the light which we derive from this rapid survey of the past, let us endeavour to appreciate the character of the crisis in our colonial history in the midst of which at the present moment we find ourselves. One inference forces itself upon us at the outset. Of the reasons which have in former times prevailed for holding colonies in subjection, not one can now be considered tenable. One after another, the objects for the sake of which our colonial empire was created have, with the progress of economic and political knowledge, been given up. Let us glance at these objects in succession; and first, tribute may receive a passing mention. Tribute—for which, with ancient statesmen, dependencies of all kinds were chiefly valued, and which has been enforced in modern times by some European nations—never filled a large place in the colonial programme of England. Once indeed she made the attempt to tax her colonies for her own benefit; but the result of that experiment has not tempted her to repeat it. At present it is scarcely necessary to say, that the idea of obtaining revenue from a British colony is one which has no place in the thoughts of any British statesman. So far from this, the tables have been turned; it is *we* who are assessed to the colonies; our annual payments amounting, in average years, to some £4,421,000 annually :* what

* " Having reference to the expenditure of 1857, which is the latest account in a complete form we have in our possession, we find the imperial cost to have been £4,115,757, and the average of five years previously £4,421,577; but we should not forget that this amount, large as it may appear, is only some important portion of the whole sum. The colonies have shared, in no inconsiderable measure, in the £12,608,000 we have expended on the navy, and £1,000,000 on the packet service."—*Our Colonies, their Commerce and their Cost*, by HENRY ASHWORTH, p. 8.

[The cost has since been considerably reduced. " From a report presented to the House of Commons in 1870 it appeared that the cost of the general colonies to the British Exchequer in 1868 and 1869 was £3,620,093, but of that sum very nearly £3,000,000 was charged under the head of 'cost of regular troops,' which, by the way, had been since reduced by £1,200,000, owing to the withdrawal of troops from various colonies."— Lecture by Mr. Knatchbull-Hugessen, M.P., Under-Secretary for the Colonies, published in the *Times*, October 24, 1872.]

they will reach this year, when the New Zealand war bill is paid, is what I will not venture to conjecture.

On the other hand, commercial monopoly was long, as we have seen, a leading object with those who built up and maintained our colonial empire. "The only use," said Lord Sheffield, in a debate during the American War of Independence, "the only use of the American colonies is the market of their commodities and the carriage of their produce;" and on this basis was erected that complicated system of prohibitions, bounties, and differential duties, of which, in a former part of this address, I attempted to sketch the outline. But free trade has wholly and for ever removed the ground from this elaborate and time-honoured structure. We do not any longer ask—we certainly do not receive—from our colonies any commercial advantages which are not equally open to the whole world, which we should not equally command though the political connection were severed to-morrow.* The commercial reason for holding colonies in subjection, therefore, like the financial one, has passed away.

But another use for colonies was in progress of time discovered: they might be turned to account as receptacles for the criminals of the mother country —convenient sewers for her moral and social off-scourings. I have shown you what was the result of this elevated and hopeful view of the colonizing art. I will only now add, that penal colonization,

* "No one now really doubts," says Mr. Merivale, "notwithstanding the hostile tariff of the States, that the separation of our North American colonies has been, in an economical sense, advantageous to us."

long condemned by the best minds of the nation, as well as by a disastrous experience, has of late years—less, it is mortifying to think, from an enlightened policy than under stress of necessity—been in practice abandoned. One example, indeed, of a penal colony under British dominion still exists—Western Australia; but this remaining blot, thanks to the rough lesson we have just received from a precocious pupil in the art politic,* it seems probable will soon be removed.

Well, the object of *finance*, the object of *commercial monopoly*, the object of *gaol convenience*—all those objects, in short, which had served in former times as reasons for our colonial empire, had one after another been given up; yet the structure remained —remained, not only without support from any grounds of solid reason, but charged with an extraneous burthen of £4,500,000 sterling, spent annually in keeping it in repair. People began to ask *cui bono?* Various answers were returned. One writer said we took out the value in prestige.† According to another, the colonial empire was to be regarded as a great political gymnasium, in which the people

---

* "A sinister system of education, under which the tutor tries to force upon the pupil moral and social poison, which the pupil struggles to reject."—Professor GOLDWIN SMITH in *Daily News*.

† "The ablest of my critics tells me in good plain English that what he thinks so valuable and wishes so much to preserve is 'apparent power.' . . . . When we see through the appearance of power, and coolly own to ourselves that we do see through it, will not our enemies have the sense to do the same? Wooden artillery has been useful as a stratagem in war; but I never heard that it was useful, or that anything was risked by a wise commander to preserve it, after the enemy had found out that it was wooden."—*The Empire*, p. 32.

of this country might practise the art of governing nations, and cultivate the "imperial sense"—an endowment which, it was alleged, was worth the money. Or, again, the Imperial Government was a kind of incurious Providence, ordering things aright by a masterly inaction—a power, "whose purely nominal but beneficent suzerainty keeps the political machinery of the colonies in working order." So much virtue, it seems, there is in a name. Just two years ago, a high authority propounded a more tangible doctrine. The political connection was justified by Mr. Merivale on the ground that colonies are valuable as a field for emigration;* the implication, of course, being that the condition of dependency constitutes an attraction for emigrants. In the keenly felt need of a working theory of empire the idea was eagerly taken up. The *Times*, of course, welcomed the opportune discovery. Even the cautious *Economist* became enthusiastic in contemplating "the amount of vivifying hope inspired in our working classes here by the knowledge that they can at any moment take refuge in a world of comparative plenty within the limits of the British Empire." The theory wanted nothing but a basis in fact: in this, however, it was deficient.

The emigration returns give no evidence of the alleged preference of our emigrating classes for countries which are still under British rule: on the contrary, the immense majority of those who emigrate from the British Isles pass, by choice, *outside* the limits of the British empire. Even of those who

* Paper on "The Utility of Colonization," read before the British Association, 1862.

emigrate, in the first instance, to British dependencies, a large proportion subsequently leave them, and pass into independent countries. The stream of emigration from Canada to the United States has lately become so large that the Canadian people, like ourselves, have become apprehensive of depopulation, and only the other day * a select committee was appointed by the Canadian Legislative Council to report on the best means of at once attracting emigration and stopping this drain. Now we may explain these facts as we please; but facts they are; and in the presence of such facts, it does seem somewhat preposterous to put forward the preference of our emigrating classes for British rule as a reason for maintaining our colonial empire. Would there not, in truth, be more colour of reason in the converse of the argument?

We have not yet exhausted the motives to imperial rule. The change in our commercial policy has, as we have seen, disposed of one—the principal—ground on which, in modern times, the theory of colonial empire has been sustained—the supposed advantages of commercial monopoly. But is it certain that this change, while removing one, has not furnished us with another and a more valid reason for maintaining our supremacy? If empire was justifiable on the principles of commercial monopoly, is it not, now that those principles are exploded, justifiable for the enforcement of free trade? Having adopted free trade for ourselves, have we not a right—is it not our duty as an imperial nation—to see to it that the same beneficent principle

* 16th May, 1864.

which we have established at home, shall also be the law throughout the widely scattered regions over which we have planted our race? There is no doubt that, some twenty years ago, as the approaching triumph of free trade menaced the foundations of the received colonial doctrines, this view presented itself to the minds of some of our most enlightened statesmen;* and eminently just and reasonable as the end aimed at is, and holding out, as it does, the prospect of large blessings to the community of nations, such an object might seem not altogether unworthy of being made the logical basis of imperial rule. But here we are met by another principle equally reasonable, equally just, and far more imperative—a principle which also, after full consideration, we have deliberately adopted—the principle of colonial self-government. Are we prepared, frankly and in good faith, to give effect to this principle? If so, the question seems to be resolved. Self-government means government in accordance with the views of the persons governed. If the colonists, therefore, desire a free-trade policy, under a *régime* of self-government,

---

* "This advantage," says Sir C. Lewis, writing in 1841, "is at present a substantial one; but it is an advantage which is founded exclusively on the perverse folly of independent states in imposing prohibitory and protective duties on one another's productions.... When civilization shall have made sufficient progress to diffuse generally a knowledge of the few and simple considerations which prove the expediency of the freedom of trade, and when consequently independent states shall have abandoned their present anti-commercial policy, the possession of dependencies will no longer produce the advantage in question. The advantage consists in possession of a specific against the evils arising from an erroneous system of policy. Whenever the errors of the policy shall be generally perceived, and the system shall be exploded, the specific against its evil effects will be valueless."—*Government of Dependencies*, pp. 229, 230.

free trade will be adopted, whether they are nominally our subjects or not. If not, then, our imperial pretensions notwithstanding, free trade will be set at nought, and protection will be established. This is, in fact, what in some instances has happened. Canada has employed the legislative powers which she received from Great Britain to lay protective duties on British manufactures. Canada has led the way, and Australia bids fair to follow in her steps.

And now I think we may see where it is that the course of our colonial history has at length landed us. People are asking whether we are to retain or part with our colonies. It appears to me that to discuss this question now is much like discussing the propriety of locking the stable door after the steed has gone forth. No doubt, the British colonies still, in strict constitutional doctrine, owe allegiance to the British crown: to withhold this allegiance would be rebellion. But bring the question to any practical test, and let us see what the value of this much-prized supremacy amounts to—in what tangible circumstances Great Britain impresses her will upon her colonies; and, on the other hand, what the attributes of sovereignty are which these communities do not possess—which they do not at this moment actually exercise.

I have just adverted to our failure to maintain in them the principle of free trade—so just and reasonable a claim. Again: in conceding to them self-government, it was hoped that the mother country might yet reserve to herself the control of the colonial waste lands—" territories," said Mr. Wakefield, " which the nation had acquired by costly efforts, as a valuable national property, which we have every right in justice, and are bound by every consideration of prudence, to use for the greatest benefit of the people of this country." But one of the first uses which the emancipated legislatures made of their newly acquired power was to possess themselves of this national property —a possession in which they have not been since disturbed. Once more, it was thought not unreasonable that, having undertaken their defence, we should have a voice in determining the amount of military force they should maintain. But here too our expectations have been falsified. For the last two years the Home Government, backed by the *Times*, has in vain employed alternate entreaties and threats to induce the Canadians to augment their military force. Thus in their commercial policy, in their territorial policy, in what we may call their foreign policy (since the view taken of their military requirements would depend upon their opinion of external dangers), the colonists, in the teeth of example, advice, and remonstrance — remonstrance rising sometimes almost to menace—have deliberately pursued their own way.

And now look at what is going forward in British North America. Some half-dozen colonies have appointed deputies to meet and decide upon a constitution under which they propose to coalesce into a nation. That, in a word, is the scope of this movement; and if that be not an act of the highest sovereignty, then it is difficult to imagine what sovereignty means. The Canadian leaders indeed assure us, as I observe from intelligence quite recently received, of their firm purpose that the North American colonies shall remain integral portions of the British Empire; but they do not tell us in what particulars they are prepared to defer to imperial authority. They will probably be content, as hitherto, to receive our advice, on the condition of being permitted to decline it when it happens not to coincide with their own views, and they will doubtless have no objection to receive our assistance in fighting their battles. On these or some tantamount terms, they are content to remain for ever loyal subjects of the British Crown. But what does a good cause gain by professions of "ironical allegiance?"* Disguise it as they will, under whatever constitutional figments and sounding phrases, the work on which they are engaged is the same work which some eighty years ago was consummated on no remote scene—when the thirteen united colonies, having achieved their independence, met together to do that which is now the business of Canadian statesmen—to make themselves a nation.

My case might seem here complete; but within the last week intelligence has reached this country which furnishes a fresh illustration of the nature of our imperial rule so apposite to my present theme, that,

---

* How much more really dignified is language like the following:— "We have come to feel that we can no longer call upon the people of England to tax themselves for our benefit; we have arrived at that time of life when it is humiliating to have everything done for us, and when we ought to assume burdens and not shrink from responsibilities of a national character. Out of this Union a colossal power will arise on the American continent, with one foot on the Pacific, another on the Atlantic." (The Hon. Mr. Archibald, leader of the Opposition in Nova Scotia, at the Montreal dinner.)

though at the risk of prolonging unduly this address, I am unable to resist the temptation of bringing it before you.

I just now stated, as you will remember, that Western Australia formed at present the single instance among all our colonies of a convict settlement. For some years this circumstance has been a source of constant discussion between the Home Government and the other—that is to say the Eastern —Australian colonies. As I have already remarked, transportation from a certain point of view has undoubtedly something to recommend it. The mother country by its means certainly gets rid of a very undesirable portion of her population; while for the emigrant, if his object be simply to make a fortune with all convenient speed, and return to his native country, or migrate elsewhere, it is beyond doubt an advantage—more especially in a very sparsely peopled country—to be assured of a constant supply of able-bodied labour. On the other hand, if the colonist intends to make the colony his country and home, it seems equally natural that he should object to the practice of letting loose periodically upon the infant community gangs of the picked ruffians of the parent state. Whether the former considerations have influenced the Western Australians I do not undertake to say; but it is certain that a large number amongst them have welcomed this species of immigration. On the other hand, the Eastern colonies have long vehemently protested against transportation in every form. Now, here perhaps it will occur to you that, the case being so, there is no reason that both parties should not be satisfied: but at this point a hitch occurs. The Eastern colonies, two of which are the gold-producing districts of New South Wales and Victoria, offer far greater attractions to the convict class—as to other classes—than the bare and unpromising desert to which the convicts are sent; and, accordingly, so soon as the term of their sentence is expired, large numbers migrate to the Eastern colonies. The colony which profits by their services is thus, so soon as those services cease to be profitable, relieved of their presence—a circumstance which we may well believe does not detract from the popularity of the system in this colony. It seems that, according to the evidence of Mr. Newlands and Mr. Torrens, both for a long time magistrates of Southern Australia, and the latter a member of the Legislative and Executive Councils, "within three years after the resumption of transportation to Western Australia, over one thousand conditionally pardoned and ticket-of-leave men found their way from that colony to Adelaide, and the result was a rapid increase of violent assaults, robberies, and burglarious crimes."* Now I think it must be confessed that such a state of things constitutes a very substantial grievance. But sentiment is also mixed up with the opposition of the Eastern Australians to the continuance of this system. "Generations," they say, "are springing up which will call Australia their birthplace, and will make it their home. To them it is fatherland, and they see clearly enough that a great career lies before it." "For this reason,"

* Letter of Mr. M'Arthur in the *Daily News*.

adds an eloquent colonial writer, "we are jealous of the fair fame of the land; and we are unwilling that colonies which contain within themselves the seeds of great nations, should have their name and history associated with convictism in any form. We ask, and we have a right to ask, why should we in this colony, who from the first have strenuously resolved that the convict element should have no place here, have the scum of England's moral impurity thrown down at our next door?" The outside world will make no nice distinctions between Eastern and Western, free and penal, Australia. They will only know that convicts are deported to Australia, and the word for them will cover all the colonies. "Therefore," say the colonists, "we suffer in reputation by even the remotest contact with the evil thing."*

I confess it seems to me that language such as this does honour to the people from whom it proceeds, and expressing, as it does, the unanimous feeling of communities which do not number less than a million and a half of people, ought to have weighed for something against the eager demand for convict labour of a few thousand Western Australians † hastening to be rich. But it seemed otherwise to the British Government. Last summer the determination was taken to continue transportation to Western Australia on the same scale as formerly. The Home Government and the people of the Eastern colonies have thus been brought into distinct collision; and now I beg

---

* *The South Australian Register*, 26th March, 1864.

† The number of inhabitants in Western Australia, excluding convicts and their families, is, according to Mr. Torrens' computation, 6,000.

you to observe the illustration this has furnished of the value of our imperial rule.

By the last Australian mail a minute has arrived from the Victorian Government, in which its Chief Secretary, after premising that it has been forced upon the attention of himself and his colleagues that further remonstrance is useless, goes on to say—" The time has arrived when it is incumbent upon us, in the exercise of our powers of self-government, to initiate legislation, in connection with the colonies whose interests are alike affected, for our common protection." He then announces that the Victorian Government has invited the co-operation of each of the other colonies interested, with a view to framing a measure "prohibitive of all intercourse whatever with Western Australia," "in order that her position as the only convict colony may be distinctly marked:" further, he gives notice that the Victorian Government will, at the expiration of six months from the 1st November, cease to contribute to the annual mail packet subsidy, unless upon the condition that the packets shall not touch at any port in Western Australia.

Such is the point at which this painful controversy has arrived. And now can anyone doubt what will be its termination? Absolute unanimity, it seems, prevails on the subject in all the Eastern colonies. Under these circumstances, is it conceivable that the Home Government should persist in forcing on a quarrel with our own kindred in such a cause— that they may have the privilege of discharging at their doors the scum of our criminal population? Of course no such fatuous act will be committed. Of course the Home Government will succumb. But what a comment does this supply on "the beneficent suzerainty!" In North America the British colonies have initiated action among themselves to form a new state. This may be an act of sovereignty, but it is, at all events, a neutral act; but how shall we characterize a proceeding in which colonies meet together to concert measures distinctly and avowedly to nullify the policy of the imperial state? Supposing these colonies were formally independent, what other course would they, in like circumstances, pursue than that which they are now actually pursuing—namely, look out for alliances amongst communities similarly affected, to counteract a policy which aggrieved them?

Look, then, at the position in which we stand. We have abandoned all the objects for the sake of which our colonial empire was founded. We are unable to impress our will upon our colonies in any particular, however in itself reasonable, or just, or apparently necessary for their safety or ours. Wholly irrespective of our wishes, they enter into alliances, unite and separate, dispose of their lands, recast their constitutions, and even combine for the avowed purpose of thwarting our designs. When things have reached this pass, it seems rather idle to ask—Are we to retain our colonies? Retain our colonies! What is there left to retain? Retain the privilege of spending yearly £4,500,000 sterling on their protection, and receive in requital prohibitive tariffs and "ironical allegiance"! But I shall not be guilty of the presumption of venturing further into an argument which has already been exhausted by the writer who has made this subject his own. Two years have just passed since Professor Goldwin Smith, in a series of letters, which for argumentative ability, masculine eloquence, and satiric *verve*, have rarely been equalled in the literature of politics, forced this subject on the attention of the people of this country —forced it on their attention, let me say, with true patriotic boldness, at a time when "leading" journalists thought only of tabooing it as an inconvenient topic, and judicious politicians gladly avoided a question from which, while no political capital was to be gained, much unpopularity might easily be incurred. Professor Smith may congratulate himself upon a triumph speedier and more complete than often falls to the lot of political innovators. Before six months had passed, the Ionian Islands, if not in deference to his teaching, at all events in perfect conformity with the policy he had just propounded amid the all but universal protests of the Press, were conceded to Greece amid the not less general applause of the nation. This, it must be owned, is a singular testimony to political forecast; and the whole course of events in the two years that have since elapsed, has but served to strengthen it. Already some of our statesmen of greatest promise have given in their adhesion to his views;* and the "leading journal,"

---

* For example, Lord Stanley, in his recent speech at King's Lynn, thus expressed himself:—"In British North America there is a strong movement in progress in favour of federation, or rather of union in some shape. In Australia I believe the same feeling exists, but not so deeply; and though it has not assumed a practical form, I think that tendency ought to be encouraged in both one and the other case (hear, hear). *We know that those countries must before long be independent states.*

which rebuked him with even more than its wonted loftiness, now, with characteristic versatility, adopts his opinions as those "which have constantly found utterance in the *Times*." *

The British Empire—let me here state for what it is worth the conclusion to which serious reflection has guided me—the British Empire, such as it has

We have no interest except in their strength and well-being."—*Times*, 20th October, 1864.

* "The power we desire to exercise [over the North American colonies] is *entirely a moral one*, and, strong or weak, the dependency that wishes to quit us, *has only solemnly to make up its mind to this effect*. . . . . The Admiral was severe on those who entertain the opinions which have constantly found utterance in the *Times*, that the colonies and the mother country will cease to be united when the common interest ceases."—*Times*, 15th October, 1864.

A union between political societies, based upon community of interest, to be dissolved at the wish of either party, and to be enforced exclusively by moral sanctions—this (by whatever name it may be called) constitutes in fact an alliance between independent nations, not the relation of an imperial to a dependent state. (See Austin's "Jurisprudence," vol. i. pp. 208, 209, and Lewis's "Government of Dependencies," pp. 2, 3.) Such was the relation subsisting between the states of ancient Greece and their independent colonies; such is that into which any two sovereign states of Europe may at any time enter, without derogation from the sovereignty of either; and such, in fine, has been that which has been contemplated and distinctly described by those who have advocated "colonial emancipation."

The form in which, two years ago, the above opinions "found utterance in the *Times*" was as follows:—". We may as well declare at once, for the benefit of Americans and Spaniards, Russians and Ionians, Sikhs and Sepoys, that England has no thought of abandoning her transmarine possessions;" and then, with a delicate allusion to the moral force doctrine, "So far from believing in her own decline, England believes that she was *never more powerful than now, or more capable of holding what she has won*."—*Times*, 4th February, 1862. It is true the writer, at the conclusion of a long tirade conceived in this spirit, adds the remark:—"No one, we believe, in this country desires to keep them against their will." But this is merely a specimen of the self-stultification into which writers fall, who, without any clear and self-consistent view, charge themselves with the task of finding arguments in defence of prevailing prejudices.

hitherto been known in the world, has reached its natural goal. That British power, or that the influence of British ideas, will in consequence suffer declension, is what at least I, for one, do not believe. Contemplating our career, as a whole, it seems to me that we have outgrown the restraints and supports of our earlier state, and are now passing into a new phase of existence. Instead of a great political, we shall be a great moral, unity;* bound together no longer indeed by Imperial ligaments supplied from the Colonial Office, but by the stronger bonds of blood, language, and religion—by the common inheritance of laws fitted for free men, and of a literature rich in all that can keep alive the associations of our common glory in the past. Thus sustained and thus united, each member of the great whole will enter without hindrance the path to which its position and opportunities invite it; while all will co-operate in the same work of industrial, social, and moral progress; exchanging freely—let us hope, in spite of some present indications to the contrary—exchanging freely our products and our ideas—in peace good friends and customers, and firm allies in war.

---

* "If people want a grand moral unity, they must seek it in the moral and intellectual sphere. Religion knows no impediment of distance. The dominions of science are divided by no sea. To restore, or pave the way for restoring, the unity of long-divided Christendom, may seem the most chimerical of all aspirations, yet perhaps it may be less chimerical than the project of founding a world-wide state."—*The Empire*, p. 86.

II.

THE REVOLUTION IN AMERICA.*

It is with feelings of no ordinary diffidence that I appear before you this evening—diffidence inspired at once by the distinguished audience in whose presence I find myself, and by the topic which I have undertaken to treat. For I am not ignorant that I now address an audience whose ears have become familiar with strains of eloquence, such as I can have no pretensions to utter; and I know that I have to deal with a topic, not only of extreme importance and delicacy, but one respecting which the sympathies of the public have already taken a decided course, and that course in a direction, I deeply regret to think, the reverse of that in which my own sympathies run. So strongly, indeed, do I feel the force of this consideration, that, were I to consult my own taste merely, " the Revolution in America " is certainly not the subject which I should have selected for this occasion. It has, however, been intimated to me that it is the wish of your Association that I should address you

* A Lecture delivered before the Dublin Young Men's Christian Association, October 1862.

upon this question; and, under these circumstances, I do not conceive—the question being one to which I have given some study—that I should be justified in resisting your flattering request. I propose, therefore, to bring under your notice this evening the Revolution in America. I undertake the task—I say it with the most unaffected sincerity—with a profound sense of my own utter inability to do it justice, but still with a hope that I may say enough to induce some of those who hear me to reconsider their opinions; and I do so in the full confidence that I shall receive at your hands that indulgence which an honest attempt to speak the truth on an important subject seldom fails to meet with in an Irish assembly.

It will, I think, conduce to a clearer apprehension of what is to follow, if here, at the outset, I state frankly the conclusions which I have myself come to respecting the matter in hand. I hold, then, that the present convulsion in America is the natural fruit and inevitable consequence of the existence of slavery in that continent; and, as slavery has been the cause of the outbreak, so I conceive slavery is the stake which is really at issue in the struggle. I hold that the success of the North means, if not the immediate emancipation of slaves, at least the immediate arrest of slavery, and, with its immediate arrest, the certainty of its ultimate extinction; and, on the other hand, that the success of the South means the establishment of slavery on a broader and firmer basis than has hitherto sustained it, combined with a menace of its future indefinite extension. I hold, moreover, that the form of society which has been reared on slavery in the Southern

States is substantially a new fact in history—being in its nature at once retrograde and aggressive; retrograde as regards the human constituents which compose it, and aggressive as regards all other forms of social life with which it may come in contact—a system of society which combines the strength of civilization with all the evil instincts of barbarism. Such, I conceive, is the phenomenon now presented by the Southern Confederacy: and the struggle which we witness is but the effort of this new and formidable monster to disengage itself from the restraints which free society in self-defence was drawing around it, in order to secure for its development an unbounded field.

These, in few words, are the conclusions at which I have arrived on this momentous matter. I shall now proceed to state, as succinctly as I can, the considerations by which I have been led to them.

I maintain, then, in the first place, that the war has had its origin in slavery; and, in support of this statement, I appeal to the whole past history of the United States, and to the explicit declarations of the Confederate leaders themselves. What has been the history of the United States for the last fifty years? It has been little more than a record of aggressions made by the power which represents slavery, feebly, and almost always unsuccessfully, resisted by the Free States, and culminating in the present war. The question between North and South is constantly stated here as if it was the North which was the aggressive party—as if the North had been pursuing towards the Southern people a career of encroachment and oppression, which had reached its climax in Mr. Lincoln's election; and as if the act of secession were but an act of self-defence, forced upon a reluctant people whose measure of humiliation was full.

Now the facts of the case are precisely the reverse of this. It is not the North, but the South, which for half a century has predominated in the Union. It is not the South, but the North, which has drunk the cup of humiliation. Southern men and Northern nominees of Southern men have filled the President's chair, have monopolized the offices of state, have represented the country at foreign courts, and have shaped the whole policy of the Union. The whole course of domestic policy in the United States, from the passing of the Missouri compromise to its repeal, and from its repeal to the conspiracy of secession, hatched under Mr. Buchanan's government, and carried out by men who had sworn allegiance to the Union, has been directed to the same end—the aggrandizement of Southern interests and the consolidation of Southern power. And such as its domestic policy has been, such also has been its foreign policy. That policy is written in the Seminole war, in the annexation of Texas, in the conquest of half of Mexico, in lawless attempts upon Cuba, in the invasion of peaceful states in Central America, in the defence of the slave trade against the vigilance of British cruisers. Wherever we turn, there is the same restless and aggressive spirit at work, employing now intrigue and now violence, now conniving at filibustering raids, and now waging open war, and always in the same cause—the cause of the South and of slavery. It is to this end that for half a century the whole power and influence of the United States have been directed; and let us observe with what results. In 1790, three years after the Union was established, the Slave States comprised an area of 250,000 square miles; in 1860 that area had grown to 851,000 square miles. In 1790 the number of slaves in the Union was less than three-quarters of a million; in 1860 that number had increased to upwards of four millions.

Such has been the material progress of the Southern institution; and still more striking has been its progress as a political and social power. When the Union was founded, slavery was dying out in the North, and was looked upon as doomed in the South. It was tolerated, indeed, in consideration of the important interests which it involved, but tolerated with shame. The very name excluded from the public documents, and the thing itself absolutely prohibited in those districts in which it was not already actually established—it was, in all the circumstances of its treatment, branded as plainly at variance with the fundamental principles of the Republic. This was the position of slavery, in a moral and political point of view, when the Union was founded; but what is its position when the Union is dissolved? No longer content with a local toleration as an exceptional and tabooed system, it claims a free career over the area of a continent; it aspires to become the basis of a new order of political fabric, and boldly puts itself forth as a model for the imitation of the world.

The struggle, therefore, which now convulses America, is not the struggle of an oppressed people rising against its oppressors, but the revolt of a party which has long ruled a great republic to retrieve by arms a political defeat—the rising of the apostles of a principle, which has long been working its way to supremacy, to consummate a long series of triumphs by a last effective blow.

I have said that the purpose of the Southern revolt is to establish a new order of political edifice, of which slavery is to be the basis. This statement is, I am aware, vehemently denied in this country; but on this point it is for yourselves to decide between the declarations of the Confederate leaders, addressed to their own countrymen, and those of writers who on this side of the Atlantic, and before an English audience, advocate their cause. I hold in my hand a paper of rather curious significance : it is entitled the " Philosophy of Secession." It is from the pen of an eminent Southern, the Hon. L. W. Spratt of South Carolina, a gentleman who has for some years taken a prominent part in the political affairs of the South. Mr. Spratt is the editor of the *Charleston Mercury*, one of the most influential papers in the South, if not the most influential. He represented Charleston in that South Carolina Convention which first gave the watchword of secession; and the confidence reposed in him by the people of South Carolina may be inferred from the fact, that he was one of the commissioners appointed by that—the leading secession State—in the most critical juncture of its history, to expound its views before the other insurgent Conventions. The Hon. Mr. Spratt, occupying this position, may, I think, be taken to speak the views of the South with some authority. I ask you, then, to attend to Mr. Spratt's exposition of the cause at stake in the present war.

"The South," says Mr. Spratt, "is now in the formation of a Slave republic. This, perhaps, is not admitted generally. There are many contented to believe that the South, as a geographical section, is in mere assertion of its independence; that it is instinct with no especial truth—pregnant of no distinct social nature; that for some unaccountable reason the two sections have become opposed to each other; that, for reasons equally insufficient, there is a disagreement between the peoples that direct them; and that from no overruling necessity, no impossibility of co-existence, but as a mere matter of policy, it has been considered best for the South to strike out for herself and establish an independence of her own. This, I fear, is an inadequate conception of the controversy.

"The contest is not between the North and South as geographical sections, for between such sections merely there can be no contest; nor between the people of the North and the people of the South, for our relations have been pleasant, and on neutral grounds there is still nothing to estrange us. We eat together, trade together, and practise yet in intercourse, with great respect, the courtesies of common life. But the real contest is between *the two forms of society* which have become established, the one at the North and the other at the South. Society is essentially different from government—as different as is the nut from the bur, or the nervous body of the shell-fish from the bony structure which surrounds it; and within this government two societies had become developed as variant in structure and distinct in form as any two beings in animated nature. The one is a society composed of one race, the other of two races. The one is bound together but by the two great social relations of husband and wife and parent and child; the other by the three relations of husband and wife, parent and child, and master and slave. The one embodies in its political structure that equality is the right of man; the other that it is the right of equals only. The one, embodying the principle that equality is the right of man, expands upon the horizontal plane of pure democracy; the other, embodying the principle that it is not the right of man but of equals only, has taken to itself the rounded form of a social aristocracy. . . . . Such are the two forms of society which had come to contest within the structure of the recent Union. And the contest for existence was inevitable. Neither could concur in the requisitions of the other; neither could expand within the forms of a single government without encroachment on the other. . . . . The slave trade suppressed, democratic society has triumphed. More than five millions from abroad have been added to their number; that addition has enabled them to grasp and hold the government. That government, from the very necessities of their nature, they are forced to use against us. Slavery was within its grasp, and, forced to the option of extinction in the Union, or of independence out, *it dares to strike, and it asserts its claim to nationality* and its right to recognition among the leading social systems of the world. Such, then, being the nature of the contest, this Union has been disrupted in the effort of slave society to emancipate itself." *

The object of the South, then, is to found a Slave republic—a republic which has taken to itself "the rounded form of a social aristocracy." But there is one feature in the prospective policy of this Slave aristocracy upon which the "Philosophy of Secession," as expounded by Mr. Spratt, throws so strong a light, that I must avail myself of one more quotation before taking leave of his able essay—I mean the position taken by the Confederacy with reference to the African slave trade. We all know that the Mont-

* " The new constitution has put at rest for ever all agitating questions relating to our peculiar institution—African slavery as it exists among us—the proper status of the negro in our form of civilization. *This was the immediate cause of the late rupture and present revolution.*" (Mr. A. H. Stephens, Vice-President of the Southern Confederation.)

gomery Convention, in drawing up the Southern constitution, introduced a clause prohibiting this trade. There are writers in this country who would have us believe that this prohibition is conclusive as to the views of the Southern leaders on this subject. But, knowing something of the history of this Southern party, and of the circumstances under which this constitution was drawn up, I confess that I, for one, have always had considerable doubts as to the *bona fides* of this prohibition, and these doubts have not been removed by the speculations of Mr. Spratt. "Then why adopt this measure?" he asks. "Is it that Virginia and the other Border States require it? They may require it now, but is it certain they will continue to require it? . . . . It may be said that without such a general restriction the value of their slaves will be diminished in the markets of the West. *They have no right to ask that their slaves, or any other products, shall be protected to unnatural value in the markets of the West.* If they persist in regarding the negro but as a thing of trade—a thing which they are too good to use, but only can produce for others' uses—and join the Confederacy, as Pennsylvania or Massachusetts might do, not to support the structure, but to profit by it, it were as well they should not join, and we can find no interest in such association." . . . . And then, referring to what was well understood to be the other reason for the prohibitory clause—the desire to conciliate European support—Mr. Spratt thus expresses himself:—

"They (the European nations) will submit to any terms of intercourse with the Slave Republic in consideration of its markets and its products. An increase of slaves will increase the market and supply. They will pocket their philanthropy and the profits together. And so solicitude as to the feeling of foreign States upon this subject is gratuitous : and so it is that our suppression of the slave trade is warranted by no necessity to respect the sentiment of foreign States. . . . . I truly think we want more slaves. We want them to the proper cultivation of our soil, to the just development of our resources, and to the proper constitution of society. Even in this State I think we want them ; of eighteen million acres of land, less than four million are in cultivation. We have no seamen for our commerce, if we had it, and no operatives for the arts ; but it is not for that I now oppose restrictions on the slave trade. I oppose them from the wish to emancipate our institution. *I regard the slave trade as the test of its integrity. If that be right, then slavery is right, but not without;* and I have been too clear in my perceptions of the claims of that great institution—too assured of the failure of antagonist democracy, too convinced the one presents the conditions of social order, too convinced the other does not, and too convinced, therefore, that the one must stand while the other falls—to abate my efforts or pretermit the means by which it may be brought to recognition and establishment.

"Believing, then, that this is a test of slavery, and that the institution cannot be right if the trade be not, I regard the constitutional prohibition as a great calamity. . . . . I was the single advocate of the slave trade in 1853 ; *it is now the question of the time.*" *

* " Now, if that," said the Hon. Andrew Jackson Hamilton, of Texas, in a recent speech at New York, referring to Mr. Spratt's essay, "was but the sentiment of one Southern man, addressed to a trusted agent of the State of Louisiana, then a sitting member in the Convention, there might be but little practical significance in it. If it had been reprobated by the public press in that section, or condemned by the public voice, there might be little significance in the fact that such sentiments were promulgated to the world. But when you bear in mind that that letter was reproduced in the leading prints of the South, and spoken of in terms of commendation, and that up to this hour no man has lifted his voice in criticism against any of the positions there assumed, then it is significant. I have heard the echoes of those sentiments in the streets, in the hotels, in the parlours, and at the festive board."

So far the representative man of the leading secession State—the exponent of the "philosophy of secession." And now I will ask you to observe how fully these doctrines have been accepted by the men who have been entrusted with the actual guidance of this movement. Mr. A. H. Stephens, the Vice-President of the Confederacy, thus states the principles on which it has been founded:—

"The ideas entertained at the formation of the old Constitution," says Mr. Stephens, "were that the enslavement of the African race was in violation of the laws of nature; that it was wrong in principle, socially, morally, politically. *Our new government is founded on exactly opposite ideas;* its foundations are laid, its corner-stone rests, upon the great truth, that the negro is not equal to the white man; that slavery—subordination to the superior race—is his natural and moral condition. *This our government is the first in the history of the world based upon this great physical, philosophical, and moral truth.* It is upon this that our social fabric is firmly planted; and I cannot permit myself to doubt the ultimate success and the full recognition of this principle throughout the civilized and enlightened world. . . . . This stone which was rejected by the first builders 'is become the chief stone' in our edifice."

We are told by those who, in this country, advocate the immediate recognition of the South, that we should not be deterred from this course by the circumstance that the South is a slave power. "A slave power!" they exclaim. "Was not the United States a slave power? Is not Spain a slave power? Is not Brazil a slave power? And have we not recognized these? Why, then, should we now become all at once so scrupulous?" This is the position taken by the admirers of the South in England; but it is evident it is not the position taken by the statesmen who now govern the South. "*Our new government,*" says the Vice-President of the Confederacy, "*is founded upon exactly opposite ideas*" to those which presided at the founding of the Union. "This *our government is the first in the history of the world based upon the great physical, philosophical, and moral truth*"—the lie embodied in slavery. In other words, slavery has before existed, but it has never before been propounded as a fundamental principle of social and political life; it has never before been preached as a gospel; it has existed, but it has never before been taken as the corner stone of an empire. This it is which, as set forth by its own Vice-President (whose statement of the case I prefer to English glosses)—this it is, I say, which separates the Southern Confederacy from all previous, and from all existing, examples of communities tolerating slavery, which renders it a new fact in history, and constitutes it unequivocally the one Slave Power in the world.

I say, then, that the present convulsion in America has originated in the exigencies of slavery; and that the stake at issue in the struggle is the existence of a Slave Empire, founded upon principles of policy now propounded for the first time in the history of the world. A year or two ago I should have thought that, having established this, I had sufficiently established my case; and that a dozen men in the British Islands could not be found who would express open sympathy with a body convicted of such designs. But really it seems to me that a singular change has, in relation to this subject, passed over the minds of my countrymen. I do not mean to say that there is any considerable number of persons in these countries, much less that there are any among my present audience, who regard slavery with positive favour; but I do say that public feeling on the subject is not what it used to be. I find a disposition in high quarters—among eminent public men, and some of our most influential organs of public opinion—a disposition to evade this aspect of the case, or, where it is met, to palliate it—a tone of apology, in short, assumed towards slavery to which British ears have not hitherto been accustomed. "The Negroes," says the *Saturday Review*, in a recent number (Oct. 11, 1862), "have been slaves for generations. They are used to slavery, and, for the most part, contented with it. They are plentifully fed, for food is cheap and abundant; and even their legal allowance is more than they can possibly eat. They are well housed—as racehorses or hunters are well housed in this country—because they are costly chattels. They are well clothed as the climate requires. In a word, the vast majority of them have no grievance whatever except in the fact that they are slaves"— a grievance, it would seem, which is not worth speaking of; for, says this elevated moralist and edifying public instructor, "that grievance is one which few of them are thoughtful enough to feel."

This is the language in which slavery is now discussed by writers who command the ear of cultivated England. The slaves are well off—well fed, clothed, and housed, and what more would you have?* They have no grievance whatever except in the fact that they are slaves, which after all, it seems, is not a grievance, since they are not thoughtful enough to feel it; in other words, it comes to this, that four millions of the African race,—a race capable—as we know from the testimony of competent witnesses to their condition in our own West India Islands, from the results of the mixed schools in New England, and from occasional instances which come under our observation in this country—not merely of feeling the obligations and performing the duties of rational creatures, but of receiving a very considerable amount of intellectual cultivation,—that four millions, I say, of these people, thus capable of human destiny, have, under the system of the South, been reduced to a condition in which they are simply brutes, with the instincts of brutes, and with no aspiration beyond the aspiration of the brute. This is the cool admission of a writer whose object is—for this is the important point—not to discredit, but to do honour to, Southern slavery,—of a vehement admirer and thorough-going

---

* In truth, however, the facts are very far from being as the apologists of slavery represent them. Commenting on the 38th section of the South Carolinian Act of 1740, which requires the owners of slaves to provide them with sufficient clothing, covering, and food, the Hon. Judge O'Neal, of South Carolina, a slaveholder and advocate of slavery, but more alive to its evils, it would seem, than some Englishmen, remarks:—"This provision is a very wise and humane one, except that the penalty is entirely too slight. I regret to say that *there is in such a State as ours, great occasion for the enforcement of such a law, accompanied by severe penalties.*" It seems then, that, in the opinion of those who are best qualified to judge, some other security for the physical comfort of the negro is needed, than the self-interest or the humanity of the master. No such remark as the above would be applicable to the treatment of racehorses and hunters in this country.

partisan of the Southern Confederacy, who seeks, by the description which I have quoted, to conciliate public favour towards the institution which he thus describes. But my present hearers will, I doubt not, disclaim the morality of the *Saturday Review*. Public sentiment on this as on many other subjects has not yet, thank God, reached the high level of that adventurous guide.* Still it is important to note the extreme line that the wave has yet touched; and if opinion still falls short of the sentiments I have quoted, I think most candid persons will admit that it has, at least, been moving in that direction. No doubt, it is common to hear the disclaimer—" Of course we don't approve of slavery!" but I think it will generally be found that this is but the prelude to a discourse showing how much is to be said for the institution, and winding up with a warning as to the dangers of premature emancipation. Yes! the bugbear of "premature emancipation" is fast becoming to the popular mind more frightful than the fact of ripe and flourishing slavery; and the danger which Englishmen are now learning above all others to dread, is, lest slaves should be liberated one moment too soon. This, it seems to me, is becoming the prevalent feeling with reference to slavery; and I cannot, therefore, deem it superfluous to call attention for a few moments to the character of the institution towards which this feeling of toleration, if not

---

* Since the above was written, I find that this journal has made another step forward. It now ranks the emancipation of slaves with the most horrible crimes. "They (the Democratic party) will have no emancipation, no confiscation, no murders in cold blood."—*Saturday Review*, Nov. 22, 1862.

of countenance and encouragement, is rapidly growing up.

What, then, is the character of slavery as it exists in the Southern States of North America? It is a system under which men and women, boys and girls, are exposed like cattle in the market-place, and are bought and sold. It is a system under which a whole race of men is deprived of all the rights and privileges of rational creatures, and consigned to a life of hopeless, unremitting toil, in order that another race may live in idleness on the fruits of its labours. It is a system under which, if we are to believe its admirers, the Negroes are perfectly contented, but from which they are constantly escaping in spite of the terrors of fugitive slave laws, of bloodhounds and man-hunters—a paradise, if you will, but a paradise from which its denizens escape to the dismal swamp*—a paradise to which no

---

* "The dismal swamps are noted places of refuge for runaway negroes. They were formerly peopled in this way much more than at present; a systematic hunting with dogs and guns having been made by individuals who took it up as a business about ten years ago. Children were born, bred, lived, and died here. Joseph Church told me he had seen skeletons, and had helped to bury bodies recently dead. There were people in the swamps still, he thought, that were the children of the runaways, and who had been runaways themselves all their lives. What a life it must be: born outlaws; educated self-stealers; trained from infancy to be constantly in dread of the approach of a white man as a thing more fearful than wild cats and serpents, even starvation. . . . I asked if they were ever shot. 'Oh, yes,' he said, 'when the hunters saw a runaway, if he tried to get from them, they would call out to him that if he did not stop they would shoot; and if he did not, they would shoot, and sometimes kill him. But some on 'em would rather be shot than took, sir,' he added simply. A farmer living near the swamp confirmed this account, and said he knew of three or four being shot in one day!"—OLMSTED, *Seaboard Slave States*, pp. 159, 160.

fugitive Negro, who has once escaped from it, has ever yet been known to return. Under this system a human being, convicted of no crime, may, in strict conformity with the law, be flogged at the discretion of his fellow, and may even die under the lash without entailing any penalty on his murderer. Under this system human beings may be, and within the last ten years have been, in several instances, burned alive. All property is for the Negro contraband; the acquisition of knowledge is for him a penal offence. The marriage tie receives no legal recognition, and no practical respect. Nay, it is worse than this! Those consequences, which in civilized communities form the natural restraints on unlicensed desire, are here converted into incentives; for the relation between father and son is, in the presence of slavery, less sacred than that between master and slave; and the mulatto offspring of a white father is not a child but a chattel: instead of entailing responsibilities it brings to the author of its being so many dollars as a price. Yes, I say that the laws of the Southern States permit fathers to enslave and sell their children, and that there are fathers in the Southern States who freely avail themselves of this law.* Do you

---

* "It is a general custom of white people here to leave their illegitimate children of slaves (and they are *very* common) in slavery. A man of wealth and station, who enjoys the friendship of the best and most respected people, lately sold his own half-brother, an intelligent, and of course valuable young man, to the traders to be sold South, because he had attempted to run away to the Free States."—OLMSTED, *Seaboard Slave States*, p. 127.

"'There is not,' said another planter, 'a likely-looking black girl in this State that is not the paramour of a white man. There is not an old plantation in which the grand-children of the owner are not whipped

doubt it? Then account for the mulattoes, quadroons, and octoroons—many of them scarcely distinguishable in colour from Europeans—who now form so large a proportion of the whole enslaved population of the South. From what source has this European blood flowed into servile veins? From whence, but from the white caste in the South?—from the men who commit their own flesh and blood to the charge of the brutal overseer, or to the more brutal trader in human flesh. This is an aspect of the case which I would gladly have passed by; but, in the present state of opinion, the facts are too serious to be blinked; and before the people of this country, which has achieved its best renown in ridding its own lands of this curse, be committed to the countenance and support of a power, the final cause of whose existence is to extend this very evil, it is important that we should understand what the cause is that we are assisting to sustain.

We hear much in these times of the "chivalry" of the South. The Southerns, we are told, are gentlemen, and on this ground they are contrasted favourably with the shopkeepers, the traders, and the lawyers of the North. I shall certainly not deny that the wealthier classes in the South possess in a high degree those qualities which the principle of caste tends to engender—pride, courage, loyalty to the interests of their order, capacity for government, perseverance in

---

in the field by his overseer. I cannot bear that the blood of the ———— should run in the veins of the slaves.' He was of an old Scotch family. .... He said the practice was not occasional or general, it was universal."—OLMSTED, *Seaboard Slave States*, p. 602.

a fixed course of policy. Nay, even as regards the chivalry and gentility—these being points about which our notions are somewhat vague, and on which opinions are apt to differ—I shall not undertake to say that the South does not possess them. I only ask you to remember that the chivalry and gentility of the South is not incompatible with the systematic appropriation of the fruits of another's labour, with laying the whip on the shoulders of a woman—with acts, that is to say, which called down on Marshal Haynau the indignation of the London draymen; with turning one's own flesh and blood to pecuniary profit; or, to give a particular illustration, with such atrocities as that committed by a Southern gentleman on the person of Mr. Sumner. The story is an old one, and probably familiar to many whom I address, but it throws so much light on the manners of the gentle and chivalrous South, that I must tell it once again. In 1856, when opposing the introduction of slavery into Kansas, Mr. Sumner made in the Senate of the United States, as senator for Massachusetts, one of the most powerful speeches ever delivered in any legislative assembly. In this speech he denounced the policy and aims of the Slave Power in language which was plain and outspoken, but which did not pass what in this country is considered the legitimate limit of parliamentary debate. The adherents of the South were fiercely exasperated; and how did Southern chivalry take its revenge? Two days afterwards, as Mr. Sumner sat at his desk in the Senate House, the House having adjourned, engaged in writing a letter, and with his head bent over his paper, he was approached by Mr. Brooks, the representative of South Carolina. Mr. Brooks addressed him: " I have read your speech, and it is a libel on the South ;" and forthwith, while the words were yet passing from his lips, and before Mr. Sumner could rise from his seat, commenced a succession of blows on his bare head with a heavy cane. Mr. Sumner was immediately stunned, and fell upon the floor: his assailant stood over him, and continued the assault. Blow after blow fell upon his defenceless head. There were senators of the South present, and there was one senator from the North—Mr. Douglas of Illinois—a democratic politician and close ally of the South; but there was no interference. One old man, indeed, did interfere a little towards the close, but for that little he was threatened with chastisement on the spot. The scene proceeded to its close, Mr. Brooks desisting just before murder was accomplished. This is the mode in which the South avenges its grievances: this is its notion of parliamentary fence. But the important point is the mode in which the outrage was received by the Southern people. Not one press south of the Potomac condemned the act; not one public body, not one public man, condemned it. Not one word of reprobation, or even of rebuke, came from any quarter of the South. On the contrary, it was universally hailed as a proper manifestation of Southern spirit: it was recognized as a sample of the policy which the times required ; and, not the men of the South only, but the women of the South, combined to heap commendation, honour, and reward upon the perpetrator.

So far as to the character and aims of the Southern

Confederacy. Let me now endeavour to state the nature of that political movement which has brought the Free States and the South into collision. And here you will of course understand that I cannot pretend to do more than to give the barest outline of the case. At every step I encounter events which deserve description, and questions which need explanation—I leave difficulties unsolved and objections unanswered. I cannot help it. The utmost I can hope to do in the brief time during which I can venture to occupy your attention, is to touch on a few salient points of the picture, and thus to convey a general notion of the drift and meaning of the whole.

To understand the influences which now agitate Northern society, to appreciate the significance of the part which the North has already acted in this great drama and the results towards which it is tending, the first capital fact to be seized is, that the movement of which we now contemplate the results—the movement which carried Mr. Lincoln to power, and of which the success was the signal for secession—that this movement is a reaction against the influences which had previously been supreme in the Union.

As I have already stated, from 1820 down to the present outbreak, the government of the United States has, with the exception of a few short intervals, been in the hands of a party composed of Southern politicians, and of a section in the North, which, for political purposes, may be regarded as Southern—the Northern democrats. Of this political combination, I do not overstate the case when I say that its leading idea, its paramount aim, almost its single purpose, was to extend slavery, and to achieve political power by extending it. Under the influence of this party, political life had suffered a blight, such as in no country it had ever before undergone in the same space of time: political morality had deteriorated; the intellect of political men had waned; political honesty was scarcely to be found; politics had become a by-word; and, in spite of a material prosperity which dazzled the world, the United States in all the qualities which make a nation respected and honoured had visibly declined. Down to 1855 this progress towards ruin encountered no serious obstruction; but in that year the evil at length began to work its own cure. The excesses of the dominant party, the shameless doctrines which it advanced, the still more shameless deeds which it perpetrated, awoke the best minds in the United States to a sense of the fearful descent down which they were hurrying—of the certain perdition which lay ahead. A reaction in public feeling at this point took place. The Republican party was formed. From that time to the present the influences which produced this party have been gathering strength. It is this party which carried Mr. Lincoln to power, and it is the same which is now rapidly transforming the whole policy of the Republic.

It is important that we should understand the principles of this Republican party; for they are those which have shaped the Federal policy for the last two years, and may determine it for many years to come. Those principles were such as the attitude assumed by the Republicans, as the opponents of the policy of the South, naturally called for; and therefore, to appreciate the Republican position, it will be necessary to advert briefly to the course which Southern policy had previously pursued.

And first, you must bear in mind that the question at issue in the past contests respecting slavery in the United States, has not been, as is frequently supposed in this country, whether slavery should be abolished or maintained, but whether it should be restricted to its present limits or extended. From the foundation of the Union down to the present hour,—or more correctly, down to the recent proclamation of Mr. Lincoln,—no considerable politician has proposed to interfere with slavery in the States where it is already established.* All the efforts of the party opposed to slavery on the one hand, and of the Slave party on the other, have been directed exclusively to the "territories," as the field of their opposing principles. And here I must interrupt my statement for a moment, to explain, for the benefit of those who have not paid much attention to American politics, the peculiar signification which the word "territory" bears in the United States. In the political nomenclature of the United States, "territory" does not signify what it signifies with us—simply the area of a country, but a certain portion only of that area existing under certain conditions; these conditions being, that society in it

---

* Even the abolitionists shrunk from going this length: their programme was—the abolition of slavery in the district of Columbia, and wherever else the Federal authority is competent to abolish it; and as regards the rest,—that is, the States where slavery is already established— separation. The language of Southern politicians would indeed frequently suggest that the aim of the anti-slavery party went the length of complete abolition; but it is well known that this language is used merely for the purposes of agitation. No educated man in the South believes it.

should not yet have been organized under a distinct local government subordinate to the general government of the United States, and called a "state" government. A "territory," in short, is a portion of the domain of the Union which is not yet a "state." Thus in the political discussions of the United States, "territory" is always opposed to "state;" a "state" being for all local purposes under its own government, while a "territory," having no local government, comes directly for all purposes whatever under the control of the Central or Federal authority.* The "territories" are in short the unsettled portions of the public domain—those vast regions which, beyond the line of the States, stretch away to the Pacific. Now it is this portion of the domain of the United States which has always formed the battle-ground of the contending forces of slavery and freedom; and I have now to call your attention to the series of pretensions advanced by the Slave party in its attempts upon these possessions.

When the Union was founded, as I have already intimated, the Slave interest was content with a merely local toleration. Over the districts owned by the state authorities it was permitted, at the discretion of those authorities, to extend itself; but from that which was properly the public domain—from that portion of the country which belonged, not to the particular States, but to the Central Government—slavery was

* Constitution of the United States, art. iv. sec. 3. "With respect to the vast territories belonging to the United States, Congress has assumed to exercise over them supreme powers of sovereignty. Exclusive and unlimited power is given to Congress by the Constitution, and sanctioned by judicial decisions." *Kent's Commentaries,* vol. i. p. 422.

absolutely excluded. What renders the case more striking is, that the whole of this land, then known as the "North-western territory," had been ceded to the central authority by a Slave state—the State of Virginia; while the first resolution providing for its government, and which contained the anti-slavery clause which was subsequently enacted, was brought forward by a native of the same state, Jefferson, himself not merely a. Southern, but a slaveholder. If in those times the Slave party entertained the pretension which they have recently advanced, of making slavery a *national* institution, and securing for it protection in all parts of the Union, this would have been a favourable opportunity for advancing such a claim. But no such claim was advanced. On the contrary, the leading statesman of the leading Slave state took the initiative in proposing that slavery should be for ever excluded from all the "territories" of the Union. Jefferson's resolution was lost; but within three years the celebrated Ordinance of 1787, containing the anti-slavery clause, was passed, and passed unanimously, securing to freedom the whole of the vast region to which it applied. It thus appears that, at the opening of the United States history, the Slave party was content with a local toleration. It advanced no pretensions on the "territories" of the Union.*

At an early period in the present century, however,

---

* " In the territories north-west of the river Ohio, and as separate territories were successively formed, Congress adopted and applied the principles of the ordinance of the Confederation Congress of the date of the 13th July, 1787. That ordinance was framed upon sound and enlightened maxims of civil jurisprudence."—*Kent's Commentaries*, vol. i. pp. 423-4.

we find a change in this state of things. With a vast extension of the cotton cultivation, Slave interest in the Republic rapidly grew; new Slave states were created; and by 1818 the pretension was openly advanced to carry slavery without restriction into the "territories." The form in which this pretension was brought forward was in the demand for the admission of Missouri to the Union as a Slave state. The demand called forth strong opposition in the Northern States; a violent political contest ensued; and the result was a compromise—the celebrated "Missouri compromise"—under which the Slave party gained its immediate object,—the admission of Missouri, but on the express condition, that in future, slavery should not be introduced into the "territories" north of a certain parallel of latitude. This was the first great achievement of the Slave party. It amounted practically to a division of the then "territories" of the Republic between freedom and slavery. In this position the question remained till about the year 1850, at which time the entire of the territory which, under the Missouri compromise, fell to the share of the South having been appropriated, the determination was formed to repeal the Missouri compromise, with a view to the extension of slavery into the portion of the territory reserved by that compact to the Free States. The Missouri compromise, therefore, was denounced by the South as "unconstitutional;" and the doctrine was advanced that the proper arbiters for determining the question of slavery or no-slavery in the "territories," were, not the Federal Government, but the settlers. To this doctrine was given the appropriate name of "Squatter Sovereignty;" and a bill embodying it was introduced and passed in 1854,—a bill, by which the unsettled lands were virtually thrown open to be scrambled for by the contending parties. This was the second step accomplished by the Slave Power in its career of aggression. The "territories," which had originally been the exclusive field of freedom, and which had afterwards been divided between the opposing claimants, were now thrown open to slavery throughout their whole extent.

The prospects of slavery were now promising, yet the hoped-for results were not realized. The measure of 1854, though it threw open the "territories" to slavery, did not go the length of establishing slavery in those domains: it left this to be decided by the settlers; and on actual trial it was proved that, in the business of colonization, the Slave States were no match for the Free. The experiment was made, as is well known, in Kansas, and, in spite of the most unscrupulous use of every expedient which intrigue and armed violence, backed by the connivance of the Federal Government, then in the hands of the Southern party, could furnish, the defeat of the Slave party in its attempt to seize the "squatter sovereignty" was ignominious and complete.

There was need, therefore, once again to reconsider the situation. The doctrine of "squatter sovereignty" was accordingly without hesitation put aside, and in its place a new doctrine was propounded. A slave, it was said, is by the Constitution recognized as property; but property is property in one part of the Union as much as in another, and the first duty of government is to protect property, and to protect it wherever its jurisdiction extends. From these premises the conclusion was drawn that it was the duty of the Federal Government to protect slavery in all parts of the Union—in the "territories" as well as in the states, and in the Free States as well as in the Slave.

This was the last and culminating pretension of the Slave Power: it amounted to no less than a demand to convert the whole Union into one great slaveholding domain. Not only was this pretension advanced, but an important step was taken towards making it good. By dint of packing the courts of justice with Southern partisans, a decision was obtained from the Supreme Court of the United States—the notorious Dred Scott decision—which fully bore out the views of the Slave party. It was laid down, first, that there was no difference between a slave and other kinds of property; and secondly, that all American citizens might settle with their property in any part of the Union in which they pleased.

Something more, however, than a judicial decision was required to make good the designs of the Slave party. It had need of a government which should be prepared to act upon the principles thus enunciated. This it was which they resolved to obtain at the last presidential election; and it was because they failed in this object that secession was proclaimed.

You have now before you the career of aggression against which the Free States, under the lead of the Republican party, at length rose in resistance; and in view of this you will understand the position which this party assumed. As the aim of the South was slavery-extension, so the ground taken by the Republican party in its opposition to the South was the non-extension of slavery. I say the *non-extension*, not the *abolition* of slavery; for the Constitution had guaranteed slavery in the States where it already existed, and it was no part of the policy of the Republican party to violate the Constitution. Slavery, therefore, in the States was not directly threatened; but the doctrine of the Dred Scott decision was repudiated, and it was declared that for the future slavery should be excluded from all the "territories" of the Republic. This was the ground taken by the Republican party: it was on these principles that Mr. Lincoln was raised to power: and it was because these principles triumphed that the South seceded.

But here it will perhaps occur to some of those whom I address, that this Republican policy, after all, scarcely deserves the importance which I have attributed to it. Proposing merely to confine slavery within its present domain, it leaves the existing body of the evil, it will be thought, absolutely untouched— nay, under the Constitution, protected against all external assaults; so that, even supposing the Republicans triumphant, slavery would still remain erect and unassailable; and this view of the case may suggest the suspicion that such consequences as those which followed the Presidential contest can scarcely be due to a cause apparently so disproportioned to the alleged result as the policy which I have described.

But it will not be difficult to show that the Republican policy involves far more than at first meets the eye, and contains, in fact, quite enough to account for the explosion which followed its successful assertion. It is a fact, familiar to the people alike of the Free and of the Slave States, that for the profitable working of slavery, as it exists in the Southern States, a constant succession of fresh soils is a fundamental necessity. This is a consequence of the methods of cultivation practised under slavery—methods of cultivation, through the effect of which the soil, after a short series of years, becomes impoverished, necessitating the emigration of the planters with their slaves to new fields. Hence it follows, that, if slavery could only be confined permanently within its existing limits, a radical change in its industrial system would, after some time, be forced upon the South—a change which would involve, as its consequence, a substitution of free for servile labour. Now this would entail social as well as economical consequences, and would, in fact, be equivalent to the downfall of the social aristocracy of the South. Against this the whole body of slave-holders will, it may well be believed, strive as a single man. To accept the Republican policy would be for the slave-holders to sign the death-warrant of their system, and, with it, of their power. But, further, in addition to the economic effects of the Republican policy, it would have had certain political consequences, which, perhaps, were still more vividly present to the minds of the Southern leaders. Under the Constitution of the United States, the Senate is the most powerful branch of the Legislature. Representation in it is in proportion to States—each State, whatever its size or population, sending just two senators to Congress. Under these circumstances, supposing slavery to be confined permanently within the States where it at present exists, the representation of the Slave States in the Senate could never exceed its present number; and inasmuch as, with the growth of population in the Northern States, the number of Free States is constantly increasing, it is evident that, under the operation of the principle of restriction proposed by the Republican party, the political influence of the Free States would rapidly preponderate in the general government. Moderate, therefore, and almost timid, as seemed the programme of the Republicans, it nevertheless involved consequences for the South of the most serious moment. By prohibiting the creation of new Slave States, it repressed effectually the political influence of the Slave party in the Union; while, by confining slavery within its existing confines, it provided for its ultimate extinction even in those States where it is now established.*

Reverting, now, to the history of the movement, which we have carried up to the point at which the civil war broke out, I have to ask you to follow me while I indicate the course of the Northern policy, under the lead of the Republican party, since that time.

When the news of the impending outbreak first reached this country, the feeling of the public here,

---

* All this is fully recognized by the advocates of the South. "Although," says the Hon. James Williams, "it is not to be supposed that the object of the great body of Americans who are enlisted in that (the Anti-Slavery) conflict is primarily to achieve a triumph of their policy in the Republic, yet such would be the effect of a successful effort to impair by degrees, and finally to destroy, the institution of slavery in the Southern American States."—*The South Vindicated*, p. 53.

as you will doubtless remember, though not of a very energetic character, on the whole, went with the North. It being understood that a contest was about to break out between the Free and Slave States, it was at once assumed (naturally enough, considering that we were not at that time acquainted with the antecedents of the contest) that the North was taking up arms to put down slavery. A very short time was sufficient to dispel this illusion. One of Mr. Lincoln's first acts, upon entering on the government, was a declaration that he had no intention to interfere with slavery where it was established. By this avowal the flow of public sentiment favourable to the North was at once arrested. It was now assumed that the war was quite unconnected with slavery; and after a short period of hesitation, our sympathies, under the skilful management of certain Southern engineers, set steadily to the Southern side.

In view now of the facts of the case, as I have just recalled them to your recollection, I ask you if our early expectation was not unreasonable? And I will not shrink from also asking you if our later conclusion was not unjust? We expected that the North should at once have thrown itself into an anti-slavery crusade. Was this a reasonable expectation? Universal emancipation—the abolition of slavery in the States where it had been established—had never been any part of the Northern programme. On the contrary, the Republican party, of which Mr. Lincoln was the representative, though embarked in a policy which aimed at the immediate restriction, and threatened in its ultimate results the very existence, of slavery

—a policy which those who were most concerned, the slaveholders, at once recognized as fatal—had always disavowed this design,—had always declared its determination to abide-by the Constitution. I might perhaps even go further than this, and with the fuller knowledge of the case which we have since acquired, I think I might ask you, whether, at the stage of the business which we are now considering—while civil war was yet but pending, while the chance still remained of accomplishing the desired object by peaceable and constitutional means—it would have been wise, whether it would have been justifiable, to have resorted at once to revolutionary measures, and to have put forward a manifesto which must inevitably have had the effect of rendering peaceful emancipation impossible?

But, secondly, I will ask you if our later conclusion was not unjust? It is true, the North did not take up arms directly and explicitly to abolish slavery. It took up arms to defend the Constitution—the Constitution under which the American people had grown from three to thirty millions, and under which those thirty millions, but for this slavery-born conspiracy, might long have lived together in harmony and peace; it took up arms to defend the Union—the Union which gave to the American people the status of a Great Power in the world; it took up arms, finally, to chastise a band of conspirators, who sought to retrieve by civil convulsion a political defeat. These, and not the abolition of slavery, were undoubtedly the motives which inspired the Northern rising. Nevertheless it is still, I maintain, true that the destruction of slavery was comprised in the programme of the North. It is often said here, the North would gladly have given up everything — would have surrendered the whole cause of freedom—if it could only thereby have bribed the South to return. It would indeed have given up much: it was prepared to make—it actually did make—humiliating—I am forced to say it—disgraceful concessions. Nay, there are people in the North who would undoubtedly have gone all needful lengths, and, for the sake of the commercial gains arising from the Southern connection, would have gladly accepted the yoke of a Southern dictator. There are people there who would still do this. All this is too true. But let us do the North justice. There are others, and these the most numerous—the party in whose hands the government is, fortunately for the interests of mankind, at present placed, who refused to exist upon these terms, who, from first to last, have stood firmly by what has been throughout the grand stake of the struggle—the destination of the "territories." The offer of returning to the Union on the terms of receiving the "territories" was twice made by the South, and was twice rejected—let that never be forgotten: it was made, first, when the Crittenden compromise was tendered; and it was made, secondly, on the occasion of the interview of the Southern deputies with Mr. Lincoln, immediately before the breaking out of the war. A strong light has recently been thrown upon that meeting. One of those very Southern deputies, Mr. Ex-Governor Moorhead, is now in England, and has given his version of what then took place; and what is the story of this Southern Ex-Governor? He ridicules Mr. Lincoln's attitudes, which, it seems, were ungainly; he tells us of some uncouth and decidedly bad jests perpetrated by the President; but, as to the real business of the hour, his testimony is, that not one word was said at that critical moment about free trade; not one word about the Morrill tariff; it was all about slavery, and the discussion was ultimately brought to this point—would the "territories" be abandoned? Give up the "territories" to be overrun by slave-holders and slaves, and the Union may be restored; but refuse this, and the Union shall be severed. In that critical hour the Illinois rail-splitter might be forgetful of the graces and sugared amenities of diplomatic intercourse, but he stood firm by the grand principle of the Republican party.* Where slavery now exists, there, he said, it may remain, so long as it can sustain itself, but beyond that limit it shall not move. This was Mr. Lincoln's position, rather than abandon which he took the chance of disruption of the Union and civil war; and in this resolution he has been backed up by the vast majority of the Northern people. Therefore,

---

* "He" (Mr. Lincoln) "said that he was willing to give a constitutional guarantee that slavery should not be molested in any way directly or indirectly in the States; that he was willing to go further and give a guarantee that it should not be molested in the district of Columbia; and that he would go still further, and say that it should not be disturbed in the docks, arsenals, forts, and other places within the slave-holding States; but as for slavery in the territories, that his whole life was dedicated in opposition to its extension there; that he was elected by a party which had made that a portion of its platform, and he should consider that he was betraying that party if he ever agreed, under any state of the case, to allow slavery to be extended in the territories."—*Speech of Ex-Governor Moorhead.*

I say, it is not true that the North was willing to surrender everything if the South would only return to the Union. The North always stood firm by its Republican programme—a programme, which, modest and reasonable as it seems and is, really goes to the heart of the matter, and contains a principle, which, if made good, will ultimately stifle the monster of slavery in its own lair.

Well, I say, and I have always said, that, whatever might have been the ostensible, or even the actual, issues joined, the war was always in its essence an anti-slavery war. And now I will ask if experience has not borne out that opinion. I ask you to look at the measures which have been passed within the present year by Mr. Lincoln's government. In March last the first overture towards a settlement of the question was made. Mr. Lincoln addressed Congress, inviting it to join him in an offer of co-operation in a plan of emancipation, to be made to the legislatures of the Slave States—an invitation which both Houses of Congress accepted by large majorities. A little later, an Act was passed abolishing slavery in the District of Columbia—a tract which falls exclusively under Federal legislation, and therefore affords a sure index of the policy of the Federal Government. Later again, we encounter a still more important Act—that which at once gave effect to the cardinal principle of the Republican programme—the exclusion for ever of slavery from the "territories." And, lastly, we can point to the recent treaty with Great Britain, conceding what all the previous Governments of the United States refused—the right of searching Federal ships, and thus at once rendering effectual what has hitherto been little more than an idle protest—our blockade of the African coast. These have been the achievements of the North under the present Government; and, in the face of these, will anyone tell me that the policy of the North is not an anti-slavery policy? If it be not, I wish to know what is. I do not say that in this policy the North has been disinterested. I do not say that it is governed exclusively or principally by philanthropic views. I do not say that, as a nation, and as distinct from the small number of righteous men who are the salt of the nation, it cares a jot about the negro. I know too well that this is not the case. But granting all this in the fullest sense, are we to wait till some heroic nation arises to wage mortal combat with the Slave Power in the name of simple justice? Are four millions of negroes to wear their chains till the growing virtue of mankind culminates in a people sublimely regardless of all but the loftiest aims. Is it this that practical England waits for? Or rather, when the interests and instincts of a people conduct them towards humanity and justice, shall we not cheer them forward in the good path, and recognize in their advances, albeit urged by no better than vulgar impulses, that coincidence of right with well-being by which Providence governs the world? And, after all, if we but look at the facts without prejudice, the North has done that of which assuredly a nation may be fairly proud—that on which, I venture to think, future times will look back with other feelings than that scornful and horrified wonder, which, for the most part, is all our critics here can find for it. In the midst of a career of unbounded material prosperity—prosperity in which, had it so pleased, it might long have continued to riot and to rot—it has arrested its course; it has shaken itself free from the frightful night-mare which had so long bestridden it; and, for the sake of great social and political ends, has committed all its best and dearest interests to the chances of a terrible war.

I have now traced the course of this American Revolution up to a recent time. Within the last month, however, the policy of the North has undergone a radical change. The anti-slavery measures which I have just now instanced—the proposal to co-operate with the State Governments, the abolition of slavery in the District of Columbia, the exclusion of slavery from the "territories," the treaty with England for the suppression of the slave trade—all these measures possess the same character—they are all strictly constitutional. Thus the Constitution assigns legislation respecting slavery in the States to the State Governments; and, accordingly, it was through the State Governments that Mr. Lincoln proposed to deal with slavery in the States. On the other hand, the legislation for the District of Columbia, and for the "territories," is entrusted by the Constitution to the Central Government; it was open, therefore, to the Government to deal with slavery there by a direct measure; and this accordingly was the course which was adopted. And so also of the treaty with Great Britain for the suppression of the slave trade; it was a measure which came distinctly within the competence of the central authority. These measures, then, were all strictly constitutional; but, to give them effect, there was need of something more than an Act of Congress. The South had taken up arms to establish a Slave empire; and nothing short of military defeat would induce it to accept terms of compromise, which were absolutely destructive of its designs. The military defeat of the South was therefore the primary and essential condition of the success of the new policy on which the North had entered.

I confess I am one of those who thought that this condition—the defeat, not the permanent subjugation of the South—might have been accomplished without departing from that constitutional policy which Mr. Lincoln had evidently from the first marked out for himself. But highly as I was disposed to rate the military prowess of the Confederacy, formidable as I thought it,—and I did think it very formidable;—I confess its achievements have exceeded my expectations; and, after the experience of the present year, I see no prospect of the fulfilment of that indispensable condition to the success of an anti-slavery policy—the military defeat of the South, except through an appeal on the Northern side to principles more powerful than any which have yet been invoked. It has been well said, that, while the South has enjoyed the full advantage of the evil principle of slavery, the North has only availed itself partially, and with hesitating nerve, of the good principle of freedom. The cause of slavery, decidedly asserted, and logically carried out, has rallied the whole Southern population to the standard of secession almost as a single man, while the North, substantially fighting in the cause of freedom, but fettered by the Constitution, has hitherto shrunk from a bold appeal to those sentiments which freedom inspires. To give a practical illustration of the disadvantage under which the North labours from this half-hearted course:—while the South does not hesitate to avail itself of the services of negroes, as *slaves*, whether on the plantation or in the camp, the North has hitherto declined to take advantage of the same services, as the services of *freemen*.

On such terms, freedom is no match for slavery. Experience has proved it. What then? Is freedom to succumb? Is the North to lay down its arms? Is it to accept a peace dictated by a triumphant Slave Power, and are the fairest portions of the New World to be made a field for the propagation of the greatest curse which mankind has yet known? I say for my part, emphatically, No! Before Freedom is pronounced defeated, let her at least have a fair chance: let her use both her hands; let her put forth all her powers; let her oppose to the demon of slavery the whole force and virtue of her own fair essence. And this is the truth which bitter disaster has at length brought home to the North. Hitherto slavery, broken loose from the Constitution, has been encountered by freedom clogged with the trammels of the Constitution. These trammels have now been flung aside; and freedom and slavery now for the first time find themselves face to face in the deadly combat.*

---

* It will be said that I am here doing more than justice to Mr. Lincoln's policy, since the proclamation offers freedom to the slaves of "rebels" only. It is true that the proclamation is open to this remark; nevertheless, a candid critic will acknowledge, that it is making severe demands on the self-denial of a government to require it, when having at its

But this is to encourage a servile war! This is to sanction indiscriminate massacre! This is to inaugurate a series of Cawnpores! So says the *Times*. For my part, I have no faith in such predictions. I distrust the source from which they proceed. I cannot forget that the same authority, which now tells us that the negroes are ready to rise in ruthless fury on their masters, but the other day assured us that they were perfectly satisfied with their present condition, that they were well cared for, and were as loyal as they were comfortable. I cannot forget that the same censor, who now denounces the Northern Government for proclaiming emancipation, only a year ago denounced the same Government, with scarcely less emphasis, for not proclaiming emancipation. I cannot forget that the same seer, who now indulges his imagination in pictures of the horrors which liberty is to produce,

disposal so powerful a war measure as the offer of security for their principal property to the loyal, to refuse to take advantage of this expedient. And, secondly, it is only fair to remember that the proclamation does not stand alone, but is rather the complement to the offer of compensation made by Congress to the loyal slaveholders some months before. No inference can be more unjust than that drawn by the *Times* from the terms of the proclamation, that, because the operation of that measure is confined to the slaves of rebels, *therefore*, the Northern Government contemplates holding in perpetual bondage all the rest of the negroes. Mr. Lincoln knows well that, if the Slave Power—the political system based on slavery—be once broken, the chief inducement for maintaining slavery will be at an end; not only this, but the prospect of new fields for Slave labour being by the same stroke cut off, the economic reasons for maintaining the institution will also disappear. In the event of the success, complete or partial, of the proclamation policy, it is, therefore, as certain as any future contingency can be, that in the former case, the whole body of slaveholders, in the latter, those who remained in the Union, would close with the offer of compensation, and thus, by the combined operation of the two measures, emancipation within the limits of the Union would be complete.

has from the commencement of this crisis to the present hour uttered prophecy after prophecy, only to see prophecy after prophecy falsified by the event. I cannot forget that the denunciations which we now hear, proceed from the same generous critic who levelled black insult at Free America in the darkest hour of her fortunes. I say, therefore, that I distrust the source from which these vaticinations proceed. For my part, I neither believe that the negroes are the contented and loyal beings which they are described in the columns of one day's *Times*, nor yet the ruthless savages which they are depicted in those of the next. I believe it would be much nearer the truth to say, that they resemble the harmless cattle of our fields,* with an intelligence somewhat more

* I have been pained to find that this expression has been understood as countenancing the slaveholder's dogma of inferiority of race. I gladly seize the opportunity of a new edition to disclaim any such intention. What I meant by the illustration was to give an idea of the stolid and helpless condition of mind to which, *as a matter of fact* (as I believe), the plantation negro has been reduced under Southern rule, without expressing any opinion as to what he is capable of becoming under different treatment. I have great pleasure in quoting the following from the pen of one who is himself a living refutation of the calumny which I was supposed to have endorsed :—

"The impression which this statement (the passage in the text) is calculated to make, is quite inconsistent with our own knowledge of the average intelligence of the American slaves. Of course all negroes are not equal to Robert Small, who captured and made off with a rebel steamer under Fort Sumpter; nor are they all equal to Jeff. Davis's coachman ; nor are they all as well informed as is the writer of this article ; but they are certainly far above 'the harmless cattle in' our fields.' The negro has a head as well as a heart, and the former is not much worse, nor the latter much better than the same of other men. Our hearts are often praised at the expense of our heads. Our submission is often attributed to our gentleness, when it should be referred to our wisdom. White men do not fight without something like a reasonable probability of whipping somebody, at least a chance of escape from being badly

developed and an instinct of self-interest somewhat surer; and, unless driven to desperation by such measures of atrocity as we find described in the telegram of to-day, in which seventeen negroes are said to have been hanged for no other offence than being in possession of Mr. Lincoln's proclamation— I say, unless driven to desperation by measures of atrocity such as this—the probability is they will act much as cattle would act, to which a door of

whipped themselves, and some such prudence as this accounts for the fact that no insurrection has yet broken out among the slaves, and that none is likely to break out among them. They have shown their good sense by maintaining a masterly inactivity. They know that naked hands are no match for broad swords, and that grubbing hoes would be sure to go down before cannon balls. The South was never better prepared for insurrection than now—and the slaves know it. They have no need to prove their ability to fight, by rushing into the whirlwind of uncertain and irregular war. They are now taking their places in the ranks of regular troops, and distinguishing themselves for all the qualities valuable in the soldier. They can afford to bide their time. When slavery is abolished, the motive for insurrection will have passed away. The black man will be far less likely to bathe his hands in the blood of his master, than to bathe his master's feet with tears of gratitude for freedom. The maligners of the negro have affected surprise that negroes have committed so few acts of violence since the commencement of the war. They often ask, Why don't the negroes rise? and because they have not risen, they are denounced as cowardly and indifferent about liberty, and contented with their lot as slaves. Could any imputation be more unjust in view of all the circumstances? At the very beginning, and throughout the first year of the war, M'Clellan, Buell, Butler, Halleck, and the Government at Washington, were careful to assure them that in any such attempt they would be met and suppressed, not only by the rebel, but by the loyal army. To use the language of the now defunct Commanding General-in-Chief, 'they would be put down, and put down with an iron hand.' Both Governments, both armies, however hostile to each other at other points, were cordially united in the policy of keeping the slaves securely in their chains. In the presence of this notorious fact, how hollow and hypocritical is the pretence of surprise that the negroes, unarmed, without money, means of concert, and two tremendous armies of well-armed men ready to overwhelm them, have not hazarded an insurrection!"— *Douglas's Monthly*, Rochester, New York State.

escape was suddenly opened from barbarous treatment by cruel masters. When the opportunity offers, they will probably fly to the Federal lines. This is what their instinct will naturally teach them; it is what they did when the war commenced; but then the war was conducted according to the principles of the Constitution; and the fugitives from slavery, with a punctiliousness of constitutional honour which, perhaps, has no parallel in history, were sent back to serve the masters, against whom those who dismissed them were fighting. But this can happen no more. The attempt to carry on war on constitutional principles has been definitively abandoned. The proclamation has superseded the Constitution. The Federal lines will henceforth become for the negro a sure harbour of refuge; and, judging from what has already occurred, and from what we know of human nature, the result will probably be a grand "stampede" of all the negroes within reach of that retreat. That is the practical result which I expect from the proclamation; and it is obvious with what consequences it will be fraught. Let the North but maintain its ground for a sufficient time on Southern soil, and the industrial system of the Confederacy will crumble beneath its feet. The blood-cemented edifice will be undermined, and will totter to its fall. That, I say, is what the proclamation appears to me calculated to effect: what will actually happen is what no human eye can foresee. That isolated instances of outrage and murder will occur is indeed but too probable. The devil does not leave the body without rending it. Nay, if the infernal policy, of which to-day a specimen is recorded, is pursued, it is indeed fearful to think of the consequences which may be in store for that wretched country—consequences by which even the predictions of the *Times* may, for once, be fulfilled. But if this be the course which events are to take— if Southern slave-masters, in their guilty fear, are to commence a wholesale carnage of innocent men, then, I say, their blood be upon their own head; and as they have sown the wind, let them reap the whirlwind.

But, once again, there is a lion in the path. What is to be done with these four millions of negro slaves? I answer this question by another —what is to be done with the eight millions of negro slaves, which, if the policy of the South be successful, these four millions will in twenty years become? I know not what plan the North may adopt. I do not pretend to be able to produce a scheme in which an acute pro-slavery critic may not find a flaw; but I hold that, whatever be the difficulties of the case, these difficulties will not be diminished by postponing the remedy. Besides, this is not the first time that the attempt has been made to frighten England from the path of duty with the bugbear of emancipated negroes. The most frightful picture of negro freedom which the prolific imaginations of Southern sympathizers have yet conjured up, might easily be matched from the storehouse of predictions uttered by those who, at the last great emancipation struggle, played the diviner's part. Notwithstanding these gloomy auguries, however, emancipation in the West Indies has been a brilliant success. From the morning of emancipation down to the present moment,* although the black population always far outnumbered the white, not one attempt at insurrection has been made, not one barbarous outrage has been committed; and the descendants of those negroes who, we are told, would only work under the lash, are now the industrious denizens of a thriving community. In the midst of the clouds which now lower around us, I take comfort from that fact. I am unable to reason out the consequences; I cannot penetrate the gloom; but I am convinced that the slave system in America is the greatest curse which has yet darkened the earth, and I believe that the blow which effectually breaks it up must be a blessing.

Finally, I shall be asked, where is this carnage to end? To what purpose is this tremendous sacrifice of human life? Is the conquest of the South possible? and is its permanent subjection to the North either possible or desirable? I, for my part, have never thought so, and I do not think so now. The restoration of the Union in its former proportions appears to me, I confess, absolutely chimerical; and, if I mistake not, indications may even now be discerned that this conviction begins to force itself on the minds of the Northern leaders. But, granting that the South cannot be permanently conquered, does it follow that it is impossible to defeat its present design? Does it follow that it is impossible to stay the plague of slavery—to recover large districts in the Border

* [It will be remembered that this was delivered in 1862.]

States, already substantially free—to throw back the destroyer behind the barrier of the Mississippi? The impossibility of this has not yet been proved, and, until it has been proved, I for one cannot raise my voice for peace. Another year of war such as has now been passed, or rather of war waged on possibly a grander scale, and certainly with far fiercer passions, is indeed an awful prospect; but the future of a Slave Power, extending its dominion over half a continent, consigning a whole race of men to utter and hopeless ruin, menacing civilization on all sides—this is a prospect which to my mind is more fearful still.

In the foregoing remarks I have endeavoured to set forth what appear to me the grand principles in conflict in the American Revolution; and the scope of my remarks has gone to show that the cause of the North is substantially the cause of humanity and civilization. I should, however, be thoroughly misconceived, if it were supposed that I was not fully sensible of much that is open to censure in the conduct of the Northern people. There has been, no doubt, much incompetency, much hesitancy in the path of duty, no small amount of hectoring, many acts of petty tyranny, and, on the part of one general, some effusions of brutal insolence.* Nay, I will go further than

---

* For it is only fair to remember that "brutal insolence" is the worst that can be charged even against Butler—the one shameful exception to the general military administration of the North. Sanguinary he is not, only two executions having taken place during his occupation of New Orleans, of which one was the execution of a Federal soldier for plundering Confederate property. "It is not," says Ex-Governor Moorhead, "that the proclamation has been actually carried out, but it is the disgrace which he has attempted to heap upon the whole female population there."

this; and I do not scruple to say that the principles held by one large party in the Northern States, are, in my judgment, as detestable as any which prevail in the councils of the South. I mean the Northern democratic party—the party which has long been the lacquey of the South, and is now anxious to resume its menial duties—the party which, by the inhuman spirit it displays towards the coloured race, as in Illinois and Wisconsin, brings dishonour on the Northern cause—the party which the *Times* is now straining every nerve to support. I say that, so far as this Northern party is concerned, I can find no distinction between it and its Southern patrons, unless it be the distinction between the bold unscrupulous tyrant, and the sycophant, no less unscrupulous, who, for the protection of his countenance and the bribe of his pay, is content to do that tyrant's bidding. Into these incidents—the eddies from the main current of the movement—I have been unable to enter. I have been obliged to confine myself to the few salient facts which mark the general direction of the tide. And, with those facts in view, I ask you, can you feel any doubt as to what that direction is? Have I not said enough to show that, amid much that is dark and discouraging in the present aspect of American society, a process of regeneration is at work, that a dawn of promise has been disclosed, that a grand and healthy reaction has set in. For the last forty years the course of the United States as a nation has been a retrograde course. That is what we all recognize. And to what are we to attribute this decline? To democracy? I am no admirer of American democracy; but in all the worst features of the past political life of America I can trace the working of a principle, the reverse of democracy. Democracy has supplied the machinery of government, but that machinery has been worked by a Slave Power, and for the purposes of slavery. Democracy in America has never yet had a fair chance. No, I trace the national decline to something with which, where it exists, anything but decline is impossible—to complicity with a great sin. There may be other causes, but I believe that this is the grand and fundamental cause. Slavery, acting on an extraordinary material prosperity, has sent a rot through the whole body politic. But the crisis of the disease has arrived. Symptoms of returning health begin to show themselves. The principle of evil has, indeed, still a strong hold of its victim, but it is visibly relaxing its grasp. If you require proof, look to the progress which anti-slavery sentiment has made within the last year—look to the practical results of that progress in the benevolent mission to Port Royal to provide for fugitive negroes—look, lastly, at the feeling which the proclamation of emancipation has called forth. The friends of slavery predicted that the proclamation would shiver the North into fragments. On the contrary, it is rapidly uniting all that is best and most hopeful in the Northern people, rallying them to a common principle, and, in the fire of a noble enthusiasm, welding them into a single mass. At such a time as this, is it for England to see only the difficulties of the problem—to be nice in scrutinizing motives, and, in her anxiety lest emancipation should be accomplished in some unorthodox fashion—lest it should be dictated by some principle less sublime than the purest philanthropy, to throw the whole weight of her splendid influence into the scale of the slaveholder? I cannot think so. I cannot believe that this unnatural infatuation for a Slave Power is destined to be a permanent attachment. It is but a transient passion, the offspring of pique and anger, from which ere long she will shake herself free. Yet a little, and she will resume her older and better character, as the England of Clarkson and Wilberforce, the emancipator of slaves, the champion of the oppressed, and the friend of freedom, in every form, and in every quarter of the globe.

III.

INTERNATIONAL LAW.*

IT is now about two and a half centuries since Grotius, in his great work, gave to the world the first clear outline of a scheme of international jurisprudence. The subject has since engaged the thoughts of many very learned and of a few very able minds. The relations and mutual pretensions of nations have, moreover, during this period, been submitted—with the growth of international trade, the collision of international interests incident to the peopling of a new continent, and a succession of wars—to the ordeal of a long and diversified experience; and the practices thus established and mutual concessions thus obtained have, under the manipulation of Prize Courts and diplomatists, been wrought into a tolerably compact and coherent system. Yet, notwithstanding the progress made in the practical art of administering international affairs, and notwithstanding the existence of many valuable treatises in the nature of digests and expositions of the actual international code, or of portions of it,—of such works, for example, as those of

* *Fortnightly Review*, November 1865.

Ortolan, Wheaton, Kent, Manning, and others—it must, I think, be admitted that little has yet been done for the philosophy of international law. Bentham, Austin, and the two Mills have indeed given us some valuable analyses of fundamental juridical ideas; Mr. J. S. Mill, in particular, has in detached essays offered some pregnant suggestions; and more recently Mr. Maine, in his not less profound than learned work on "Ancient Law," has incidentally thrown a clear light on some recondite points in the development of international jurisprudence. Yet a work treating international law as a whole, in a philosophical spirit, and with reference to the altered conditions in many important respects of international intercourse, is still, I think it must be said, a *desideratum* in philosophical literature. Upon such questions, for example, as the true nature of international law, its proper sanctions, its authoritative exponents, the grounds of its obligation, the limits of civilization within which its rules may be justifiably enforced—how utterly vague, unsatisfactory, and fluctuating are the views of even its professed cultivators! There are those, no doubt, who will tell us that all this is of little consequence. Practice, we know, precedes theory; and those people will probably add that it does not much matter if theory ever follow. But, with due respect, I must contend that it does matter; that, albeit the first essays in every path of art must needs be made somewhat blindly and on trust, for continuous and sustained progress, theory *is* necessary: a survey of the ground passed over, an observation of our actual position with reference at once to the goal in view and to the state of other but kindred arts, are important conditions in order to a fresh and effective start. It seems to me that the study of international law has just reached that stage at which a resort to the chart and the compass becomes necessary; at which, without this assistance, we are in danger of returning on our course, and wandering through the mazes of exploded systems and obsolete ideas; at which, therefore, the most effective service that can be rendered to the course of international jurisprudence, even in the most strictly practical sense, will consist in a determination of its proper character, its ultimate aim, its relation to other connected departments of human speculation and action—in a word, in setting forth a true philosophy of international law. To the ability and learning requisite for such a task the present writer makes no pretension; his purpose at present does not extend beyond an attempt to discuss a few fundamental problems in the light of modern facts and of some recent contributions to ethical and juridical science, and with a view to exhibit, by way of illustration, the mode in which an improved philosophy of this branch of study may be made conducive to the work of practical reform.

It has already been intimated that the proper nature of international law is still a subject of controversy. On the part of Bentham and his followers, and, not less by a very different school, Savigny and those who accept his teaching, a distinction in character has been recognized between the rules which regulate international intercourse and the municipal code of a State. On the other hand, there are writers on international law who do not perceive, or refuse to acknowledge the relevancy of, this distinction. Dr. Phillimore and Dr. Twiss, for example, have in recent publications contended that international law is "law" proper—law, that is to say, in the same sense in which an Act of Parliament is "law." Now I am anxious, so far as possible, to avoid verbal controversy, and I shall therefore content myself with observing that there are at least two distinctions in the case, which, whatever we may think of their importance, cannot, as facts, be gainsaid. International law, unlike the civil code of a State, does not proceed from any determinate source generally recognized as authoritative; and, secondly, it is not enforced —in this respect also differing from the civil code of a State—by any definite and regularly applied sanctions. These distinctions, I repeat, whatever opinion we may hold on the verbal controversy, must as facts be admitted. And this negative position gained, it remains to inquire what, then, *is* the source of international law, and what *is* the character of its sanctions?

To the former question, the answer given by Bentham, and since his time more precisely stated by his disciple Austin, must, I think, be allowed to be satisfactory. International law is merely the formal expression of the public opinion of the civilized world respecting the rules of conduct which ought to govern the relations of independent nations, and is consequently derived from the source from which all public opinion flows—the moral and intellectual convictions of mankind. That this is the true character of international law may be shown as well historically as on abstract grounds—from its genesis in the writings of publicists and the decisions of international tribunals, no less than from the nature of the case, by reference to the sphere of its operations as affecting the conduct of independent States. Whence, for example, did Grotius derive that body of doctrine which he gave to the world as the " Law of Nations "? From two sources, he tells us,—the " Law of Nature," and the agreement of mankind as evidenced in the testimony of the learned. But what are the law of nature and the testimony of the learned, in connection with the topics to elucidate which they are appealed to by Grotius, but the views of social morality entertained either by Grotius himself, or by other eminent writers in times past and present—in a word, the opinion on international subjects, actual or prospective, of the civilized world? Subsequent writers on the law of nations have, for the most part, followed substantially the method of Grotius. The actual law of nations they have taken from the existing opinions and practices of mankind; while the law of nature—that is to say, their own views of the highest social morality—has supplied them with the ideal to which they have sought to elevate the actual usage—an ideal which has from age to age been ever varying with the progress of ethical speculation. Prize courts, again, congresses, and other international tribunals—the actual administrators of the international system—have followed more or less implicitly the customs of the times and the rulings of the publicists; while the decisions of these tribunals have in turn furnished precedents from which new rules have been evolved.

and the law of nations further extended and enriched. The staple of the "Law of Nations" is thus public opinion—public opinion embodied in usage, expounded and generalized in the treatises of publicists, interpreted and enforced in international courts. And, indeed, from the nature of the case, what else than public opinion could international law embody? What but moral control can sovereign Powers, consistently with their sovereign character, acknowledge and undergo?

And when, in the second place, we ask what are the sanctions of international law, it is plain, from what has been already said, that they can be only such as opinion has at its disposal, and may, therefore, best be gathered by observing the action of social opinion in the sphere within which we are most familiar with its operation—the sphere of private life. Opinion, it is obvious, may enforce its behests by either of two means—by physical coercion, or by moral suasion. In the early stages of social progress opinion makes its energy felt chiefly, or at all events largely, through the former means. A violation of the minor morals of life—a disregard in any form of the rules prescribed by social opinion—is commonly followed by personal chastisement or by forcible expulsion of the offending party from the society whose rules he has set at naught. But as society advances, a recourse to violence comes to be less needed in proportion as the moral elements in the human character grow in power. Praise and blame are gradually substituted for the coarser sanctions of the earlier state. Already this process has been carried so far in the more advanced nations of Europe and America, that these—the moral sanctions of opinion—are now found adequate in the main to all the ends of social intercourse. In Great Britain and the Free States of the American Union, they may be said to have absolutely superseded all other modes of enforcing social morality so far as it lies outside the sphere of municipal law; while even in continental countries, the resort to physical violence in support of social conventions is becoming rare, and is evidently doomed to give way before the better influences of the times. Now this being the history of the sanctions of opinion in the social life of individuals, the question occurs, how far we are justified in anticipating a like development in the social life of nations.

And here it is, at the first glance, obvious that, at all events up to the present time, mankind has nowhere, even in the most advanced nations of Christendom, reached the stage at which the physical sanctions of opinion can, in international affairs, be safely dispensed with. Not to refer to America, the present state of Europe, garrisoned over its whole extent with immense standing armies, at the cost of financial embarrassment and of industrial and commercial depression to the States which maintain them, sufficiently refutes the notion—a refutation which might be supplemented at pleasure from the events of current history. But the mere fact that opinion in international affairs is not yet powerful enough to serve as its own sanction, by no means proves that it may not become so; and the question for the philosophical publicist is, not simply what is now the efficacy of public opinion in the affairs of nations, but what, in the advance of civilization, public opinion is capable of becoming. Is a state of mutual distrust and suspended hostility destined to be the normal and inevitable condition of independent States? or may we reasonably look forward to a time when, in the intercourse of nations, as has already happened in the intercourse of individual men, submission to opinion may supersede the necessity of violent expedients, and "the kindly earth may slumber, lapt in universal law"?

In an essay on international law by the late Mr. Senior, published originally some twenty years ago in the *Edinburgh Review*, but revised by him just before his death, one view, perhaps the prevailing one, on this question, is stated with Mr. Senior's usual emphasis:—

"The fear of physical evil," says Mr. Senior, "to the persons and properties of the members of the community is the principal restraint on the conduct of nations. . . . On the other hand, nations are not restrained by fear of the loss of honour; for honour, in the sense in which that word is applied to individuals, does not apply to them. It consists in the absence of certain imputations which exclude a person tainted by them from the society of his equals. But as a nation cannot be excluded from the society of other nations, a nation cannot lose its honour, in the sense in which honour is lost by an individual. Never has the foreign policy of France been more faithless, more rapacious, or more cruel, than during the reign of Louis XIV. For half a century she habitually maintained a conduct, a single instance of which would have excluded an individual from the society of his equals. At no time was France more admired and even courted. At no time were Frenchmen more welcome in every court and in every private circle.

"What are often called injuries to the honour of a nation are injuries to its vanity. The qualities of which nations are most vain, are force and boldness. They know that, so far as they are supposed to possess these qualities, they are themselves unlikely to be injured, and may injure others with impunity. What they most fear, therefore, is betraying timidity, which is both an index and a cause of weakness. But timidity, which excludes a man from society, makes a nation only the more acceptable. To call, therefore, any manifestation of cowardice, however gross, a loss of national honour, is illogical. It implies the double error of applying to a nation a liability which is peculiar to an individual, and of inferring a result, which, even if that liability existed among nations, would not follow from the supposed cause."
—*Historical and Philosophical Essays*, vol. i. pp. 147, 149.

If this statement correctly represents the moral conditions of international life—if nations are not only not sensible of the feeling of honour, but incapable of becoming so—the question just proposed for consideration must of course be resolved in the negative. But, not to dwell upon the obvious inadequacy of Mr. Senior's definition of "honour"—a definition which confounds the feeling itself as a principle of conduct with a particular, and by no means an essential or invariable, sanction of the conduct which it prescribes—it would not be difficult to show that the same line of argument might with equal plausibility be used to disprove the existence and efficacy of private honour. Never, he tells us, was the foreign policy of France more faithless and rapacious than during the reign of Louis XIV., when France was universally courted and admired; but what were the private morals of high society in France, and we may add in England, during this time? What is the kind of life disclosed in such books as the Memoirs of Grammont and St. Simon? Yet because Sedley and Villiers were "admired and courted" by the society of the court of Charles II., are we to conclude that honour has no existence amongst men?—that the horsewhip and the pistol are the only effective restraints upon social immorality and insolence?

With most readers of the passage I have quoted, the difficulty, I apprehend, will be not to refute Mr. Senior's reasoning, but to understand how such reasoning could have proceeded from a man of the world. The statement, for example, that "to call any manifestation of cowardice, however gross, a loss of national honour, is illogical," is as extravagantly at variance with the most widely-felt sentiments and the most ordinary language of mankind, as if it had proceeded from the merest recluse and bookworm. It is a curious example of that mingled cynicism and love of paradox which gave so marked a bent to Mr. Senior's mind. How little the views here advanced affected his general judgments on international affairs, is shown by other passages in the same volume. Referring to the part acted by Great Britain in reference to the slave-trade, he remarks that an impartial observer, contemplating her conduct, "would admire the self-devotion with which England had encountered offence, misrepresentation, expenditure of treasure and life, and even the chances of war, in the hope of preventing evils with which she is acquainted only by report, and of civilizing, or at least improving, nations of which she scarcely knows the names. He might doubt whether the means adopted were wise. He might know, indeed, that their failure has been most complete and most calamitous; but he could not deny their generosity." (Vol. i. p. 56.) And again, discussing the conduct of England in the affair of the "Russo-Dutch Loan," he remarks :—" We have little doubt that, if the question could have been submitted to a legal tribunal, judgment would have been given against Russia. But as the decision rested with England, she thought that it became her to decide against herself. She has continued her payments as if no severance between Holland and Belgium ever occurred." (Vol. i. p. 81.) Is not this precisely the motive from which, in private life, a man of decent feeling would act in an analogous case?

The truth is, that in the seventeenth century public opinion was, in its influence on the internal no less than on the external affairs of nations, still in a rudimentary state; and the progress which it has since made in the former of those spheres is highly noteworthy for its bearing on the question we are now considering. More particularly is this the case as regards the efficacy which opinion has since attained in that province of internal affairs which is concerned with political life. For, without at all overrating the present state of political morality in this and other countries, we may yet safely affirm that, even within the memory of living men—the fact will of course be still more apparent if we extend our comparison further back—it has undergone a vast improvement, an improvement which is due entirely to the growing influence of public opinion. And if opinion has been powerful enough to accomplish this reform in the conduct of internal politics—to restrain gross cupidity and self-seeking in public men, and to enforce a decent consistency and moderation on political parties—why should we be less sanguine of its efficacy in the wider field of international morality? The passions which impel nations into conflict are not stronger than those which, in domestic controversies, actuate statesmen and parties: the interests involved in international contests are rarely so palpable or direct as those which depend on the issues of internal political strife. Why should a force which has been found regulative of the former influences prove impotent in controlling the latter?

And the reasonableness of sanguine expectation upon this head will be the more evident when we reflect on the causes which have led to the more rapid growth of public opinion in domestic than in international affairs. The condition of a public opinion is, that there should be a public, conscious of common objects, and capable of interchanging ideas. This condition has already for a considerable period been pretty fully realized in the domestic life of most civilized states; it has followed in the wake of popular education, a free press, good roads, and improved postal communication. But in their bearing upon international society, these agencies are only just coming into operation. It is not strange, therefore, that public opinion in this wider sphere should still be immature and weak. The rapidity, however, with which it is forming—under the influence of expanding commerce, increasing study of the modern languages, railways and steam navigation—is one of the most prominent and remarkable facts of the present time. It would be easy to adduce evidence of this from patent manifestations in contemporary history, such, for example, as the enhanced and constantly growing interest taken by the British public in questions of foreign policy—a phenomenon which, it is said, finds its parallel in other European countries. One instance of this kind deserves special attention in connection with the present argument.

The anxiety of the people of the Free States of the American Union to obtain the sympathy of foreign nations, but more especially that of the people of Great Britain, in their struggle with the insurgent slaveholders, has been a subject of general observation. By a certain class of writers this susceptibility has been regarded as an indication of weakness in the national character, and has been made the mark of a good deal of flippant ridicule. That a great people should be so sensitive of its fame with foreign countries as to keep up through its press a standing controversy in defence of its conduct,—that it should send deputations across the Atlantic charged, not with soliciting aid from foreign governments, but with convincing foreign people of the justice of its cause,—that it should wince under harsh criticisms, chafe at ungenerous taunts, while it equally welcomed every expression of disinterested approval, or even of discriminating appreciation,—all this has seemed infinitely undignified and ridiculous to a certain order of minds. I own, however, that the phenomenon seems to me one of most hopeful augury; forming, as it does, the most signal and cogent evidence which the world has yet received of the growth of an influence on which more perhaps than anything else depends the possibility of any important amelioration in the future relations of independent States. It is an example on a grand scale of an international sentiment precisely similar in kind to that which, through its influence on individuals, has been the chief instrument of such improvement as has yet been attained in the domestic life of nations—the desire to stand well in the estimation of our fellows--the sense of discomfort and mortification which is felt under the consciousness of their disapproval. I shall be told, perhaps, that the instance which I have taken illustrates rather the weakness than the strength of international public opinion, since the people of the United States have not suffered themselves to be turned from their object by even the strongly expressed opinion of Europe. But, in the first place, it is by no means clear that the verdict of Europe has been unfavourable to the cause of the United States. The ruling classes in England, and the ruling clique in France, have doubtless favoured the slaveholders' cause; but the heart of the English masses, and the convictions of no small number of the most thoughtful and cultivated Englishmen, have gone with the Free States; while the liberal party in France has almost to a man taken the same side; as has also, I believe, in the main, the liberal party in Germany. It matters not, however, for the present argument, on which side the larger number of votes has been cast. It is not desirable in international, any more than in private affairs, that people should substitute their neighbours' convictions for their own. What is wanting is, not that independent nations should take their policy —more especially in regard to domestic concerns—from other nations, but that they should show themselves alive to the moral judgments respecting their policy which other nations form—that they should recognize the obligation of justifying their moral position in the eyes of civilized mankind. This is that which the people of the Free States have exhibited in a degree hitherto quite unparalleled, and by doing so have given to the world a hopeful presage—may we not say an encouraging earnest?—of the growing power of public opinion in international affairs.

There thus seems reason for believing that all the leading currents of modern civilization are setting steadily and rapidly towards the formation of a body of international opinion which, judging from the efficacy that opinion has already developed in analogous departments of human life, there is ground for hoping may ultimately, and at no remote date, become an effective check on the conduct of nations. If this view be sound, the direction which our efforts should take for any radical improvement in the principles by which the conduct of nations should be governed is not doubtful. International law must have its sanctions; and for these the alternative lies between fleets and armies and the moral restraints of opinion. If the enormous armaments which now weigh upon the physical and mental energies of Europe are ever to be largely and permanently reduced, this will only be when the nations of Europe feel secure that those instruments may be safely dispensed with, which will happen then and no sooner than when international opinion is felt to have become strong enough to perform their part.* I have endeavoured to show that this is not an impossible consummation; and this being so, the course for the advocates of peace and reform would seem to be clear; it will lie, not in declaiming against establishments, the evils of which are felt, but felt also to be necessary, but in cherishing the growth of that innocuous agency which is destined one day to take their place—in cultivating a sound international opinion.† I have adverted

* With singular want of appreciation, as it seems to me, of the drift of modern tendencies, Dr. Twiss, the most recent writer in England on "The Law of Nations," positively refuses to regard any other sanctions of international law than the physical, apparently for the reason that the fact that international law carries a physical sanction, constitutes a ground for regarding it as "law proper." In truth, the criterion wholly fails in its purpose, unless Dr. Twiss is prepared to consider social conventions also as instances of "law proper;" these in most parts of the world being, quite as much as international law, upheld by the sanctions of physical force. Dr. Twiss, in contending for this view, deprecates the opposite doctrine of Austin (according to which international law is "positive morality merely") as tending to weaken "the ascendency of Reason over the Will." But what can be better fitted for this end than a philosophy of international law, which puts altogether out of sight the moral forces in international affairs?

† In entire conformity with the practical course here advocated, as well as with the general line of reasoning pursued in this paper, is the following suggestion from a journal distinguished at once for the firmness and moderation of its tone on foreign questions, on the most important international question now pending. The *Daily News* (October 18, 1865) writes:—"It must be admitted, of course, that 'Her Majesty's Government is the sole guardian of its own honour.' But the honour of a nation is not more precious than the honour of an individual. And in these days how is it that matters affecting personal honour are settled? There was a time when it was thought that satisfaction for an imputation against a man's personal honour was only to be had by resorting to the sword or a pair of pistols. But the days of duelling are past. In these times recourse is had either to a court of law, or more commonly to the kind offices of mutual friends. And even officers in the British army and

to the various circumstances in modern society which favour the growth of this power. Its efficacy for the purpose in view, however, will depend not on its strength merely, but even more on the unity of its direction. Nations must agree upon their mutual duties before opinion can have any effect in enforcing them; and for agreement the most important condition is a simplification of international questions. Now it happens that the present time

> navy readily acquiesce in this modern system. Nor are there many who fail to acknowledge its advantage. It is, perhaps, difficult to understand why so excellent a system should be confined to private life. . . . Let the case of the American Government be submitted by themselves to the most eminent statesmen and jurists in France, Italy, Germany, Russia, and the other countries. Let the wisest and ablest men in Europe and America be asked their opinion upon the case made by Lord Russell on the part of the British Government, and by Mr. Adams on the part of the American Government. There is no danger that the oracles would remain silent, and it is obvious that the opinions thus obtained must carry weight which would be almost irresistible. To whichever side the majority of those consulted inclined, it would be well-nigh impossible for the other side to maintain its position. It is not assumed that either Government will agree beforehand to be bound by the preponderating opinion; nevertheless, it can scarcely be supposed that the people of America, or the people of England, would permit their ministers to enforce claims thus condemned by the general consent of the leading statesmen and jurists of the civilized world. . . . . . Let an appeal be made to the civilized world. If the opinions delivered by the eminent men who may be consulted are unanimous, or even if the majority in favour of either side is very considerable, the matter may be considered settled. If the opinion of the civilized world is with England, the British Government and the British people will be justified in resisting the claims made upon them. If, on the other hand, that opinion is with the United States, the concessions we may have to make will not only be without danger 'to neutral nations in all future wars,' but we shall have the assurance that we have maintained the peace without sacrificing the national honour."
>
> [The course actually taken in the Treaty of Washington was in its essential character that which is here recommended; the chief difference being that the two Governments *did* "agree beforehand to be bound by the preponderating opinion."]

offers singular facilities for an advance towards this end, in the steady liberation of commerce from the complicated restraints of the obsolete system of protection, and in the recent progress of ethical and juridical philosophy. The elucidation of this aspect of the subject, however, if it is to be attempted, must be reserved for another paper.*

---

* [This purpose the writer was unable to carry out.]

IV.

FRAGMENTS ON IRELAND.

1.—*THE AGRICULTURAL REVOLUTION—PROTECTION AND FREE TRADE.*

THE feature in the present* industrial condition of Ireland which first strikes the eye of the most casual observer, is probably also that which is most pregnant with consequences for good or evil to her future fortunes—the extensive conversion of tillage-land into pasture, now rapidly proceeding over the greater portion of its surface. It may not be generally known that this is the direct reversal of a change through which the industry of the country passed rather less than a century ago. Ireland was then mainly a pastoral country. Subsequently, more than half her cultivable land passed under tillage, mostly under potatoes and grain; and she is now reverting to the condition of pasture once more. It would almost seem as if the sarcasm of Moore expressed the literal truth, and that the history of Ireland represented in a miniature scale "the grand periodic year of the Stoics, at the close of which everything was to begin again, and the same events to be all reacted in the same order."

* [Written in 1866.]

But before accepting this view,—before the present step can be pronounced to be retrogression,—that which preceded it must be shown to have been progress; and this, I apprehend, would be a quite impossible feat. In fact, the movement in question was a violent diversion of Irish industry from its natural course—a diversion from which have directly flowed no small part of all the most serious evils which Ireland has since endured. It will here be worth while to consider briefly the causes and consequences of that movement which committed Ireland for a time to the *rôle* of a grain-producing country; for it will be found to throw some light on the converse phenomenon now presented to our view, the character of which it is so important to understand.

The causes which kept Ireland, down to the middle of the eighteenth century, in the condition of a pastoral country are sufficiently on the surface: they lay partly in the character of her climate—"that country," said the poet Spenser, in the sixteenth century, "is a great soyle for cattle, and very fit for breed: as for corne it is nothing natural"—partly in the low civilization of the bulk of her inhabitants, who, thanks to the wretched misgovernment of England, had, down to the period we speak of, scarcely risen above the primitive mode of living in which the conquerors found them. The penal code, too, apart from its general effects, worked with an especial force in this direction; for, while the great majority of the people were precluded by law from possessing any substantial interest in land, that mode of industry, in the absence of a strong bias the other way, would naturally be preferred which involved the least outlay and needed the least security. These standing causes were further enforced by an incident which occurred about a century ago, and of which we have recently been painfully reminded—the cattle murrain which ravaged England in 1760 and the few following years. The high price of meat, which followed upon this pestilence, encouraged in Ireland the enclosure for grazing purposes of land formerly available as commons for the peasantry. The operation would seem to have been conducted on an extensive scale; for it seems to be agreed that it furnished the occasion for the outbreak of "White-boys" or "Levellers"* which occurred about this time.† But the stimulus thus given to pastoral industry was quickly counteracted. A group of causes—the same which in a few years changed England from a corn-exporting into a corn-importing country—were now coming rapidly into play, and soon not only arrested the movement towards an extended pasture, but gave a powerful impulse to the cultivation of grain. The most important of these causes was the start taken by England in the latter half of the eighteenth century in manufactures and population, coinciding as this did with a remarkable succession of bad seasons—causes of dearness which, before many years, were powerfully seconded by the corn laws, and ultimately by the French wars.‡ Under the influence of these events the price of corn rapidly rose. The prospect of increased rents was as welcome to Irish

---

* Of fences, not of social distinctions.
† Lewis on "Irish Disturbances," pp. 8, 9.
‡ Tooke's "History of Prices," vol. i. chap. 3, §§ 4 and 5.

as to English landlords; and a series of measures passed about this time in the Irish Parliament, in the nature of bounties on the inland carriage and exportation of grain and prohibitions on its importation, attest their eagerness to improve the occasion. As the result of the whole, the industry of the country received that impulse towards the cultivation of cereals which continued down to recent times.*

He would have been a bold speculator who should have ventured a century ago to have called in question the wisdom of the course on which the country was then entering; for undoubtedly it was in its first effects advantageous, according to obvious standards, to every class in the community. It would be plainly so to landlords and middlemen; and it was not less certainly so to the masses; for it created a rapid increase in the demand for their labour, which continued without abatement for some generations. The brief glimpse of prosperity which dawned at this time on the political fortunes of Ireland—it was the era of the Volunteers—was felt also in her material condition; and for a time plenty actually reigned in Irish cabins.†

---

* The movement was in full progress when Arthur Young visited Ireland. The rapidity with which it proceeded may be judged by the returns which he furnishes of the sums paid in bounties on the inland carriage of corn under the Act of 1762—"one of the most singular measures that have anywhere been adopted." These, it seems, rose in the interval between 1762 and 1777 from £4,940 in the former year to £61,786 in the latter. Young further remarks that "the increase of tillage has by no means been in the poor counties by breaking up uncultivated lands; on the contrary, it has been entirely in the richest counties in the kingdom, which confirms the intelligence I received on the journey, that it was good sheep land that had principally been tilled."—*Tour in Ireland*, Part II. § xviii.

† A statement to the contrary effect is quoted by Sir C. G. Lewis, in his work on "Irish Disturbances," from a speech of the Irish Attorney-

"Generally speaking, the Irish poor," said Arthur Young (his visit to Ireland, it will be remembered, was in 1777), "have a fair belly-full of potatoes, and they have milk the greatest part of the year. . . . Mark the Irishman's potato bowl placed on the floor, the whole family upon their hams around it, devouring a quantity almost incredible, the beggar seating himself with a hearty welcome, the pig taking his share as readily as the wife, the cocks, hens, turkeys, geese, the cur, the cat, and perhaps the cow—and all partaking of the same dish. No man can often have been a witness of it without being convinced of the plenty, and, I will add, the cheerfulness that attends it." It does not give us a high idea of Young's philosophy that he should have contemplated this scene apparently with the most unmixed satisfaction, and even contrasted it favourably with that presented by the cottage homes of England. "An Irishman and his wife are

General in 1787. "As to the peasantry of Munster," said the Attorney-General, "it is impossible for them longer to exist in the extreme wretchedness under which they labour. A poor man is obliged to pay £6 for an acre of potato ground, which £6 he is obliged to work out with his landlord for 5*d*. a day." But one or two statements of this kind (and this is all which Sir C. Lewis's research has discovered bearing on the period under consideration) cannot be allowed to weigh against such undisputed and indisputable facts as the extensive conversion of pasture to tillage which at this time occurred, combined with an unparalleled increase of population. Between 1767 and 1793 the population of Ireland must have nearly, if not quite, doubled itself, a feat only possible on the condition of an abundant supply for its physical wants; and that this supply was forthcoming we have the strongly confirmatory, albeit negative, evidence, afforded by the fact that *agrarian* disturbances, strictly so called, ceased in Ireland about the year 1772, and did not recommence till 1806. The "Peep-of-day-boys" and "Defenders," who quickly developed into "Orangemen" and "United Irishmen," and whose struggles culminated in the rebellion of 1798, were, as Sir C. Lewis points out, organizations of a religious and political, not at all of an agrarian character. See Lewis on "Irish Disturbances," pp. 22, 23, and 36-41.

much more solicitous to feed than to clothe their children; whereas in England it is the reverse. . . . In England a man's cottage will be filled with superfluities before he possesses a cow. I think the comparison much in favour of the Irishman. A hog is a much more valuable piece of goods than a set of tea-things; and though his snout in a crock of potatoes is an idea not so poetical as—

> 'Broken tea-cups wisely kept for show,
> Ranged o'er the chimney, glistened in a row,'

yet will the cottar and his family find the solidity of it an ample recompense."* History has not sustained this verdict. The type of decency has proved to be of more value in the long run than gross abundance in which the barn-door fowl, the pig, and the wife share upon equal terms.

Such a state of things contained precisely those conditions which are favourable in the highest degree to the growth of population. All the moral checks on increase were absolutely removed; while the physical checks were scarcely felt to operate. "They say of marriage," says Bishop Doyle, "as of other changes in life, that it cannot make them worse, but it may give them a help-mate in distress, or at least a companion in suffering." † Thus, the more abject the Irishman's

---

* "A Tour in Ireland," Part II. pp. 21–26.

† It is but just to Dr. Doyle to add that he admits this to be "a weak plea," and he would only excuse "the weakness by which it is dictated." He very sensibly says :—" Let, then, the condition of the poor be altered ; enable them to acquire a competency ; give the parent some means of providing for his daughter ; give to her a better education and a deeper sense, not of propriety alone, but of politeness and social decency, and you will delay marriage, and thereby retard the increase of population without infringing on virtue."—*Letters on the State of Ireland*, by J. K. L. pp. 110–112.

condition, the more eagerly did he rush into marriage. We shall, therefore, not be surprised to learn from Arthur Young that "marriage is certainly more general in Ireland than in England; I scarce ever found an unmarried farmer or cottar. In England," he continues, "where the poor are in many respects in such a superior state, a couple will not marry unless they can get a house, to build which, take the kingdom through, will cost from £25 to £60. . . . But in Ireland the cabin is not an object of a moment's consideration; to possess a cow and a pig is an earlier aim; the cabin begins with a hovel that is erected with two days' labour, and the young couple pass not their youth in celibacy for want of a nest to produce their young in." And, as if the inducements to reckless multiplication were not already sufficiently strong, an Act of the Irish Parliament passed in 1793—the Act for giving the franchise to forty-shilling freeholders—brought political passions to reinforce the animal feelings; for by this measure the political influence of landlords was made directly to depend upon the number of human beings amongst whom their estates were divided. What wonder under such circumstances that population should have increased in Ireland at a rate unheard of in old countries! We unfortunately possess no accurate returns of the population of Ireland anterior to the Census of 1821; and a paper recently published * rather throws doubt on

---

* "Observations, by W. H. Hardinge, M.R.I.A., on the earliest known Manuscript Census-returns of the People of Ireland," published in the "Transactions of the Royal Irish Academy," 1865. According to the document brought to light by Mr. Hardinge, the total population of the country in 1659 would be almost exactly half a million. Sir William Petty's

the estimates usually received. These, however, inasmuch as they are based on a constant criterion—the number of registered births—may still be taken for the purpose of comparison; and the illustration they afford of the results of the social life just described is sufficiently striking. In 1672 the population of Ireland, according to these estimates, was 1,320,000; nearly a century afterwards, that is to say in 1767, it stood, according to the same authority, at 2,544,000—thus falling short of doubling itself in that period; but in 1792 it had increased to 4,088,000, and in 1805 to 5,395,000;—in other words, on arriving at the period when the extensive cultivation of cereals began, the rate rapidly increased; the numbers more than doubling themselves in thirty-eight years. From this point—the beginning of the present century—though at a less rapid rate (for the growing numbers were already treading close upon the means of support)—the population continued to advance, culminating in 1846, when the catastrophe which had been maturing through a century suddenly fell.

What is the lesson taught by this retrospect? Not, certainly, that an increased demand for the labour of a people is an evil; and just as little that cheap and abundant food is a curse. The language used by some writers on the subject of the potato * would

estimate for 1672 is 1,100,000; Shaw Mason's, quoted by Mr. Thom, 1,320,000. These numbers are not reconcilable with any possible rate of human increase.

* Mr. McCulloch's tirade against the potato is well known. Even Professor G. Smith takes leave of common sense in his horror at this excellent root. "Raleigh had introduced the potato . . . . . the gift, than which the Archfiend could scarcely have offered anything more deadly," &c.

not be more than adequate, if, as Judge Longfield somewhere remarks, potatoes ate men instead of feeding them. At the worst, the use of potatoes permitted the population to become somewhat more numerous than it otherwise would have been. The true sources of the calamities which followed lay, *first*, in the purely artificial character of the economy under which the Irish now came to live; and *secondly*, in the entire absence of any standard of comfort or decency—of anything in short but mere physical necessity—to regulate the growth of the people. By the former of these causes, the well-being, or rather the existence of the people came to be identified with methods of industry entirely unsuited to the country where they were established, and sure to be swept away with the progress of civilization; and owing to the latter, the numbers supported by such precarious means were multiplied to the utmost limits compatible with human existence. The failure of the potato precipitated the disaster, as the failure of oats or maize might have done, had either of these been the main subsistence of a people reduced to the extreme verge of poverty; but the seeds of it were in the nature of the industrial system, and the habits of the people; and free trade, even without the assistance of famine, would inevitably have undermined the fabric.

Such, as it seems to me, were the leading causes —tracing them no further at present than their social and industrial manifestations—which brought Ireland to the condition in which the potato famine found her. The phase through which she is now passing exhibits a reversal of all the causes from which that condition grew. A natural agriculture is taking the place of one, the result of artificial methods, kept in existence only through the same forcing legislation which gave it birth. Education and intercourse with other countries are slowly, but we hope effectually, generating in the Irish people ideas of decency and comfort—in the last resort the only effectual safeguard against the evil of excessive numbers. The opening of the earlier movement was marked by a temporary rude abundance, which was followed by an extraordinary increase of population: that of the present has been signalized by frightful but temporary distress; and a decline of population, not less notable than the previous increase, has now set in. These are the salient points on the surface of Ireland's present condition, and they indicate with sufficient accuracy the main direction of her industrial course.

* * * * * *

The famine of 1846 is commonly taken as the turning-point in the industrial history of Ireland. In fact it has proved so, because the famine precipitated free trade; but it is not less true that free trade would of itself have entailed, though without the frightful aggravations incident to the sudden failure of a people's food, all the consequences of a permanent kind which we trace to that calamity. All the leading incidents of the industrial economy of Ireland as it stood in 1846 were identified with the maintenance of its tillage system; and of that system free trade sounded the inevitable doom.

If these pages should find readers who cherish the tradition of Protection, they will doubtless regard this statement as a concession fraught with discredit to the doctrine of commercial freedom. Here, it will be urged, is the admission of a Free-trader that free trade has, in one instance at least, involved, if not accomplished, the destruction of a nation's industry. At whatever cost of odium to the doctrine in question, I am bound to accept the inference as substantially fair. It is, I hold, indubitably true that the cultivation of cereals in Ireland on the scale on which it prevailed anterior to 1846 depended upon Ireland's being secured in the monopoly of the English markets; and this condition free trade forbade. Whether England was on this account bound to exclude her own people from procuring their food where they could get it cheapest—bound to set limits to her own development in order to find a market for products unsuitable to the Irish soil—is the question which Free-traders have to meet. For my part I meet it by denying the obligation. Further, it is a part of my case that the sacrifice it involved would have been not less injurious to the country in whose behalf it was made than to that which was called to undergo it.

I regard it as a truth placed now beyond the reach of controversy that the population of Ireland in 1846 was excessive to a most injurious degree, excessive—looking to the actually available resources of the country to maintain its people—beyond any example afforded by history. Opinions to the contrary effect have indeed frequently been hazarded, sometimes even by writers of distinction. M. Gustave de Beaumont, for example, in his work on Ireland, expressed the deliberate opinion that population in that country has never been excessive, and that there is no reason in the economic conditions of the case that Ireland should not contain 25,000,000 of inhabitants. Had M. de Beaumont reflected that, on this view of the relation of population to territory, France, whose industrial capabilities are certainly in proportion to her area not inferior to those of Ireland, ought to contain 186,000,000 people—nearly five persons, that is to say, for every one who now inhabits that country—he possibly would have paused before giving utterance to so extravagant an opinion. Speculations which lead to such results, and which rest neither on experience, nor on any recognized principles of economic science, may, I think, be left to find their proper place in the judgments of unprejudiced men. As a matter of fact, Ireland in 1846 contained a population denser than that of most countries in Europe—denser, for example, than that of France, than that of Italy, than that of the average of the United Kingdom, and than that of the great majority of the states of Germany. In three countries only in Europe has the density of population ever decidedly exceeded that of Ireland in 1846 : and these are England, Saxony, and Belgium, each commanding, besides a remarkably fertile soil, manufacturing resources far in excess of any that Ireland can yet lay claim to.*

* "Histoire de l'Émigration," par M. Jules Duval, Paris, 1862, pp. 21, 64, 156. Belgium, it seems, is the most densely populated country in Europe, and in Belgium pauperism claims one out of every five of the inhabitants. (Ibid., pp. 115, 116.)

And what was the condition of the multitudes thus crowded together upon Irish soil? The answer is to be found in the well-known Report of the Devon Commission; but it would be idle now to adduce evidence of a state of things that was long a standing reproach to the British name. Suffice it to say that the great majority of this immense population were existing in the last stage of human wretchedness. In this condition they were found by the potato famine, and the long-pending collapse occurred.

Well, what was the cure for the state of things thus brought about? How was this excess of people to be remedied? The school of politicians who adopt M. de Beaumont's view on this subject would probably reply, by a suitable development of the industrial resources of the country; and this brings us to the inevitable dilemma in the Irish case. The resources of the country had already been developed, but developed in a wrong direction. An erroneous fiscal code had given encouragement to a system of agriculture wholly unsuited to the country, but which gave an impulse to population far beyond what a natural system could support. Was her industry to be urged still further in this direction? Was the principle of Protection to be again appealed to, and England to be invited to close her markets still more completely against foreign supplies? Either this, or it became necessary to abandon the policy that had brought her to the present pass. Started on a wrong course, she had reached the inevitable goal—the *cul-de-sac* of Protection: escape could only be found in retreat. Free trade was thus scarcely a choice. But free trade once adopted, all the consequences which have since been realized followed with the certainty of the results of a physical law.

Let us glance at a few of these consequences. And first, and most important of all, free trade imperatively prescribed a large reduction in the numbers of the Irish people; for it struck at the root of the large cereal cultivation by which those numbers were sustained. An agriculture of tillage differs from one of pasture amongst other things in this, that the capital which supports it is, for the most part, circulating— exists mainly in the form of food. Consumed every year, it is every year reproduced, and is thus available as a constant fund for the support of population to nearly the full extent of its actual amount. The capital of a pasture system, on the other hand, exists to a large extent in a certain condition of the soil which yields revenue without any or with little human exertion. It is not yearly consumed to be yearly reproduced, and consequently, so far as it takes this form, it is incapable of supporting population. Now, it was a system of this kind that over a large part of Ireland was rendered inevitable by the adoption of a free-trade policy. The effect, indeed, was not felt at once. So long as the process of conversion from tillage to pasture was in operation, the demand for labour, and with it the circulating capital of the country, would be maintained unimpaired: but the conversion once effected—the land once brought into the condition in which it was destined permanently to remain—both the need for labourers and the means for their subsistence would together suffer decline. Free trade in Ireland, thus, of necessity—throwing the country back, as it did, on its natural capabilities, which were favourable to pasture—involved as its consequence a diminution in the number of its people. But other causes, founded no less than free trade in the irresistible tendencies of modern civilization, were at this time acting powerfully in the same direction.

2.—THE EMIGRATION.

Within a quarter of a century following 1846, more than two million Irishmen have left the shores of Ireland never to return. The population of Ireland under the drain, aggravated by famine and pestilence, has declined from over eight to considerably under six millions of people. And yet, despite the lowering of the head-water, the efflux continues, and, though in later years partially checked for a season, shows as yet but few signs of abatement. The phenomenon in its actual dimensions is, I believe, unique in history. Passion and prejudice apart, let us endeavour to determine the causes and probable results on the fortunes of Ireland of this momentous movement.

On approaching the problem, the solution which most naturally suggests itself is misgovernment. "When the inhabitants of a country," says Mr. Mill, "quit the country *en masse*, because its government will not make it a place fit for them to live in, the government is judged and condemned." I have no need to dispute the soundness of this position as a maxim in political ethics; but in applying it to the case in hand, I must remark that, if misgovernment have produced the spectacle which Ireland now presents, either it is the misgovernment of a former age, or else the whole political philosophy of modern times is in a wrong track. For when we turn to the history of recent legislation affecting Ireland, what is the scene that it unfolds? A long series of measures extending over half a century, moving steadily in the direction of liberty, equal justice, intellectual and moral cultivation, and industrial development. The penal code has been abolished. Class ascendency, so long rampant, has been all but overthrown. Catholics have been emancipated. Municipal corporations have been reformed. An efficient police has been organized. A system of popular education, based upon the principle of absolute impartiality between different sects, and having at its disposal the best modern appliances, has been established. This gift of primary education has been followed by a provision, founded on the same principle and carried out with the same efficiency, for the higher intellectual cultivation. A Poor law has been passed under which the duties of property towards poverty have in Ireland for the first time been recognized and enforced. Medical charities have been reformed and rendered efficient. The civil service of the United Kingdom has been thrown open to the youth of Ireland upon equal terms. Nor have material interests been overlooked. A Board has been constituted, charged with the special function of

* [I may now (1873) say "quite."]

guiding and assisting Irish industrial enterprise; under its auspices arterial drainage on an extended scale has been carried out at the expense of the State, and, in addition, public money to the amount of nearly two millions sterling has been advanced to individuals on terms below the market rate for kindred purposes. A plan for the collection of agricultural statistics—an obvious reform, hitherto attempted in vain in other portions of the empire—has in Ireland been carried into effect with complete success. Lastly, a new Land court has been erected, in which, in obedience to the teaching of a sound political economy, and conformably with the procedure of an enlightened jurisprudence, the land of the country has been brought largely into the market, broken up into comparatively manageable portions, and transferred from listless and bankrupt, to solvent and enterprising hands. These are the salient features of modern Irish legislation. I do not say they prove that Ireland is now well governed, that further legislation, and that of a radical sort, is not needed for her welfare—on the contrary, as will be seen in the sequel, my position is that such legislation is imperatively required;* but the foregoing enumeration justifies me, I think, in asserting that the misgovernment from which Ireland is suffering, so far as it is of a positive kind, is not of recent date; that the sins of modern legislation against her have, at the worst, been sins of omission: at least, if it be otherwise—if the enactments just mentioned be examples of misgovernment—then manifestly the political philosophy of the present age is at fault.

* [Written in 1866.]

But, in the next place, it must be observed that the phenomenon with which we have to deal, unless as regards the exceptional dimensions it has assumed, is not one peculiar to Ireland. Emigration on a vast scale is rather a feature of the age than of any particular country, and has been conspicuously exhibited by some of the most advanced nations of Europe. The commencement of the movement, on the scale which it has assumed in modern times, may be placed about the end of the first quarter of the present century. At that time, Great Britain, Ireland, and Germany—the countries in which emigration has since attained the greatest height—did not send forth from their collective bounds an annual aggregate of more than 20,000 persons. But from that point the tide rose, and with such rapidity and power, that within another quarter of a century, the stream of 20,000 had swollen to 500,000—a magnitude which it maintained for some six years in succession, and to which, though it has since considerably declined, there are symptoms at the present moment that it may approach once more. The proportions in which the three countries, Great Britain, Ireland, and Germany, contributed to the stream when at its highest, were not very unequal; they may be taken to be nearly as follows :—

Ireland	210,000
Germany	155,000
Great Britain	135,000

Total annual emigration from the three countries, 500,000

The contribution of Ireland to the movement, compared with its population, is obviously in excess of that furnished by the other contributories; still, it cannot be denied that theirs is also very large. Nor have the countries named been the only ones in which emigration has received an extraordinary impulse in recent years; in a less degree, but still sensibly, Spain, Belgium, Scandinavia, and even France, have felt the emigrating impulse.*

With these facts before us, we shall not be disposed to seek an explanation of Irish emigration exclusively in local causes. It is plainly part of a larger movement, the result of influences which have made themselves felt over the greater portion of Western Europe. A variety of events at once suggest themselves as connected with this dispersion of population—seasons of dearth, fluctuations in trade, gold discoveries, civil commotions, foreign wars, notably, just now (1866), an urgent demand for labour in the United States of America. Each of these events has no doubt contributed something to the general result; but causes of this kind, which have never been absent from the world, can plainly be no more than secondary,† in relation to a phenomenon, which, in its actual dimensions at least, is a purely modern one; it is, therefore, to modern agencies mainly that we must look for an explanation; and amongst these four stand out as of

* "Histoire de l'Émigration," par M. Jules Duval.
† Many will be disposed to place the Australian and Californian gold discoveries amongst the primary causes of the phenomenon in question. I have not done so, because, however considerable their effect has been in attracting emigration—and doubtless it has been very considerable—I wish to distinguish what may be regarded as accidents which produce their effect once for all, from those causes of a permanent kind, the influence of which, far from declining, must increase from age to age.

prime importance—popular education, steam, free trade, and the progress of colonization.

The influence of education in unsettling population and impelling it towards new lands, is too plain to need detailed proof. Kindling among the masses the desire of bettering their condition, it discloses to them at the same time a new world of which they had been before but dimly conscious; a world where labour is amply rewarded, where the labourer is liberally endowed with political power, where a bounteous soil offers to his grasp that most cherished object of human yearning—a spot of ground which he may call his own. The vision awakened in the school is kept alive by the newspaper, and gathers strength from the account of friends who have tried it and proved it true. The idea becomes a conviction, the conviction a resolution, and the die is cast. Popular education has thus supplied the motive, and steam and free trade have not less surely furnished the means. It would be waste of time to enlarge upon a proposition which I suppose must be admitted as soon as stated. Steam and free trade have obviously been amongst the most potent of the agencies to which the unprecedented expansion of industry and commerce in modern times is due; and the expansion of industry and commerce cannot but facilitate emigration. I have added as among modern facts bearing upon emigration the progress of colonization; for colonization is eminently one of those undertakings in which the beginning is more than half the work. Amongst the practical problems of politics, none, perhaps, is more difficult than to found a colony. Rarely has success been accomplished except through straits in which the pioneers of civilization have been called upon to endure all the extremes of suffering. But settlement once effected, the foundation once laid, the subsequent building up of colonies is an easy task. The emigrant, on his arrival, finds himself at once in the midst of the comforts of a well-ordered society, and enters forthwith into the realization of his dreams. Emigration thus becomes less repulsive as colonization extends. A wider area of choice is opened up to the dissatisfied denizens of the old world; and there exist fewer drawbacks to the golden prospects which lure them from their homes.

The result may be stated in a few words: under the old-world rule, when the masses were shut up in ignorance,—when surplus wealth, from the inefficiency of productive processes, was small,—when industry was artificially organized, and commerce fettered,—when vast regions of the globe were still in the possession of savage man,—civilization rallied to a few favoured centres, around which clustered excessive populations: but a new epoch has opened, and agencies unknown in former times have brought the unsettled portions of the earth into immediate, sensible, and practical competition with those which are already occupied. The result cannot be doubtful: there must henceforward be a greater dispersion and mixing of populations, and a greater equalization of the conditions of wealth. It will no longer be a few favoured and conveniently situated spots on the earth's surface, but the whole earth, that will be turned to the purposes of man.

Such appear to me to be the leading causes of a general kind that have given that impulse to emigration on a vast scale which is undoubtedly one of the most remarkable facts in the present condition of the civilized world. It will scarcely be denied that, so far as emigration is traceable to these causes, it is due, not to misgovernment, but to improved government, or rather in but a slight degree to government at all, and mainly to the progress of human intelligence and human well-being. The causes which I have enumerated are all inherent in the present state of civilization; and emigration, so far as it is a feature of the age, is thus a sign, not of decline but of advance — evidence, at once practical and conclusive, that the world is moving onward—

"Through the shadow of the globe we sweep into the younger day."

Nor will it be denied that these causes have all been in operation in Ireland. The national system of education—a system under which Roman Catholics and Protestants are invited to come together and receive beneath the same roof those common elements of secular and moral instruction the value of which is recognized by all Christian denominations alike—has brought knowledge on easy terms to the poorest of the peasantry. From being perhaps the most ignorant population in Europe—ignorance which was no fault of theirs, but in which they had long been compulsorily kept by an atrocious system of penal legislation—the Irish have become, in the course of a generation, educated at least up to the English popular standard. In the national schools their children have learned the English language :* they have also learned geography, and have heard, most of them for the first time, of a great country, teeming with riches, within a fortnight's sail of their coasts. What more natural than the desire to reach this land of promise? The march of industry and commerce in Ireland has not indeed kept pace with that witnessed in the more advanced European countries; nevertheless, as will presently be shown, industrial and commercial progress even in Ireland has been real and considerable; and, what is more to our present purpose, so far as the facilities for emigration are concerned, Ireland has enjoyed all the benefits of the more rapidly expanding commerce of the Empire. The increased intercourse of England with the outer world is directly available for the Irish peasant, who has thus brought within his reach the most widely ramified system of international communication and the cheapest navigation in the world. The practical result is this. In 1825 the cost of a passage to America was not less than £20. So late as 1845 the Land Occupation Commissioners considered the high rate of fares as the chief obstacle to emigration. But since that time the passage-money has been reduced to £10, to £6, to £5. In the spring of 1863 steamboats were carrying passengers from the Irish ports to New York for £4 15s. per head, and sailing vessels for £2 17s. 6d. The road thus smoothed, and aspiration thus awakened, a new accessory to the movement has been

* The number of the Irish who could speak Irish *only* was in 1822 (according to the estimate of the Irish Society) 2,000,000. In 1851 this class had (as ascertained by the Census) fallen to 319,602, and in 1861 to 163,276. (Hancock's Report, &c., p. 11.)

developed through the connection of the emigrants with those whom they had left behind. Their prosperity has at once justified their conduct in the eyes of their friends at home, and enabled them to furnish those friends with the means of following their example. It is an honourable and hopeful trait of the emigration that, through the liberality springing from family affection, it has become an entirely self-supporting movement. In 1847 £200,000, it has been estimated, reached Ireland from America with this destination; in 1853 the remittances rose to a million and a half.

It must then, I think, be admitted that there are other causes than "misgovernment" at the root of the Irish emigration: nevertheless, I do not mean to deny, under the reserve I have indicated, that "misgovernment" is also a cause. The circumstances which I have enumerated account for emigration from Ireland; they do not account for the exceptional and extraordinary dimensions which Irish emigration has assumed; they do not tell us why it has become an "Exodus." To understand this we must take account of causes of repulsion as well as of causes of attraction; of the impossibility of remaining as well as of the facilities for going: we must combine with those agencies which have affected all civilized peoples the condition in which these found the people of Ireland. That condition has been already described. The country was immensely over-populated. The overgrown population was plunged in the deepest misery. It had just been visited by a tremendous calamity; and the system of industry, under which alone the maintenance of its numbers was possible, had run its course, and was collapsing from exhaustion. Free trade was heralding a new industrial career, but one incompatible with the actual numbers of the Irish people. All things thus concurred to the same result, and Irish emigration became the portentous spectacle we have seen it.

Such has been the character of this extraordinary movement, and such, to the best of my judgment, is its explanation. It is the composite result of perfectly distinct trains of events—of decades of good, following upon centuries of bad, government—of the sudden disruption of mediæval barbarism by the grandest forces of modern civilization. But where is the movement to end? and what is its significance as regards the interests of the country from which it proceeds?

3.—*THE IRISH COTTIER.*

In his admirable "Plea for Peasant Proprietors," Mr. Thornton observes that "Ireland is one of the few countries in which there neither are, nor ever were, peasant properties." The remark well deserves consideration, and, followed up, will be found to throw light on some characteristic features of Irish industrial life.

It would seem that, in the progress of nations from barbarism to civilization, there is a point at which the bulk of the people pass naturally into the peasant-proprietor condition. In the work just referred to, this transition has been traced in the industrial history of the Jews, Romans, and Greeks amongst ancient nations, and, amongst moderns, in that of the leading nations of Western Europe; and it has been shown with abundant and interesting illustration that the *régime* of peasant properties has been constantly coincident with great physical comfort amongst the masses of the people. As Mr. Thornton observes, it was after peasant proprietorship had existed for five hundred years in Judea, that David declared he had "never seen the righteous forsaken, nor his seed begging bread;" while, on the other hand, it was not till under the later kings—when men had begun "to lay field to field till there was no place, that they might be placed alone in the midst of the earth"—that pauperism became a constant and increasing evil among the Jews. The notion of every man "dwelling under his own vine and fig-tree" was the traditional Jewish ideal of national happiness. In Roman history, to borrow another example from Mr. Thornton, though debt and poverty were never rare amongst the plebeians, pauperism as a normal phenomenon, paupers as a distinct class, did not make their appearance till towards the seventh century of the city, when the small peasant estates of the Roman Commons had been consolidated into the enormous grazing farms cultivated by slaves, which were the characteristic feature of the later Roman agriculture. From being the scene of a thriving rustic population, each man the owner of his own farm of some ten or twelve acres, Italy became a country of immense estates of absentee proprietors worked by slave-gangs; while the population which had in the early time sustained itself by industry, crowded into the cities, and chiefly to Rome, where they became the formidable rabble whom it was found necessary to support by regular largesses of corn. The connection between pauperism and consolidation did not escape the patriots of the time. It is a noteworthy fact that the practice of largesses was introduced by the same men who were also the agitators for the distribution of the public lands. To give one example more, English history illustrates the same tendency to peasant proprietorship at a certain stage of a nation's growth, and not less decisively the social value of that economy. The period when it had attained its greatest development in England seems to have been about the end of the fifteenth century, by which time the condition of villenage had very generally passed into that of copyhold tenure, while that tendency to a consolidation of estates and holdings which marked the epoch of Elizabeth had not yet commenced. To what extent the system then actually prevailed, there is not perhaps any distinct evidence to show; but two centuries later, when considerable progress had been made in the consolidation of farms, the authorities on whom Lord Macaulay relies speak of not less than 160,000 proprietors as existing in England, forming with their families not less than a seventh of the whole population, who derived their subsistence from little freehold estates. "These petty proprietors," says the historian,—"an eminently manly and true-hearted race,—cultivated their own fields with their own hands, and enjoyed a modest competence, without affecting to have scutcheons and crests, or aspiring to sit on the bench of justice." *

Of the remarkable prosperity enjoyed by the rural population of England when peasant proprietorship formed the prevailing tenure—that is to say, in the latter half of the fifteenth century—the evidence adduced by Mr. Thornton is copious and striking, and to my mind conclusive; nor is it the less instructive when contrasted with the fact that the movement towards consolidation which followed the period in question was attended with an extraordinary increase of pauperism, resulting, as is well known, in the passing of the first English Poor Law. These examples might easily be multiplied; but enough has probably been said to illustrate, if not to substantiate, our position, that in the progress of nations from barbarism to civilization the condition of peasant proprietorship naturally arises, and that the period when it has prevailed has always been conspicuous for human well-being. Now, into this phase of industrial existence the Irish people have never passed. The fact, as it seems to me, is one intimately connected with their present condition and character; and as such it will, I think, be found to repay a careful investigation.

In one of the most profound of modern works on the philosophy of jurisprudence it has been shown that the primitive condition of property is that of joint

---

* "History of England," vol. i. pp. 333, 334.

ownership—"that property once belonged not to individuals or even to isolated families, but to larger societies composed on the patriarchal model;" and that private property, as we now know it, has only attained its actual form by a process of "gradual disentanglement of the separate rights of individuals from the blended rights of a community."* This discovery—for, looking to the theories as to the origin of property hitherto current in the accepted text-books of jurisprudence, it must, as such, be regarded—if taken in connection with the known historical facts of the conquest of Ireland, will be found to throw some light upon the problem with which we are now concerned. The conquest of Ireland is popularly referred to the reign of Henry the Second and the twelfth century: in fact, as was long ago shown in Sir John Davis's well-known essay,† with the exception of the small portion of the island known as "the Pale," and some towns along the eastern and southern coasts, Ireland was not conquered till the reign of Queen Elizabeth, nor effectually brought under English dominion till that of her successor. "The Irish chieftains," says Sir John Davis, "governed the people by Brehon law: they made their own magistrates and officers; they pardoned and punished malefactors within their several counties; they made war and peace upon one another without controlment; and this they did not only in the reign of Henry the Second, but afterwards in all times even unto the reign of

---

* Maine's "Ancient Law," chap. viii.
† "Discovery of the True Causes why Ireland was never entirely Subdued."

Queen Elizabeth."* Now the condition of landed property in Ireland at the time when the conquest was consummated affords, it seems to me, an instructive illustration of what may be called the juridical principle brought to light by Mr. Maine, exhibiting property, as it does, in the intermediary condition, when the process of disentanglement had been begun, but before it was yet completed.

The following is the account given of it by the writer from whom I have just quoted, himself a member of the Commission to which was entrusted the task of accepting the surrender of Irish estates, and re-granting them according to the course of English common law:—

"By the Irish custom of Tanistry the chieftains of every country, and the chief of every sept, had no longer estate than for life in their chiefries, the inheritance whereof did rest in no man. And these chiefries, though they had some portion of land allotted them, did consist chiefly in cuttings and coshcries, and other Irish exactions, whereby they did spoil and impoverish the people at their pleasure. And when their chieftains were dead, their sons or next heirs did not succeed them, but their Tanistres, who were elective, and purchased their elections by strong hand; and by the Irish custom of gavelkind the inferior tenancies were partable amongst all the males of the sept, both bastards and legitimate: and after partition made, if any one of the sept had died, his portion was not divided among his sons, but the chief of the sept made a new parti-

---

* "Discovery of the True Causes why Ireland was never entirely Subdued." The Parliament of Kilkenny condemned the Brehon law, but this only applied to its use by the "degenerate English." "The Statute," says Hallam, "like all others passed in Ireland, so far from pretending to bind the Irish, regarded them not only as out of the king's allegiance, but as perpetually hostile to his government. They were generally denominated the Irish enemy."

tion of all the lands belonging to that sept, and gave every one his part according to his antiquity."

What struck English lawyers, to whom the duty fell of examining this proprietary system, was, as we might expect, its loose and indeterminate character. The "cuttings and cosheries"—exactions, of which the principal consisted in living at free quarters amongst their tenants,* which constituted the chief property of the Tanists—were wholly undefined, or rather defined only by custom; while the practice of redistributing the lands of the sept on the death of any of its members, which formed a distinctive feature of Irish gavelkind, seemed still more utterly irreconcilable with English ideas of property. Nevertheless, extraordinary and apparently impracticable as were these Brehon tenures, judged by the standard of modern English notions, they in fact bear a strong analogy to—indeed, I might say, are in character identical with—various modes of possession which have at different times existed amongst other nations during the corresponding stage of their growth, and of which some examples are still extant;†—a fact from which we may infer that they were on the whole not unsuitable to the social and industrial requirements of those who lived under them. Those requirements were the requirements of a people who had advanced a little beyond the nomad condition, but had not yet attained to that of settled and systematic agriculture. Spenser, writing in the reign of Elizabeth, has thus described what he calls "their Scythian or Scottish manners:"—

* "Somewhat analogous," says Hallam, "to the royal prerogative of purveyance." † Maine's "Ancient Law," chap. viii.

"Of the which there is one use amongst them to keepe their cattle, and to live themselves, the most part of the yeare, in boolies, pasturing upon the mountaine, and waste wilde places; and removing still to fresh land as they have depastured the former. The which appeareth plaine to be the manner of the Scythians, . . . to live in heards, as they call them, being the very same that the Irish boolies are, driving their cattle continually with them, and feeding only on their milke and white meats."* This being the mode of existence generally prevailing in the wilder and more remote parts of Ireland at this time, and the proprietary usages consonant to this state of things, or to one slightly in advance of this,—such as they appear in the Brehon laws,—being entirely analogous to what have been found prevailing in other parts of the world where society has attained a corresponding stage of growth, we are justified, I think, in assuming that, had the Irish people been allowed to follow the course of their natural development, what has happened in other countries would have happened in Ireland also. It is reasonable to think that the progress of population and enlarged intercourse with more advanced nations would there, too, in the absence of disturbing causes, have produced their natural effects in quickening the sentiment of property; that the exactions of the chiefs would have become more and more strictly limited; that the occasions for redistributions would have been made less and less frequent; that the common sept property would by degrees have passed more or less completely into individual possession; in

---

* "View of the State of Ireland."

a word, that the Brehon tenures would have ripened into a peasant proprietorship. But just at this time a large portion of the soil of Ireland passed into the hands of English owners; and within half a century the remainder for the most part followed the same destination. These owners took the place of the native chiefs, but with proprietary pretensions of a far different kind. The loose prerogatives of the Tanists were suddenly, by the fiat of an English judge, transmuted into the definite ownership of English law; and, on the other hand, the claims of the members of the clan—adjudged by the English courts to be no estate, " but a transitory and scrambling possession"—were absolutely repudiated. The natural development of property in the soil was in this manner violently arrested in Ireland, which has accordingly never known peasant proprietorship. It has, however, in lieu thereof, furnished the world with a type of tenure peculiarly its own. "Cottierism" is, we believe, a specific and almost unique product of Irish industrial life.

One of the most curious and unfortunate blunders which have been made about the Irish cottier is that which confounds him with the peasant proprietor under the general description of a representative of the *petite culture*. In fact the two forms of tenure are, in that which constitutes their most important attribute—the nature of the cultivator's interest in the soil which he tills—diametrically opposed: and the practical results stand as strongly in contrast as the conditions. It would be difficult, perhaps, to conceive two modes of existence more utterly opposed than the thriftless, squalid, and half-starved life of the peasant of Munster and Connaught, and that of the frugal, thriving, and energetic races that have, over a great portion of continental Europe — in Norway, in Belgium, in Switzerland, in Lombardy— and under the most various external conditions, turned swamps and deserts into gardens. And it is scarcely a less gross error to apply to the same status, after the fashion so common with political reasoners in this country, conclusions deduced from the relations of landlord and tenant in England and Scotland. True, the cottier and the cultivator of Great Britain are alike tenant-farmers: they both pay rent, which is, moreover, in each case determined by the competition of the market. But under what circumstances does competition take place in the two countries? In Great Britain the competitors are independent capitalists, bidding for land as one among the many modes of profitable investment which the complex industrial civilization of the country supplies: in Ireland they are men—we speak, it will be remembered, of the cottier class—for the most part on the verge of absolute pauperism, who see in a few acres of land their sole escape—we cannot now say from starvation, but at best from emigration and the workhouse. Is it strange that the result should be different in the two cases? and that "rent," which in England and Scotland represents exceptional profit (the appropriation of which by the landlord merely equalizes agriculture with other occupations), should in Ireland be the utmost penny that can be wrung from the poverty-stricken cultivator? How, again, does the analogy of the tenant-farmer of continental countries meet the present case? Between the "métayer" and the cottier there is the broad distinction, that, while the rent of the former is a fixed proportion of the produce, determined by custom, that of the cottier is whatever competition may make it—the competition, we repeat, of impoverished men, bidding under the pressure of prospective exile or beggary. Lastly, we must insist on keeping the cottier distinct from another class also, with whom he has been more pardonably confounded, and with whom indeed he has many real affinities—the serf of Eastern Europe and of mediæval times. Judging from their ordinary existence, there is perhaps little to distinguish the cottier from the serf. Nevertheless they are not the same. The serf is *adscriptus glebæ*: the Irish cottier, as he knows by painful experience, is bound to the soil by no tie save those imposed by his own necessities. He has unbounded freedom to relinquish, when he pleases, his farm and home, and to transfer himself to the other side of the Atlantic, and he pays for the privilege (of which, no doubt, he has largely availed himself) in the liability, to which the serf is a stranger, of being expelled from his farm and home when it suits the views of his landlord.

Such is the Irish cottier, the essential incidents of whose position are well summed up in the definition of Mr. Mill—"a labourer, who makes his contract for the land without the intervention of a capitalist farmer," and "the conditions of whose contract, especially the rent, are determined not by custom but by competition." *

I have said that cottierism is a specific product of Irish industrial life; and it will not be difficult to show that, in the position in which Ireland was placed after the confiscations of the seventeenth century, this was the mode of existence on which the bulk of the Irish people were naturally, perhaps inevitably, thrown. It has been already seen, that the circumstances of the case precluded the realization, in conformity with the analogy of industrial progress in other countries, of a peasant-proprietor *régime*. It is obvious that those circumstances were equally unfavourable to the rise of a tenant-farmer class on the modern English pattern, who might, by a steady demand for the services of the natives, have raised them at all events to the level of the Dorsetshire agricultural labourer; for disposable capital is the basis of such a class, and disposable capital did not exist in Ireland; nor could it arise in a country in which the embers of political and religious hate were still glowing, ready on the slightest provocation to burst into flame. From the advantages of the "métayer" tenure of the Continent, again, the Irish

---

* Mr. Jones's definition of a "cottier" is "a peasant tenant extracting his maintenance from the soil, and paying a money rent to the landowner." He adds, "The distinguishing peculiarity of this race of peasant tenants is that they pay a *money* rent." (Jones's "Political Economy," p. 208.) It seems to me that this definition omits the most important circumstance affecting the cottier's condition, the fact that his rent is determined by competition—a fact on which the same writer in a later passage very sensibly comments; while that which he lays down as the distinguishing peculiarity of the "cottier" is not peculiar to him, nor in fact essential to the *status*. The Indian ryot pays his rent, I believe, mostly in money; while the "money rents" of the Irish cottier used to be largely paid in labour.

were excluded by moral, but not less potent causes. *Métairie* belongs eminently to that class of institutions which are not made, but grow. Resting upon custom, it presupposes common traditions and mutual confidence and regard—conditions, which, it is superfluous to say, were not to be found in Irish industrial society. There remained serfdom, which was in effect, though not in name, the state of life into which, in the period immediately following the great confiscations, the mass of the Irish people fell. But, as we have said, serfdom, though closely allied to, is not precisely, "cottierism." To realize the latter, it is necessary to apply to the former the maxims of competition and contract; and this was what in the course of the eighteenth century happened in Ireland. Modes of action which are only suitable, which are only tolerable, in an advanced industrial civilization, where the actors stand on independent grounds and exercise a real choice, and where moreover an effective public opinion exists to control extravagant pretensions, were suddenly introduced and rigorously applied*

* "Agents, particularly of those noblemen or gentlemen who reside in England, or at a distance from their estates, who have been empowered to treat with tenants and give leases, to ingratiate themselves with their employers (that thus by their skilful management they might procure more agencies from others), have in some cases taken proposals sealed up, under promise to divulge none of the names but that of the person who offered most, whose proposal was to be accepted of. Thus the lease was given to the highest bidder, so that the present possessor had no chance for a renewal unless he offered above the value; for doubtless among so many proposers there were some who offered at random, without knowing the value of the land; and if any tenant had been a greater improver than his neighbour, or had his houses or lands in better order, he was sure to be the sufferer. These have been the methods used by some agents, to the ruin of the nation, by which means they gave landlords a nominal rent-roll, and very often paid part of their

amongst a people just emerging from the nomad state. In the lowest deep there was thus found a lower deep; and Irish serfdom merged in the more desperate *status* of the Irish cottier.*

I have hitherto dwelt chiefly upon one incident—the fundamental one, as it seems to me—in the condition of the Irish cottier—the determination of his rent by competition, he himself having no other resource than the land. But we may look at him also from another point of view, as, to borrow the definition of Judge Longfield, "the cultivator who produces almost wholly for his own consumption, and pays his rent chiefly in labour." Thus regarded, we shall have no difficulty in connecting him with that capital revolution in the history of Irish agriculture, referred to in a former passage, which marked the close of the eighteenth century, to which, though it did not originate cottierism, the principal development of the system is undoubtedly to be traced. The nature and some of the effects

rents with a mouthful of moonshine, by reason of tenants breaking and running off in arrear, whilst they themselves, by ways and means, got estates sometimes equal to those of their employer."—*An Essay upon the Trade and Improvement of Ireland.* By Arthur Dobbs, Esq. (1739).

* As I wish to be impartial, it is proper to add that the cottier condition is not absolutely without something to recommend it. "The principal advantage which the cottier derives from his form of tenure," says Mr. Jones, "is the great facility with which, when circumstances are favourable to him, he can exchange altogether his condition in society. The serf has many stages to go through before he can become a capitalist and independent farmer; and it is hard for him to advance a step in this direction. . . . . But the cottier is already the owner of his own stock; he exists in a society in which the power of paying money rents is already established. If he thrives in his occupation, there is nothing to prevent him enlarging his holding, increasing his stock, and becoming a capitalist and farmer in the proper sense of the term."—*Political Economy*, pp. 210, 211.

of this movement I have already attempted to describe. It consisted in a rapid extension of cereal and potato cultivation, which henceforth took the place of pasture as the leading industry of Ireland. In a country like England—indeed, in any of the more civilized countries of Western Europe—such a movement as the extension of tillage farming would obviously be carried into effect through an increase of circulating capital. Funds would be obtained which would be expended in paying labourers who would perform the necessary operations, and a class of workmen depending on the labour market would thus be called into existence. But Ireland was at this time almost wholly destitute of circulating capital. The landlords themselves, the middlemen, and the few large pastoral farmers, with whom the initiative in effecting the change would naturally lie, were scarcely better off in this respect than the peasantry whom they desired to employ. Under these circumstances, the course with which we are now so familiar could not be adopted. Silver and gold, food and clothing, the leaders of Irish industry had none; but such as they had, they gave. They took the peasantry into their employment, and paid them with land. The practice, far from being unknown, is precisely that which has invariably been adopted under similar circumstances, and is in fact the mode of proceeding which has at one time or another, in almost all European countries, led to the introduction of serfdom.* What distinguished the Irish

---

* "In the early and rude state of society, the expedient used by landed proprietors to get rid of the task of raising food for their labourers is as follows :—They set aside for their use a portion of their estate, and

course of action lay, as I understand the matter, mainly in these two circumstances,—first, the bargain was not struck once for all, but was liable to subsequent modification according to the reciprocal necessities of those who were parties to it—that is to say, according to the state of the market; and secondly, though in effect an exchange of land against labour, it was not struck in terms of land and labour, but in terms of money. The Irish peasant undertook to pay for his patch of land that sum of money which the competition of his fellows forced him to pay, and this sum he was allowed to work out in labour, at a rate of wages also determined by competition. Cottierism (omitting the condition of personal freedom, and regarding it simply in its economic aspect) was thus in fact serfdom reduced to a money standard, and modified by competition.* As we have already said, the system in Ireland did not owe its origin to this movement. Its roots lay in an earlier period, and are traceable to a political and social, rather than an

leave them to extract their own subsistence from it at their own risk; and they exact as a rent for the land thus abandoned, a certain quantity of labour to be employed upon the remaining portion of the estate, which is retained in their own hands."—JONES'S *Political Economy*, p. 198.

* The practice, as it stood in the latter half of the last century, is thus described by Arthur Young :—"If there are cabins on a farm, they are the residence of the cottars ; if there are none, the farmer marks out the potato gardens, and the labourers who apply to him on his hiring the land, raise their own cabins on such spots ; in some places the farmer builds, in others he only assists with the roof, &c. ; a verbal contract is then made that the new cottar shall have his potato garden at such a rent, and one or two cows kept him at the price of the neighbourhood, he finding the cows. He then works with the farmer at the rate of the place, usually sixpence halfpenny a day, a tally being kept (half by each party), and a notch cut for every day's labour : at the end of six months or a year, they reckon, and the balance is paid. The cottar works for himself as his potatoes require."

industrial revolution. But it received at the time we are speaking of, and under the circumstances we have described, its principal extension, that which has given to the *status* its modern importance in Ireland, and rendered it the type of the industry of a people. Cottierism in Ireland has thus become associated with the fortunes of cereal cultivation; and, as it has grown with its growth, so, as will presently appear, it seems destined to sink with its decline.

One cannot help remarking here on the intimate connection of the policy of Protection with the industrial fortunes of Ireland. As has been previously shown, it was mainly to Protection that the excessive multiplication of the Irish population was due; and it now appears that the same principle is not less responsible for the peculiar mode of existence to which the great mass of this vast population was consigned. The factitious demand for labour occurring at this time was due to Protection; and, in the absence alike of peasant properties and circulating capital, this demand could only be met—as in fact it was met—by calling into existence the Irish cottier.

4.—*IRISH LANDLORDISM.*

"Irish landlordism," as it has existed in the last and the earlier half of the present century, may be roughly resolved into three categories :—firstly, the great landlords,—with a few exceptions, Englishmen or of English descent, and Protestants, of whom the great majority had derived their estates from the confiscations of the seventeenth century; secondly, the owners of smaller estates, by extraction also in great part English, or at all events British, and indebted for their properties mainly to the same political revolutions; and thirdly, the class of middlemen or profit-renters, who, though themselves paying rent to landlords, were by religion, political sympathies, and habits, intimately connected, and, in their conduct and general views, practically identified with the proprietary class. Of these the first class to a great extent became absentees, managing their estates either through agents, or, as was the more common case, through middlemen—those who form the third category in the above enumeration —to whom they let the land in large portions at low rents, and who sub-divided it and sub-let it to the occupying tenantry. The second and third classes, whose revenues were not sufficient to allow of residence in England or abroad, for the most part lived on the estates which they owned or superintended.

"The principal source of all our misfortunes, and the chief cause of all our distress," said Prior,* writing in 1729, "appears plainly from the list of absentees, and the estimate of the quantity of specie they may be reasonably supposed to draw yearly out of the kingdom." Such has been the complaint of writer after writer from that period to the present time. Nevertheless there are now, I should imagine, few competent thinkers who will not be of opinion that the utmost damage inflicted by absenteeism on Ireland—

* Author of "A List of the Absentees of Ireland," published 1729.

and I am, for my part, far from thinking that this was not very considerable even in an economic point of view,* and still more in a social and political—was absolutely inappreciable in comparison with the misfortunes entailed upon the country through the proprietary who remained at home. The absentee landlords neglected their duties, and drew their rents: the resident proprietary drew much more exorbitant rents, and were at the same time the active agents of a tyranny as demoralizing and ruinous as any which the history of modern times has exhibited. "Surely the gentlemen of this country," said Arthur Young, with excellent sense, "when they complain of restricted commerce and the remittance of the rentals of the absentees to England, cannot be thought serious in lamenting the situation of their country, while they continue wedded to that internal ruin which is the work of their own hands, and the favourite child of their most active exertions. Complain not of restrictions when you yourselves impose the most enormous

---

* From this point of view chiefly through the enormous difficulty of remitting rents, owing to the harassing restrictions placed upon every branch of the Irish export trade—even the trade in corn and cattle having for some time lain under prohibition. The following dialogue between Dr. Johnson and "the famous George Faulkner" sets this difficulty in rather a striking light. Faulkner maintained that "England had drained Ireland of fifty thousand pounds in specie, annually, for fifty years. 'How so,' said Dr. Johnson; 'you must have very great trade?'—'No trade.'—'Very rich mines?'—'No mines.'—'From whence, then, does all this money come?'—'Come! why, out of the blood and bowels of the poor people of Ireland.'" (Boswell's "Johnson," vol. iv. p. 36.) As a *reductio ad absurdum* of the mercantile theory of wealth, the argument is perhaps sufficiently complete; but it does not very greatly exaggerate the truly Egyptian tyranny under which in their commercial, no less than in their political and religious interests, the Irish then groaned.

restriction ; and what are the body of absentees when compared with the absence of industry and wealth from the immense mass of two millions of subjects? I should be well founded in asserting that these evils, great and acknowledged as they are, are trifles when compared with the poverty and debility which result from the oppression of the Roman Catholics."

Industrial society in Ireland had thus, by the middle of the last century or a little later, received its definitive form—that form in which it has existed down to quite a recent date. We have already seen how one constituent of the system—the cottier element—grew in dimensions towards its close, contemporaneously with the great extension of tillage farming which was the industrial feature of the time; and I have now to observe that the same cause was not less powerful in developing the territorial economy in other directions. As tillage was extended, rents rapidly rose. I believe I should be within the mark in stating that in this period, between 1760 and the close of the French wars in the beginning of the present century, the land revenues of Ireland were augmented in the proportion of 4 to 1.* Each step in this progress would of course

* The lists of the rent-rolls of absentees drawn up by Prior and Young, at the dates respectively of 1729 and 1777, will give a rough idea of the advance down to the latter date. I subjoin a few examples which are not more than fair specimens of the general tenor of the lists. It will be borne in mind that the pace was accelerated from the commencement of the French wars.

	1729.	1777.		1729.	1777.
Abercorne . .	£2,000	£8,000	Donegal . .	£4,000	£31,000
Bellew . . .	600	4,000	Fitzwilliam .	5,000	8,000
Clanricharde.	3,000	5,000	Kingston . .	2,000	7,000
Courtnay . .	8,000	30,000	Middleton .	1,500	10,000

And see Young's "Tour in Ireland," Part I., pp. 171, 306, 315.

furnish increased scope for the multiplication of new
interests in the soil, and these took the form determined by the prevailing influences. Landlords who
formerly resided on their estates could now afford to
spend a greater or less portion of the year in some of
the fashionable centres of the Empire. Middlemen,
lessees under leases granted when prices were low and
pasture the prevailing pursuit, found their incomes
growing ; and, their ideas rising with their fortunes,
in many instances yielded, like their betters, to the
attractions of city life. Absenteeism thus increased,
and, with absenteeism, agencies and profit-renting. A
second and a third race of middlemen thus intruded
themselves between the head landlord and the occupying tenantry. The grades of the territorial hierarchy
became constantly more numerous ; the higher no less
than the lower being identified with the system of
agriculture which had now established itself in the
country. The Corn-laws soon came to aid the more
fundamental tendencies, and the commercial effects of
the French wars added a new and powerful stimulus
to the now complex influences which were impelling
Ireland on her disastrous career. In that career she
was arrested by the fearful summons of the famine
of 1846. The shock, rude as it was, extensively deranging as it could not fail to be to the entire
territorial system, might possibly not have been fatal,
had not the famine been the occasion of free trade ;
but, as I have already shown, free trade effectually
and for ever sealed its doom.

* * * * * *

The fundamental causes which involved the catastrophe of 1846 have been already considered. The immediate effect of those causes was the impoverishment of the country, and the sudden arrest of its industrial career: their secondary effect has been the development of tendencies of a new order, under the influence of which the proprietorship and occupancy of land in the country, and with these the conditions of production and the mode of distribution, have undergone, and are undergoing, extensive changes. The Encumbered and Landed Estates Courts have been the principal instruments in effecting changes in proprietorship; while changes in occupancy are taking place under the ordinary law set in motion by the parties concerned. The extent and character of the changes thus accomplished will next claim our attention.

The Encumbered Estates Court was established by Act of Parliament in 1848,* and commenced its sittings in 1849. Its object, as I believe is pretty well known, was to compel the sale of encumbered estates—that is to say, estates encumbered to one half of their value—on petition of either the owner or of any of his creditors, and to effect the distribution of the proceeds amongst the claimants. The Court continued to perform these functions down to 1858, when it was superseded by the present Landed Estates Court, which is in effect the same tribunal, constituted on a permanent footing, and with enlarged powers.† It must be admitted that the

---

* 12th and 13th Vict. c. 77.

† The main difference is that the Landed Estates Court can deal with *un*encumbered as well as with encumbered estates.

system thus established was of a character which could only be justified by the exigency of the case. It proceeded according to rules unknown to our existing system of jurisprudence; it set aside solemn contracts; it disregarded the cherished traditions of real property law. Mr. Butt does not overstate the case when he says, that the Act establishing the Encumbered Estates Court "compelled creditors to submit to a sale who had an express contract that no one should ever disturb them in their claim on the land except by paying off that claim. It forced properties to a general auction, to be sold for whatever they could bring, at a time when legislation had imposed new and unheard-of burdens upon landed property. At a time of unprecedented depreciation of the value of land, it called a general auction of Irish estates. I have always believed," continues Mr. Butt, "I still believe, that English history records no more violent legal interference with vested interests than the provisions by which this statute forced the sale of a large proportion of the landed property of Ireland, at a time when no prudent man would have set up an acre to be sold by public competition."* It would not be easy, I think, to disturb these statements of Mr. Butt, or to prove that the measure, tried by the received maxims of English jurisprudence, was not a measure of confiscation; yet it is not less certain that of all measures passed in recent times it is that one, of which the beneficial effects have been most widely and cor-

* "Land Tenure in Ireland," by Isaac Butt, formerly Professor of Political Economy in the University of Dublin, p. 88.

dially recognized. This is a fact which may perhaps be usefully borne in mind just now, when it is thought a sufficient condemnation of moderate proposals to describe them as "revolutionary." With our experience of the working of the Encumbered Estates Court, we may be permitted to think that to be "revolutionary" is, after all, not so very violent a presumption against a measure of Irish land reform.

The Encumbered Estates Court, as I have said, commenced its sittings in 1849. By 1859, when it closed its proceedings, about one-seventh of the whole landed property of Ireland had passed through its hands. The amount realized by the sales effected under its direction was upwards of £25,000,000 sterling, which, however, inadequately represents the real value of the land disposed of; a large proportion of the whole having been sold while the market was in a greatly depressed condition. Since that time the work has been taken up by its successor —the Landed Estates Court—which, in the interval between 1859 and 1865, effected sales to the amount of £12,000,000 sterling more. As the result of the combined operations of the two Courts, about one-eighth of Ireland in value, greatly more than one-eighth in area—probably one-sixth—has passed from the hands of the old proprietary into those of new men. It may be well to dwell for a moment on some of the consequences involved in this momentous change.

And, first, one immediate result has been an extensive weeding out from the proprietary of Ireland of that numerous class of needy, rapacious, deeply mortgaged "squireens," or petty gentry,—the owners of estates varying from £50 to some £200 or £300 of annual value—whose presence had long weighed as a nightmare on all efforts at Irish renovation. It would be a mistake to regard these men—albeit their final overthrow happened to be accomplished by the famine and the measures which that event rendered necessary—as the victims of this particular crisis in Irish history. Like the ruin of the Jamaica planters, which, though consummated by the Emancipation Act and free trade, had through half a century been steadily maturing under the pre-existing state of things—a state of things not very dissimilar from that which had prevailed in Ireland—the fate of this class of Irish squires had been sealed long before the famine, free trade, or the Encumbered Estates Court had been heard of. In the case of a large majority, their indebtedness dated from an early period of the century, and was, in fact, the direct result of their own reckless and extravagant habits —habits, no doubt, quite naturally engendered by their situation. So far, indeed, as their ruin could be attributed to any cause distinct from the general circumstances of the country, it might, with more justice, be charged upon their favourite system of Protection, than which it would not be easy to imagine an order of things better calculated to seduce a proprietary of easy virtue into extravagant courses.* Seasons

---

* It may be useful to recall some of the incidents of this period, which has now almost passed out of mind. The ordinary opinion connects the high range of prices in the early part of the century with the French wars. The wars, no doubt, contributed something towards the result, so far,

of extraordinary dearness, followed by seasons of no less extraordinary abundance, glimpses of prosperity succeeded by the gloom of falling markets— by such alternations, the direct result of the sliding scale, hopes were kept alive only to be disappointed; nominal revenues maintained at a pitch which was never realized in fact; and a fox-hunting and reckless squirearchy in a manner lured to their doom. The famine and the measures which it necessitated can therefore only be regarded as precipitating an inevitable catastrophe; and the Encumbered Estates Court merely gave the sanction of law to what were already accomplished facts. By such means the

that is to say, as they obstructed supplies; but, as Mr. Tooke has shown, the paramount influences in the case were the seasons in connection with the sliding scale. Thus, before the war had terminated, agricultural prices had fallen to a comparatively low level. In July 1814 the *Gazette* averages were, for—

	s.	d.	
Wheat	66	5	per quarter.
Barley	33	0	,,
Oats	23	3	,,

But by July 1817, they had reached the extraordinary rates of, for—

	s.	d.	
Wheat	111	6	per quarter.
Barley	55	4	,,
Oats	39	3	,,

From these points prices fell, at the close of 1817, to, for—

	s.	d.	
Wheat	85	4	per quarter.
Barley	45	11	,,
Oats	27	10	,,

After further violent oscillations extending over the three or four following years, the point finally reached in December 1822 was the extremely low level of 38s. per quarter for wheat, with corresponding rates for the other cereals—less than one-third of those prevailing five years before. (See Tooke's "History of Prices," vol. ii. pp. 19—23 and 77—86.)

weakest and worst of the Irish squirearchy have been effectually rooted out. `In their place has arisen a proprietary of a different order—men for the most part self-made, who have purchased land as a pecuniary investment, and whose mercantile instincts will effectually save them from the suicidal rapacity of their predecessors. The influence of these *parvenus* on the territorial system of Ireland is not to be measured by the extent of their possessions. Already there is manifest among the older proprietors a tendency to adopt the ideas of the new men. "If our lands are not to become valueless to ourselves and our children," writes one of the former class,* "we must get them into the hands of men who can and will cultivate them properly, and will earn rent for us and profit for themselves in the open market of the world"—language which betokens a vast breach with the past. Already solvent tenants, even though independent, begin to be preferred to political retainers with promises of impossible rents.

Insolvency in Ireland had not of course been confined to the minor gentry: a good many of the superior squires have accordingly made their exit through the same door; as have also some of the greater landlords. If the question be asked what, on the whole, has been the effect up to the present time (1866) on the distribution of landed property in Ireland, I think the answer must be,—that while effecting a greater equality in the size of estates, and, by consequence, a more equal distribution of wealth

* "An Irish Landlord" writing in the *Times*.

amongst landowners, the new Courts have not yet added sensibly to the number of the Irish proprietary. Several very large estates have been broken up and parcelled out amongst numerous owners ; but, on the other hand, estates of the smaller class—those which I have spoken of as varying from £50 to £200 or £300 a year in value—have, to a large extent, been consolidated; several of them having commonly passed into the hands of a single purchaser. Two opposite processes—one of division, the other of consolidation—have thus been going forward contemporaneously, resulting in a greater equality in the distribution of landed property, but leaving the total number of landed estates pretty much as before.*

* That at all events no considerable addition has been made to the number of Irish proprietors since 1849 is, I think, proved by the following circumstances. Down to 1858, when the Encumbered Estates Court closed its career, as the result of 4,000 petitions received, very nearly 3,000 distinct estates had been sold, in the sale of which the number of conveyances executed approached 8,000. Had each of these conveyances represented a distinct purchaser, the figures would no doubt indicate a considerable increase in the number of Irish landowners ; but it is quite certain that nothing like this is the fact. On the contrary, I believe there are few men who have purchased an estate in the Encumbered or in the Landed Estates Court, who have not purchased more than one ; while there are many who have purchased several; besides which the purchasers have in some instances been landlords under the old *régime*. On the whole, it would perhaps be a fair assumption to take two to one as the average proportion of conveyances to distinct purchasers ; in which case the proprietors created by the Encumbered Estates Court would be about 4,000 as against 3,000 whom the Court had displaced. There would thus have been an augmentation (down to 1858) in that part of the country which was subject to the operations of the Court, to the extent of about one-third—no doubt a substantial increase, but then it must be observed that this period embraced the sale of almost all the greater estates—of such estates as those of Thomond, Kingston, Langford, Miltown, and others of the same order ; whereas the great proportion of the properties recently sold have been far below the average standard of the country. According to a statement of Judge Longfield's, " Of the

Such have been the general results accomplished by the Encumbered and Landed Estates Courts in the state of landed property in Ireland. They may be briefly summed up as follows :—1. A large, if not complete, elimination from the Irish proprietary of its most pernicious element—the class of needy, petty squires; 2. The exclusion of insolvency generally from the landlord body; 3. The introduction into the system of a large number of self-made men, mostly belonging to the mercantile classes, who have become purchasers of land as a pecuniary investment, and are prepared to manage their properties on mercantile principles, with a view to profit; 4. A greater equalization of estates, and by consequence of wealth, amongst the landed proprietors than formerly obtained. On the other hand, the new Courts do not appear to have added materially to the number of Irish proprietors.

Turning now to the changes accomplished in the occupancy of land, and affecting the other extreme of the Irish territorial system, we find a process going forward in many respects analogous to that which we have just traced. As it was amongst the smaller gentry that the greatest havoc was made by the operations of the Encumbered Estates Court, so it was amongst the small tenant farmers that the causes affecting the condition of occupancy in the country

petitions for sale presented to the Court (in 1864), less than 10 per cent. were for the sale of estates belonging to the classes who are called landlords; the remaining 90 per cent. did not represent an average annual value of £50." Keeping these facts in view, I should be disposed to conclude that the later operations of the new system have on the whole tended to consolidation, and that the Landed Estates Court had, up to 1866, not improbably reduced the number of Irish landowners as much as its predecessor had enlarged them.

produced the largest gaps. The general character of the movement down to 1864 will be seen from the following table :—

Size of Holdings.	Number of Holdings			
	In 1841.	In 1851.	In 1861.	In 1864.
Not exceeding 1 acre	134,314	37,728	40,080	48,653
Exceeding 1, but not exceeding 5	310,436	88,083	85,469	82,037
,, 5 ,, ,, 15	252,799	191,854	183,931	176,368
,, 15 ,, ,, 30	79,342	141,311	141,251	136,578
,, 30	48,625	149,090	157,833	158,135
Total of all sizes . . .	825,516	608,066	608,564	601,771

Several observations suggest themselves on considering this table. In the first place, it appears that a large proportion of the whole effect was produced by the year 1851; in the next place, the character of the movement exhibits a change after that year—a change which becomes more pronounced in the interval between 1861 and 1864, the latest for which we have returns. Down to 1851 the noticeable fact is the immense decrease of holdings under fifteen acres in extent, coupled with an increase in those between fifteen and thirty, and over thirty acres. Thus, down to 1851 the decline in the former amounted to 379,884 : the increase in the latter to 162,434. These new farms of fifteen acres and upwards have in the main been formed by consolidation of the smaller holdings; and the reasonable supposition is that their present occupants are men who had formerly been the tenants of the smaller farms.* We must, therefore, in order to

---

* Some Scotch and English farmers were introduced in a few districts; and it is possible that some members of the trading and commercial classes who have purchased land in the Encumbered Estates Cour

arrive at the number of families actually dispossessed, deduct from the aggregate of small holdings abolished, the aggregate of larger farms created. This gives a net reduction of holdings in Ireland in the five years ending with 1851 (for the process did not commence till 1846) of 217,450. A large proportion of these, however,—probably one-third,—would seem to have been mere potato gardens, held doubtless by labourers in part payment of wages; while the bulk of the remainder would probably comprise farms varying from four and five to ten and twelve acres in extent; and their occupants would be the cottiers of whom I have spoken. The character of the change effected in occupancy, therefore, down to 1851, is very plain. The small garden farms held by the labouring classes were extensively done away with; and a sweeping reduction, which must in many parts of the country have amounted to a wholesale clearance, was made of the cottier tenantry. On the other hand, there was a large addition to the farms between fifteen and thirty acres in extent, and also to those above the latter limit.

In the following decade the process of abolishing the very small tenancies continued, but at a greatly reduced rate: the total number got rid of during the period being but 2,614 as against 222,353 in the previous five years.* It is in the farms between five

---

may have taken to farming, but the number of new farms which might be disposed of by these methods would be quite inappreciable in the aggregate.

* The number of garden farms—holdings under one acre—increased during this time, and the increase is continued down to 1864. The explanation, I imagine, is, that in the panic following the famine, numbers

and fifteen acres that the largest reductions are now found; while the compensating additions occur exclusively in the farms over thirty acres; those between fifteen and thirty acres, which had largely increased in number previous to 1851, having, so far as appears from the table,* remained stationary. On the whole, during this time 10,537 small holdings have been abolished; while an addition has been made of 8,743 to the farms over thirty acres in extent.

Passing to the period 1861 to 1864, the tendency developed in the preceding decade becomes more marked. The reduction in the two classes of holdings above the very smallest proceeds at a somewhat accelerated and nearly uniform pace; but now for the first time there is seen a considerable decline in the farms between fifteen and thirty acres in extent. The reduction in these farms during this period of four years amounted to 4,673. But a still more significant feature is the form in which the compensating increase has taken place. As in the former decade, it occurs exclusively in the farms over thirty acres in extent; but there is evidence in the returns to show that the new farms, added to the list since 1861, have been on a greatly larger scale than those which formed the additions to the earlier returns. In

of labourers, in their eagerness to emigrate or reach the towns, threw up their small holdings, but that afterwards, as a more normal state of things ensued, it has been found convenient, so far as labourers are concerned, to return to the old practice.

* This result, no doubt, is attained by an increase in the earlier years of the decade, compensated by a diminution in the later. *Down to* 1851 this class of holding was in process of rapid augmentation : *from* 1861 it has rapidly declined.

the decade 1851 to 1861 the average size of what we may describe as the new consolidated farms was about eighty-five acres : in the period 1861 to 1864 the average size of farms in this category would be about 411 acres.* Such a result is significant, and justifies the assertion that in recent years the movement of which we have been tracing the course has in a great degree changed its character. In its early stage the results were visible in an extensive abolition of the cottier holdings, under which there lay a considerable proportion of the whole cultivable surface of Ireland—holdings, which, as they disappeared, were replaced by farms of moderate size. Of late years, on the contrary, but little comparatively has been done in reducing the number of the very small tenancies. The smallest of all, indeed, have quite recently rather remarkably increased ; while a large proportion of the farms now disappearing are farms much above the smallest class, ranging from fifteen to thirty acres, and such as in any European country but England would be regarded as medium-sized tenancies. This class of farms was rapidly increasing in number a little more than ten years ago, but is now undergoing a rather rapid decrease.† Such is the

---

* This result, though not expressed in the returns, may be deduced from them by an easy calculation.

† Yet the contrary is constantly asserted. W. R. G., for example, writing in the *Pall Mall Gazette*, tells us : " These "—that is to say, farms between fifteen and thirty acres—" are precisely the holdings which are already greatly on the increase, which are multiplying steadily and even rapidly, and the multiplication of which is notoriously and provably contemporaneous with, and probably a main cause of, that marked improvement in Irish agriculture, both in kind and quality, to which all observers bear testimony. The holdings of from fifteen acres to thirty increased between 1841 and 1864 from 79,342 to 136,578, or nearly twofold." The

destructive portion of the process; while the constructive part consists in forming out of the *débris* a very small number of very large farms— 15,668 farms being abolished, most of them of moderate dimensions, in order to create 302. And there is another feature in the recent changes which also deserves attention. In the period 1851 to 1861 no less than 88 per cent. of all the land used in the formation of the larger holdings, or for increasing the size of the smaller, was obtained from reclamations effected during the time: in the period since 1861 the material out of which the new farms have been made has been obtained exclusively through the suppression of the smaller holdings: some land indeed has during this time even passed out of cultivation altogether. These are indications which those familiar with the working of the *grande* and *petite cultures* will recognize as probably not unconnected with the fact I have just been insisting on—that a large farm system has begun to take the place of one of moderate size in the agricultural economy of Ireland.

It will be instructive to compare these changes in the occupation of land with the course during the same time of the emigration. The emigration on its

writer might have added that the farms in question increased in even a greater degree between 1841 and 1851, namely from 79,342 to 141,311. The fact is, so far as the returns inform us, the total increase occurred *before* 1851, since which time there has been a constant decline. The decline was apparently slow down to 1861, but since that time it has been rapid; the total number falling in three years from 141,251 to 136,578. So much for the assertion that farms between fifteen and thirty acres are in Ireland "multiplying steadily, and even rapidly."

* The average emigration of the previous five years had been 61,000: it rose in 1846 to 106,000.

modern scale of magnitude commenced in 1846 :*
it reached its full flood in 1849 : for three years in
succession it carried away rather more than a quarter
of a million of human beings; but from 1851 the
energy of the movement abated. By 1856 it had
fallen to the greatly reduced total of 92,000 persons :
from that point, after some fluctuation, it declined still
further, and, during the five years ending with 1862,
remained at an average level of 74,000. Since 1862,
however, the movement has received a new impulse.
The stream, notwithstanding the lowering of the head-
water, has suddenly swollen to something like its old
proportions. In 1863 the numbers emigrating were
117,000; in 1864, 114,000; in 1865, 101,000; and in
the present year it is computed the numbers will be in
excess of those of 1865. Taking the last three years
for which we have returns, the average emigration from
a diminished population is no less than 50 per cent.
greater than the average of the preceding five.

The general results to which these various indications lead may be thus provisionally summed up.
Two processes, one affecting the occupation of land,
the other the population, are seen proceeding in
parallel lines. Up to a certain point they advance
together; then they decline; and then, after an
interval, they are found once more in full action. The
double movement in the first period of its manifestation flows directly from the two capital evils of the
time—the extreme subdivision of cultivation, and its
concomitant, excessive population. But by the middle
of the last decade,—the mass of the very small holdings having been then got rid of, and the population

greatly reduced,—the impulse derived from these causes seems to have nearly spent its force. From that point the growth of a more stable and healthy condition of society might have been looked for. In fact, however, but a few years pass when the industrial agitation is revived; the changes in the occupancy of land become more frequent—the movement this time being directed against farms, not of very small, but of moderate dimensions, and issuing in the creation of others of colossal size; and contemporaneously the emigration recommences on the grand scale. Such are the general results; and they justify me, I think, in regarding the later stage of the movement as due to causes distinct from those which gave it its original impulse. What those causes are I shall hereafter inquire. But meantime the result at which we have arrived suggests the expediency of considering the Irish industrial movement from 1846 to the present, not, in the way it is usually considered, as a connected series of consecutive events flowing from an original impulse, but as resolvable into two perfectly distinct periods;—the first commencing with 1846 and reaching —we may say without pretending to strict accuracy —to 1856; the second commencing a few years after that date, and continuing to the present time.

Adopting, then, this division of our subject, we find the first period distinguished, as has been already said, by a vast destruction, amounting, as it must have done, in many places to a wholesale clearance of small holdings. The number of these destroyed down to 1851, uncompensated by the creation of larger farms, was 217,450; and the work continued, though at a greatly diminished rate from that point. By 1856, this number must have been considerably enlarged; and, as each holding abolished represented a family dispossessed, it is probable that not less than a million and a quarter of human beings' had by this year abandoned their hold upon the land of the country. Of these some few have found employment on large farms in their neighbourhood; a larger number probably in the towns of the empire. A portion of the whole have thus passed permanently into the ranks of daily labourers; but the vast majority no doubt have either emigrated or died. Let us now glance briefly at the actual agencies and immediate influences by which these remarkable results have been brought about.

In the days which succeeded the first shock of the famine, while the strain of the calamity was at its height, the removal of tenants from their holdings, and the emigration which followed, proceeded at the bidding of the most imperative of all laws—that of physical necessity. To give up their holdings was then for a very large number of the cottier tenants not a matter of choice. There were not on their farms the means of support, even if they held them, as for some time many did, rent-free. Thousands, therefore, without any other compulsion than that imposed by the calamity itself, abandoned their lands, glad to escape to the towns or less suffering districts where a chance of obtaining employment might be supposed to exist. As for landlords, they were, for the most part, in these transactions little more than passive, stunned for a while like others by the suddenness and overpowering nature of the disaster.

That period, however, of panic and general prostration was not of long duration. After a little, the owners of the soil, recovering their self-possession, began to deduce the lesson of the crisis. That lesson was very obvious. The evils of sub-division, sub-letting, and over-population had been brought home to Irish landlords in a manner they were not likely to forget; and thenceforward, to prevent the growth of sub-interests in the soil, to remove the hopeless portion of the smaller tenantry, and to consolidate the vacated farms, came to be regarded as cardinal maxims in the management of Irish estates. At the same time, the period of mortal struggle once over, the dread of positive starvation once removed, the peasant's passion for the land quickly revived. Thereupon ensued an inevitable conflict between interest and obvious policy on the one side, and, on the other, the natural instinct of a race to cling to the soil of its birth. From this point few tenant-farmers in Ireland gave up their holdings without a struggle. A certain amount of landlord pressure became necessary to induce the tenant to relax his hold on the land. But in what form was this pressure applied? And what is the moral judgment which the conduct of Irish landlords in applying it calls for from their countrymen? To these questions, which have of late been much canvassed, the course of the investigation now requires that I should attempt an answer.

Before considering what landlords have in fact done, let us endeavour to determine what, in the actual circumstances of Ireland at the time we speak of—the reader will remember that I am now concerned with the period 1846 to 1856—it was their duty to do. The conditions under which they were called to act were these. Their estates were extensively broken up into a great number of small cottier holdings, the majority not exceeding a very few acres in size; and these were burdened with a population greatly in excess of what the available means of subsistence in the country could maintain. The props which had sustained the cottier system hitherto had, in consequence of the events of 1846, completely given way. Corn, extracted from an exhausted soil, and sold at free-trade prices, could not be depended on to pay rents; and, after the experience of 1846, it was obvious that the people must look elsewhere for their staple food than to the potato. A change in the system of agriculture, involving an extensive substitution of grass and roots for grain, and a more scientific rotation of crops, was demanded by the plainest requirements of the case; and such a change could not be carried into effect by the existing race of cottiers, or on farms of the dimensions which they cultivated. It followed that an extensive abolition of the smallest class of holdings, and simultaneously a large reduction in the population, were indispensable conditions for the extrication of the country from its perilous position. Amongst those who accept this view of the position of affairs, there will not, I should think, be much difference of opinion as to the duty which it imposed on those who were called to act. Plainly, the course which the case prescribed—and not for landlords alone, but for all Irishmen in proportion to their means and opportunities—was to assist in promoting those ends which the best interests of the entire community manifestly required, not forgetting, however, in doing so, the paramount obligation to alleviate, as far as possible, the inevitable evils of the transition. I cannot therefore agree with those persons who appear to hold that the mere act of dispossessing tenants of their land, and furthering the emigration of Irishmen, involves of necessity something disgraceful and unpatriotic—something of which an Irishman would have need to be ashamed. On the contrary, my view of the situation would lead me to hold that, where due consideration was had for the circumstances and feelings of those concerned, where the legal powers with which the owner of the soil is invested were exercised under the restraints of humanity and justice, the effort of a landlord to induce hopelessly struggling tenants to give up their land and emigrate, was a wholesome exercise of authority, and one, whatever may have been the private motives of the actor, in itself, and having regard to its consequences alike to the country and the emigrant, emphatically commendable. On the other hand, I am equally indisposed to admit what seems to be assumed in the reasoning of another class of disputants, that the mere inevitableness of the event, regarding the question from the point of view of economic principle, or its desirableness, taking a wide view of the interests of the country, constitutes a sufficient justification for all that may have been done in contributing towards its realization. The danger of a ship's foundering in a storm would not serve the sailors as an excuse for anticipating the catastrophe by throwing the passengers overboard; and as little are acts of positive inhumanity, in driving men and women from their homes, to be palliated by the plea that these cruelties were committed in the cause of industrial reform. The upshot, then, of these various considerations is this, that the right or wrong of a landlord's conduct, in the circumstances in which Ireland was placed at the time we are considering, would depend, not exclusively on the direction and object of his efforts, but on these, taken in connection with the mode in which his authority was exercised. To promote a movement which, while it benefited himself, was manifestly for the good of the community at large, was plainly a duty: in doing so, to keep his conduct within the limits prescribed by a due consideration for the interest and feelings of those who were most seriously affected by his reforms, was also a duty, and one, I venture to think, still more imperative, as involving obligations with which no circumstances could dispense. Such appear to me to be the moral principles applicable to the case. Let us now turn to the question of fact.

I do not suppose it will be denied by any candid Irishman that the conduct of many Irish landlords, in the trying ordeal through which they have passed, has been such as would stand the test of the maxims I have just laid down. That there have been landlords in Ireland who, placed in circumstances of unparalleled difficulty, have admirably done their duty, is not, I think, a matter of controversy. The point which has been raised is whether there has been any considerable number who have failed in their duty; whether the Irish peasantry have to any large extent—to such an extent as would influence sensibly the temper of the whole people and the course of events in Ireland—been treated with harshness and inhumanity by those who were invested with the powers accorded by the law to the owners of the soil; whether they have been driven in large numbers from their farms and homes, and thus forced to swell the tide of emigration. This is the issue which has been raised; and on which a candid consideration of the evidence compels, I think, an affirmative decision.*

That evidence consists chiefly in the records of evictions,† of which the first that have been published are for the year 1849. From that year down to 1856, the termination of the period now under consideration, the number of evictions which took place in Ireland amounted to 52,193; the number of persons evicted, to 259,382. During the same years the numbers emigrating were 1,479,916. The persons evicted, therefore, bore to those who emigrated the proportion

---

* To prevent misapprehension, I wish to explain. In maintaining this affirmative, it is not intended to assert that the emigration would have been sensibly less, had no evictions occurred. The causes which necessitated a reduction of the population—at least, during the first decade of the movement—were of far too imperative a kind to be evaded, and, doubtless, had the pressure been relaxed in one direction, it would have been felt in some other. But because evictions may not have increased the mere volume of the tide, it does not follow that they have not affected its character and course, or produced on the social condition of the country effects of an important kind.

† These I take from Dr. Hancock's "Report," which I believe gives the only accurate returns extant. Those obtained later, by Lord Belmore, are the returns, not of "evictions," but of "notices of ejectment," with respect to which documents it is well known that they may be served for many other purposes than the dispossession of a tenant; and even where actions of ejectment are commenced with this view, a subsequent settlement of the rent frequently puts an end to the action.

of 17·5 per cent.; in other words, not far from one in every five of the multitudes who then swarmed across the Atlantic had been driven by positive physical violence from his home. This, it must be admitted, is an impressive fact; but to give it its due significance, it should be considered that virtually eviction was carried on to a far greater extent than the recorded returns would indicate. No eviction appears in those returns which has not come under judicial cognizance, and been actually carried into effect by the executive authorities; whereas it is notorious that a mere "notice to quit" will frequently do all the work of an eviction, and that a single example of the rigour of the law will naturally reduce many tenants to submission, just as a single agrarian murder will spread consternation amongst all the landlords of a district. Bearing this in mind, it must, I think, be allowed that the proportion of the whole emigration of this time due either to eviction or fear of eviction must have been very considerable.

But it is alleged that two-thirds [*] of these evictions took place for non-payment of rent. Granting that the fact was so, does this constitute their moral justification? Before answering this question, it may be well to recall what an eviction, as conducted in Ireland, commonly is. Most frequently, then, the evicted tenant has for himself and those dependent on him absolutely no means of support, or place of shelter, outside his farm. The evictions, moreover, having

---

[*] The statement of Lord Dufferin. His lordship's statement would seem to refer to evictions during the last ten years; but in the absence of other evidence, I take the same proportion for the earlier period.

almost invariably taken place for the purpose of consolidating farms, even where non-payment of rent may have been the occasion and legal ground, the pulling down of the tenant's house has been an almost constant incident in the scene—an incident, too, which is generally performed in the sight, if not over the heads, of the retiring family, who are thrust forth, it may be in mid-winter, frequently half-naked and starving. In the rare instances in which they have saved enough to procure them a passage to New York, they will probably emigrate at once : where this is not the case, they will cower, often for days and weeks together, in ditches by the roadside, depending for their support upon casual charity. Of course they have the alternative of the poorhouse, but this they do not readily, or at all events at once, accept. After a while some of them retire thither; others throw themselves on the labour market; ultimately the great majority—all except the very old—emigrate.

This being what is meant by an eviction in Ireland, the question might be raised, whether the strict enforcement of contracts for rent by such means, in such times as Ireland has lately passed through, be altogether reconcilable with that Christian charity of which we all make such loud profession; whether, when a great national convulsion has made the performance of contracts impossible, the exaction by landlords of the tenant's pound of flesh is the precise duty which in that crisis they owe their country ; in a word, whether the bare plea that rent is written in the bond, ought, under all circumstances, to be taken as a complete discharge from responsibility for any amount of misery inflicted in enforcing it;—this, I say, is a question which might be raised; but for the present I have no need to entertain it. It will suffice to call attention to the admitted fact that for a large proportion of the evictions there did not exist even this technical justification.

For it is admitted that one-third of the evictions were not grounded on this reason. Well, one-third of the evictions down to 1856 would be 17,397, and would represent a population of 86,988, who were thus, by admission, turned adrift, while prepared to pay the rent for which they had contracted. And these, be it remembered, are the recorded evictions only. How many people, over and above these 87,000, were involved, on no stronger reasons, in the same fate, through the simple expedient of a notice to quit, we have no means of knowing; but that they must have borne a large proportion to those actually evicted cannot be doubted. Moreover, it should be observed that the evictions recorded as, technically, "for non-payment of rent," would inevitably be greatly in excess of those to which this description could properly be applied for the purpose of the present controversy. There is an ambiguity in the expression "non-payment of rent." In the condition of Irish tenure as it has long existed over large portions of Ireland, there are generally at least two rents payable in respect to the same portion of land: there is the rent of the middleman, and there is the rent of the occupier. Now the occasion on which evictions in Ireland have most commonly taken place has been furnished by the determination of middlemen's leases. Suppose this determination to have occurred through non-payment of rent by the middleman, and that the landlord coming into possession finds his estate extensively in the hands of small occupiers holding from year to year, whom he proceeds to evict,—the evictions will in this case be recorded as having taken place for "non-payment of rent," although it may be that every one of the persons thus turned out is willing and prepared to pay the rent in consideration of which he was admitted to his farm. As none, however, are prepared to pay the middleman's rent, which most probably accrues from a very large district, and this is the only rent in respect to which the landlord was a contracting party, "non-payment of rent" is recorded as the ground of the eviction. Keeping in view how frequently middlemen's leases have lapsed through default on the part of the middlemen, and again how frequently this has been the occasion for wholesale evictions, I think we must come to the conclusion that, as against the victims of these proceedings, the persons actually turned adrift, the plea of non-payment of rent, whatever it may be worth, has a much more limited application than appears from the printed returns.

I shall here perhaps be asked—What is the bearing of this discussion? To what purpose bring to light scandalous transactions long past, and which cannot now be undone? In the first place, unfortunately, wholesale clearances by means of eviction and for the purpose of consolidation are not yet quite obsolete in Ireland,* and still less is that state of feeling between

* [The reader will bear in mind that this was written before the passing of the Act of 1870.]

the owner and the occupier of the soil of which such evictions have been the natural fruit. But further, the part taken by Irish landlords in connection with the Irish emigration is a portion of history, and one of which the due recognition is, I hold, quite indispensable to the right understanding of present events.

Not a few public writers feel much difficulty in accounting for the persistent hatred manifested by a portion of the Irish people for the English name. Such a state of feeling is regarded as incomprehensible, in presence of the many and great benefits conferred on their country by modern legislation, and of the good disposition towards Irishmen which is known to animate most English statesmen; and, as generally happens in like cases, the phenomenon is therefore commonly referred to some ineradicable vice or flaw in the Celtic character. It might help those writers to a solution of their difficulty, if they would reflect on the condition of mind in which the victims of the violent expulsions just described must have crossed the Atlantic. Is it strange if, in after years, the picture of the sheriff and his posse, with crowbar and torch, and the smoking ruins of their hovels tumbling to pieces over their heads,—if the nights spent in the ditch by the wayside, and all the wretchedness of the tramp to the port,—if these things should find a more permanent place in their imagination than the advantages of Catholic Emancipation, Corporate Reform, the National Schools, or the Encumbered Estates Court? Men leaving their country full of such bitter recollections would naturally not be forward to disseminate the most amiable ideas respecting Irish landlordism and the power which upholds it. I own I cannot wonder that a thirst for revenge should spring from such calamities; that hatred, even undying hatred, for what they could not but regard as the cause and symbol of their misfortunes—English rule in Ireland—should possess the sufferers; that it should grow into a passion, into a religion, to be preached with fanatic zeal to their kindred, and bequeathed to their posterity —perhaps not the less effectually that it happened to be their only legacy. The disaffection now so widely diffused throughout Ireland may possibly in some degree be fed from historical traditions, and have its remote origin in the confiscations of the seventeenth century; but all that gives it energy, all that renders it dangerous, may, I believe, be traced to exasperation produced by recent transactions, and more especially to the bitter memories left by that most flagrant abuse of the rights of property, and most scandalous disregard of the claims of humanity—the wholesale clearances of the period following the famine.

V.

OUR DEFENCES: A NATIONAL OR A STANDING ARMY?*

THE war of 1870, which has already unmade and made emperors, which has shaken one nation to its centre and consolidated another, has also brought some well-worn platitudes to the proof. What have become of our peace-at-any-price principles? of the doctrine of non-intervention, as interpreted by Manchester? How completely do we now miss in able leaders the customary assurance winding up all discussion on foreign topics, that, come what might, under no circumstances could England be drawn into war. The common form has disappeared, and has given place to an entirely different refrain. The picture of the secure watcher gazing from his serene height on the tempest-tossed bark below is less familiar than it was some six months ago. In early July England's interest in European politics was that of the gods of Epicurus in human affairs. Before the month passed, indeed, the revelation of the Benedetti treaty showed that anger could find a place even in the placid bosoms of

* *Fortnightly Review*, February 1871.

Englishmen. But the unwonted emotion was appeased by the new Belgian treaty. The course of the war, removing all danger on the side of that Power from which danger was most apprehended, reassured us, and by October we had begun to settle down into the comfortable conviction, that, behind our "streak of silver sea," the *rôle* for us in Europe could only be a moral one. Let others maintain armies and seek aggrandizement or glory in barbarous warfare; ours the purer ambition, sitting aloof from the distractions of less favoured lands, to weigh the merits of our neighbours' quarrels, award by our verdict the meed of honour or disgrace, and shape that opinion which rules the world. "Happy England!" which thus, safe from the dangers of Continental neighbourhood, may yet share in all the honours of the grand drama! We had begun, I say, to settle down into this conviction, when the Gortchakoff circular rudely disturbed our self-gratulations, and showed us the sort of paradise we were living in. We, whose interest in European affairs was either none at all, or that of the impartial and disinterested spectator, were suddenly discovered to be the principal, if not the sole, guardians of European public law. Having pronounced judgment, it belonged to us also, it seemed, to carry the sentence into effect. Nor—so strictly were our obligations interpreted—was it permitted to go behind the form in order to look at the substance, nor yet to take account of the joint nature of our responsibilities, shared as they were by others equally or more interested and equally bound with ourselves. It was sufficient that the law was so, that our signature was to the bond. Such, or nearly such, was the language very generally held by the London press in the end of November under the stimulus given to our national self-respect by the Russian manifesto; and it would seem in the main to have correctly reflected the passing mood of the public. To this complexion have our peace-at-any-price professions come, and such is the practical issue from our oft-repeated resolves to withdraw wholly from the Continental scene. I say such is the practical issue from those professions; for who does not see that the present overwrought susceptibility of the nation is but the natural and inevitable reaction from past ignoble avowals? No doubt we meant but a small portion of what we said, or what was said on our behalf; but professions of faith are not necessarily without practical consequences because they are insincere. They may be believed by others; and those who uttered the platitudes, or who suffered them to pass, thinking them, perhaps, a graceful homage to becoming aspirations, may find themselves forced into courses such as they would never have dreamed of entering on, were it not for the real or supposed necessity of dissipating delusions they have themselves sedulously built up.

But, not to enter now on controverted ground, one truth, at all events, comes out with sufficient distinctness from the heated utterances and more or less wild pretensions of the last month. England is not going to retire from the field of European politics. She means to take part in the controversies of nations; a part other than that of impartial spectator and serene arbiter of disputes in the issue of which she has no share. Englishmen may differ as to the precise occasions which would warrant and call for a resort to arms; but as a nation they recognize that such occasions may arise. Not only do they desire to pursue, undisturbed from without, their internal development: they would also speak their mind freely on the great issues of Europe, unassailed, or at all events unaffected, by those insolent warnings of which Belgium, for instance, was but the other day made the object. Nay, further, if I do not greatly misinterpret the present signs, they would wish, in certain not impossible contingencies, to be ready to strike an effective blow in the cause of the independence of nations. And, desiring the end, they desire the means. They would have a force sufficient, not merely to secure them against attack, but also to give weight to their voice in council, and, if need were, value to their co-operation in the field.

Such seems to me the practical conclusion deducible from the crisis we have just passed through. And now how does our material position accord with our political pretensions? Our foreign policy, we have been told by high authority, must govern our armaments. Taking the former to be such as has been indicated, what is the state of our preparations in presence of the Powers whose forces we may any day be called upon to confront?

The facts of our military position (for I put aside the question of the navy as foreign to the subject of this paper) must now be familiar to most readers. The entire aggregate of our military establishment of all arms, comprising colonial and West India corps, depôts of Indian regiments and other accessory establishments, amounts, *on paper*, to just 115,000 men.* Of these the numbers in England amount to 82,000; and of this force, the proportion which would be available to put in line against an enemy, after the necessary deduction for Ireland, for garrisoning our fortresses and for various subsidiary services, is, according to Mr. Trevelyan's calculation, which has not, so far as I know, been disputed, from 35,000 to 40,000 men—little more than the strength of a single Prussian army corps. In addition to these, we should have, as a reserve, our militia, yeomanry, and volunteers, the value of which, in the present state of their organization and equipment, if opposed to the trained and fully equipped troops of the Continent, I leave to military critics to determine. These, at all events, even on the most favourable supposition, could only come into action as a second line; and in effect the net available outcome of our military resources at the present time, in the event of our being engaged in a struggle with a Continental Power of the first rank, would be represented by 40,000 men, as against, for example, the 250,000 which France six months ago was able to place in line of battle on her frontier, or the 500,000, supported by a reserve of still greater dimensions, which Prussia sent to the front. What the tangible force actually forthcoming out of the enormous military resources of Austria and Russia would be, I will not venture to conjecture; but, as set down on paper, the regular armies, including reserves, of these two Powers

* I take these figures from Martin's Statesman's Year Book.

appear respectively as 830,000 and 1,135,000 men.* Such would be our military position in the presence of a Continental Power of the first class. But then we are told of the excellent quality of English troops, and how a French general congratulated himself there were so few of them. They would certainly need to be of high quality, considering the odds against which they would have to fight; and they certainly ought to be of high quality if cost of maintenance affords any criterion of the value of the article. For how stand the facts in this respect? Briefly thus :—while France, at an expense of £14,000,000 sterling, maintained, up to the outbreak of the war, a force available for the field of 250,000 men; while North Germany, at half this expense, that is to say, for £7,000,000 sterling, maintained an organization capable of furnishing, at fourteen days' notice, 500,000 men, and of not only keeping up this number through a most destructive campaign, but of raising it in a few months to nearly double the amount; we, at a cost equal to the larger of the sums mentioned—that is to say, at a cost of £14,000,000 †—have just contrived to keep on foot an army which, all indispensable and permanent needs being provided for, would leave us,

---

* Martin's Statesman's Year Book. Under the new military laws of Russia, of which the proposed draft has just been published, the effective aggregate for that country will, no doubt, be largely increased. It will be noticed that all the proposed reforms are in the direction of the Prussian military system.

† The total cost of the army, as set down in the last estimates, is, in round numbers, £13,000,000, but a supplementary vote was passed at the end of the session for £2,000,000 for both services, of which £1,000,000 may be assumed as taken for the army. In 1869-70 the army cost us £14,111,000, and in 1868-9, £15,455,000.

in the event of war, a force available for the field of 40,000 men. Or we may represent the case thus :— A German soldier costs the State some £29 a year; a French soldier costs the State some £41 a year; an English soldier costs the State £100 a year; so that if cost furnished any criterion of quality, the quality of the English soldier might fairly be supposed to stand high. Unfortunately in this critical age people will ask for some other evidence of the superiority of the British soldier than that furnished by the extravagant sum which he costs. But, unless they are satisfied with allusions to "the thin red line," and to the exploits of British armies under Marlborough and Wellington, I fear they will ask in vain. It will scarcely be held that the Crimean campaign is conclusive upon this question ; and it will be remembered that most of the armies of the Great Powers in Europe have been remodelled since 1856.

What we know is, that the *personnel* of our army differs from that of armies on the Continent mainly in these two circumstances :—alone among European armies, the English rank and file is recruited exclusively from a single class of the population, this class being the poorest, the most ignorant, and the least moral of the community; and alone, again, among European armies, it is commanded by officers who owe their promotion, not to proved professional qualification, not to personal merit or distinction, not even to seniority, but mainly to the strength of their aristocratic or political connection and to the length of their purse. So far as outsiders can see, these are the main differences between English and Continental armies in the matter of *personnel;* and they are scarcely of a kind to warrant us in supposing that English troops can, man for man, stand against four or five times the number of their possible adversaries. Thus, at a cost equal to that incurred by France, double that incurred by Germany, we maintain an army for practical purposes one-sixth as numerous as the army of France, one-twelfth as numerous as the army of Germany—an army composed exclusively in its rank and file of the dregs of the community,* and officered by men for whose moral, intellectual, and professional competency it is a very weak statement of the case to say we have absolutely no guarantee at all.

Such are the broad and simple facts of the case; the undisputed, the indisputable facts. Is it necessary to go further, and to spend time in discussing "the dual system of government," the half-pay list, sinecure colonelcies, army agencies, and the other mysteries of the system? Nothing, it is evident, short of absurdities and abuses without parallel in the civilized world, could explain the results; absurdities

---

* The words are not mine, but those of the *United Service Gazette:*—
"The army as a service, even with limited enlistment, has not become more popular, nor has a better class of men been induced to join. On the contrary, in both these respects it has decidedly fallen off. It is no easy matter, if any pressure prevails, to get a sufficiency of men to enlist at all, and everyone who knows anything about it will say that our soldiers are, far more than they ever were, the very scum and dregs of the population. Ticket-of-leave men abound amongst them. One-half the recruits raised are practised rogues and vagabonds; they only enlist for the purpose of getting the bounty and deserting immediately after. The numbers who are said to have done so, upon the authority of official documents, during the last year, were no less than between 20,000 and 30,000."—*United Service Gazette,* for July 1861, quoted by Mr. Edwin Chadwick.

and abuses which, whatever apology history may offer for their existence, can have no other conceivable effect than to facilitate nepotism and extravagance, to push incompetency into high places, and to provide for the ruin of the country. If we desire—I will not say to play the part of an international police for Europe—but to maintain our position as an independent State, a thorough-going and radical reform of our military system is simply imperative; and the most urgent need of the country at the present moment is to determine upon what principle this reform is to be carried out.

Fortunately the problem has been greatly simplified for us by recent experience and discussion, and two or three points may at once be taken as established in advance—established, I mean, as far as reason and experience can establish anything. In the first place, it need scarcely be said, the purchase system must be absolutely swept away. This has long been felt by all who have not given themselves over to delusion, to be an absurdity and a scandal; but the exposure it has within a few months received at the hands of Sir Charles and Mr. Trevelyan, has shown it to be at once an influence of the most malign kind on the whole range of society in contact with the army, and an obstacle in the forefront of hindrances to effective military reform. While a shred of it remains, it is plain that nothing of any moment can be done. Secondly, whatever be determined with regard to the volunteers and the militia, one condition at all events will have to be fulfilled: they must be brought into such relation to the line, as to constitute the whole in effect a single system, moulded by the same training, and subject to the same discipline. A third point might perhaps be added, so strongly does recent experience testify in its favour, and so decidedly is opinion setting towards it—the superiority for military purposes of short service over long. These are changes which we may take for granted will form articles in any really serious attempt at army reform.* But, to place our military system on a rational basis, to put our army into a condition in which it will be at once adequate to the requirements of the country, and at the same time not ruinous to our finances, much more will be needed than the correction of a few of the most palpable evils of the present system. We must go deeper, and endeavour to penetrate to the root itself of the rank abuses that luxuriate on all sides. As preliminary to this, I shall now invite the reader to follow me in a brief survey of the leading types of military organization presented by the principal countries of Europe. They will be found, with much variety of detail, to fall naturally into three groups or categories, which will be conveniently designated by the terms, Standing armies, National armies, and armies of the mixed kind—that is to say, those raised by the Conscription. For our present purpose, the best examples of the several types are furnished by the armies of England, of Prussia, and of France.

The constitution and leading characteristics of the English army result from the fact that it is a standing

* [They have all been embodied, as the reader is aware, in Mr. Cardwell's reforms of 1871.]

army supported by voluntary enlistment. As a standing army the bulk of its forces are kept constantly on foot; its reserves occupying in the system a comparatively unimportant place. Indeed, it is a question whether it be proper to speak of the reserves of the British army at all; the relation of the militia and the volunteers to the line being of a very loose and undefined character, and these forces in their actual state forming, according to competent opinion, not so much reserves, as material for reserves. The army thus maintained as a standing force is raised by means of voluntary enlistment, and this gives occasion to some of its most characteristic features. The State being thrown for the supply of soldiers on the labour market, and the soldier's vocation being, fortunately for mankind, one that with the progress of society steadily declines in public estimation, two important consequences result: first, in order to attract a sufficient supply of men to the ranks, the Government is under the necessity of constantly raising its terms,—of raising them, not merely in proportion to the general advance of the labour market, but so as to compensate the declining honour into which the soldier's trade has fallen; and secondly, the recruits, thus attracted, come more and more from the lowest and least reputable classes of the community. The system thus becomes constantly more costly; while the character of the men who fill the ranks steadily deteriorates. Again, the plan of voluntary enlistment necessarily leads to the rule of long service in the ranks. The man who enters the army under a voluntary contract, if his object be not simply to desert as soon as he receives the bounty, naturally looks to it as a permanent vocation; and engaging soldiers as permanent servants of the State involves the consequence of providing for them on the expiration of their period of service. In this way the inherent costliness of the system is enormously aggravated, through the necessity of maintaining, over and above the active army, a large force of ineffectives in the character of pensioners. These circumstances, irrespective altogether of the special abuses of the system, render a standing army on the English plan inevitably and incomparably the most expensive military instrument that can be devised; and one, moreover, which of necessity becomes more and more expensive with every fresh step in social progress. Lastly, from all these causes, it results that the army, thus maintained, is not, and cannot be, a constituent portion of the nation, but remains a class apart from it,—a class without share in the industrial work of the community, excluded from marriage, subject to a code of laws which is not that to which the ordinary citizen yields obedience, unaffected by the strongest influences of civil and political life, forming itself upon an ideal far remote from that of the society in which it exists; in a word, a class which of necessity becomes a caste. Such are the main features and necessary incidents of a standing army on the English plan.* Of the several types of military organization, it is the only

---

* The purchase of commissions I have not adverted to, because it has obviously no necessary connection with a standing army raised by voluntary recruiting; it is a factitious outgrowth, and a quite gratuitous aggravation.

one that is confined to a single country. England monopolizes unchallenged the credit of the invention.

The constitution of the Prussian army offers in every respect the most striking contrast to that which we have just considered. The foundation of the force is, not contract, but *status*; the *status* of liability incurred by every able-bodied citizen (subject to certain specified exceptions) to serve his country as a soldier in the ranks; and from the impartial application of this principle all that is really characteristic of the system directly flows. The rule of liability to service being so wide as to embrace the bulk of the able-bodied population, short service in the ranks—short at least as compared with the service exacted in standing armies—becomes a necessity of the case. In Prussia, where the capacity of the system has been strained to an extreme degree, the period is three years, as compared with five in France and twelve in England; but in other countries, where the same type prevails, a much shorter period has been found sufficient. And from this rule of short service in the ranks, results what, from a military point of view, must be regarded as the capital feature of this form of force, the immense strength of its reserves as compared with its active army. Owing to the strain put upon the system in Prussia, to which I have just referred, this characteristic is less marked in the instance of the Prussian army than in others belonging to the same group.* Yet even here it is sufficiently distinct; for though the active force on a peace footing amounts to no less than 300,000 men, the reserves

* For example, the Swiss army, to be afterwards described.

bear to this enormous force the proportion of three to one; these reserves having all passed through the same training as the active force, and being, as we have had ample proof, in all respects equally efficient. Another characteristic of the Prussian system is its cheapness, an incident which again directly results from the nature and constitution of the force. In the first place, the service being compulsory, the State is enabled to obtain recruits on its own terms instead of being compelled, as under our system, to raise its bid, not merely to keep pace with the progress of the labour market, but to compensate for the unpopularity of the service. It is true that the economy obtained by this means may, to a certain extent, be ostensible merely. Where the services of the citizen during his career in the ranks are rated at less than their proper worth, the burden is merely transferred from the nation in its corporate capacity to the individuals who endure the loss; and as this is probably more or less the case with all armies raised by compulsory recruiting, this circumstance should undoubtedly be taken account of in considering the cost of such armies. Another and less equivocal source of economy arises from the almost entire exemption enjoyed by National armies from the charge of ineffectives—a charge which forms so large an item in the budgets of Standing armies. The soldier, on his release from the ranks, instead of remaining a burden on society, passes at once to the business of productive industry and civil life, and all the economic waste, not to speak of the social mischief, arising from the maintenance of an idle class, is thus avoided. The working of the system in this respect is strikingly shown in the Prussian military budget; the cost of that vast organization, which enabled her in a few weeks' time to put a fully-equipped army of half a million of men on her frontier, having amounted to no more than an annual sum of £7,000,000 sterling, *plus*, as I have said, whatever should be added on the score of private losses resulting from inadequate payment of the troops actually under arms. These are, perhaps, the most prominent features, in a military and financial sense, of this description of force; but we must not omit to notice an attribute attaching to it, from a social and political point of view, of the greatest interest and importance. The type of military force represented by Prussia is essentially national. Including the entire potential army, line, reserve, and landwehr, the organization comprises within its sweep, in effect, the mass of the able-bodied population;* and the

* This is denied by a writer in the *Edinburgh Review* for October last, p. 486. But the facts, taken from authoritative sources, are thus stated by M. de Laveleye :—" The first datum to be taken account of is the number of young men who reach each year the age of military service, and who thus form what is called the *class*. The Journal of the Royal Bureau of Statistics of Berlin, published by M. Engel, sets down the *class* of 1855 at 147,613 men; that of 1858, at 155,692; that of 1861, at 165,162; in fine, that of 1864, at about 170,000. . . . . In Prussia, as in France, more than half the *class* is exempted for deficiency of height, of strength, or of health. In Prussia the requirements are more strict than in France on the score of the quality of the men. Thus, in 1861, out of 165,000 composing the *class*, only 69,933 were found fit to enter the army. As the contingent amounted this year to 59,431, the lot exempted only 10,502. The following year, 1862, 62,517 conscripts were taken out of 69,513 young men, so that the number of the *disponibles* dispensed by the lot from at once joining the ranks, amounted to 6,996."— *La Prusse et l'Autriche depuis Sadowa*, vol. i. pp. 56, 57. It appears from this that the Prussians are strict in interpreting the qualification "able-bodied;" but that of the "able-bodied," thus strictly ascertained,

elements of this vast aggregate are drawn, with strict impartiality, from all classes of the community. An organization of this kind may, it is possible, generate in the nation maintaining it the so-called phenomenon of militarism—how far it has in fact had this effect in Prussia I do not now inquire—but an army thus constituted cannot, in the nature of things, be a caste. It cannot but be a fair representation of the community from which it is drawn, must share its feelings and aspirations, social and political, as well as military, and be incapable of betraying its aims. Such an army may, therefore, be properly characterized as national or popular; and it is by this term that, in the following pages, I shall designate this type of military force.

The third type of military organization presented by European armies is that exemplified by the army, or what was the army, of France. As in Prussia, the foundation of the military system is here *status*, not contract; every citizen being, according to the theory of the law, liable to serve the State in the ranks of the army: but the principle is in France applied through the conscription; the persons actually called upon to serve are determined by lot; and the rule is further qualified by the privilege, accorded to those who have

from 84 to 90 per cent. go at once into the ranks, while the surplus—*i.e.* the 6 or 10 per cent. not required (as previously explained by M. de Laveleye)—are not exempted from service, but pass into the landwehr. The statement, therefore, is strictly true that the mass of the able-bodied population, as that expression is construed by the Prussian military rules, pass into the potential army of Prussia. Even, however, though this were not the case, the fact, which is not disputed, that the Prussian army is recruited from all classes of the community indifferently, would alone entitle it to be considered a National army.

the means, to purchase exemption from service. The effect of these qualifications of the strict rule is to give to the resulting force a character widely different from that which I have just described as distinguishing armies of the popular type; for the use of the lot* implies the limitation of the obligation of service to a portion only of those who are capable of discharging it; while the privilege of exemption, accorded in consideration of money payment, leads to the result of throwing the burden of service exclusively on the poorer classes of the population. And this, as M. Laveleye informs us, and as indeed we might infer from the nature of the case, is a growing tendency. "In proportion as a larger number of families attain to easy circumstances, the number of those exonerated by purchase increases, and the army is no longer recruited but from the lowest classes of the population."† Precisely similar results are recorded as realized in the Belgian army, which represents the same principle of military organization. In 1866, as we are informed by M. Fourcault,‡ the number of substitutes formed no less than a fourth of the whole annual contingent— a proportion more than double what it had reached ten years before. It thus appears that, not only in point of quantity of the aggregate potential force, but also in point of quality, the armies raised under the conscription, as it is practically operative in Continental countries, differ widely from those con-

---

* The lot is also used in Prussia; but the part which it plays in the system is quite subordinate.

† "La Prusse et l'Autriche," vol. i. p. 74.

‡ "Annales de l'Association Internationale. Congrès de Berne 1866," p. 692.

stituted on the popular principle, as represented by the Prussian army. They do not form a fair representation of the community from which they are drawn, but, like our own, are composed almost exclusively of a single class, and that the lowest of the nation; and they do not give that development to the reserves which is characteristic of the popular system. These results will be found to obtain in all countries where the conscription reigns; but in the constitution of the late French army the weak points of the system were aggravated by the political circumstances of the country. The Imperial Government of France naturally enough shrank from giving military training to the masses of the population. The army was for it quite as much an instrument for keeping down disaffection at home, as for threatening its neighbours abroad; and accordingly its efforts were directed to giving the utmost development to the active standing force, to the almost entire neglect of the potential elements. One means by which this result was sought to be attained was by employing the proceeds of the fines, payable for exemption from service, in effecting re-engagements with old soldiers on the expiration of their five years' term. These soldiers accordingly remained in the active army instead of passing into the reserve force, which was thus starved in order that the standing army might be pampered. The practical result was to furnish France with an army which, in spite of its nominally popular basis, had far more analogy with our own than with that of Prussia—in effect, with a standing army, of long service, recruited from the lowest class of the population, and without reserves. Under the financial aspect also the French system was not without resemblance to the English. The cost of the late French army amounted to some £14,000,000 sterling, almost exactly the sum with which we have contrived to maintain an army of about one-fourth the strength, but double that which went to support the far more efficacious organization of Prussia. One cannot but remark with some uneasiness, in this comparison of the French and Prussian military systems with our own, that the points in which the French system differs from the Prussian are precisely those in which ours also differs from the Prussian, though in a more extreme degree; our system exaggerating in every instance those features of organization which were peculiar to the French, and to which, it now seems tolerably plain, the collapse of that system has been mainly due.

With this sinister omen from our review of the military systems of Continental Europe, let us now return to our own position, and endeavour to estimate the extent of the danger against which we have to provide. I have already stated what I believe to be the general character of the foreign policy which the nation desires to pursue. I believe in the first place that we desire to place our national independence beyond question; so unequivocally so, as to render an invasion of this country not merely a perilous enterprise, but an undertaking so manifestly hopeless that no statesman of moderate sagacity would contemplate it. Accomplishing this effectually, we cannot be without influence in Europe, since our fleet alone would then become formidable as an offensive weapon: and a military system which would be really effective for defence, would quite certainly, in an extreme emergency, be effective for something more. We need not, therefore, for our present purpose, go beyond the question of defence, and the contingency which we have to contemplate is obviously the possibility of invasion.

Against invasion our main protection must, of course, always be our fleet, and it is satisfactory to hear that we have in this something more solid to rest upon than we find in our "thin red line." But it is admitted that our fleet may fail us. A single naval disaster, such, for example, as the defeat at Beachy Head in William III.'s time—a defeat, by the way, suffered when our position seemed strongest, our most formidable naval rival, the Dutch, being then our ally— would now, as then, lay open our coasts to the enemy. And supposing this to happen, what would be the extent of the danger we should have to face? Lord Derby tells us that at the very utmost we should have to deal with an army of 100,000 men. I must own that I fail to perceive the grounds of this particular limitation. The event occurring which we have supposed, the enemy would for a time, at all events, have free access to our coasts, and, under such circumstances, with armies on foot of from 500,000 to 1,000,000 men, with converging railway systems at his command, with an adequate transport fleet in readiness, it is not apparent why double or treble the number named might not in a few weeks be placed upon our shores. We have lately seen in the results which followed the capitulations of Metz and Strasburg, what enormous forces may be suddenly rendered disposable by the liberation of armies engaged in merely subsidiary operations, when war is carried on upon the scale it now assumes. Had we, for example, at the time those capitulations happened, been at war with Germany, what would have prevented her—with a month's command of the sea, and with such preparations as Count Von Moltke would have known how to make to meet this contingency—from placing the army of Prince Frederick Charles on the coast of Kent? It may be that warfare carried on by entire populations is "essentially retrograde;" but retrograde or not, this *is* the danger against which we have to provide. And it seems to me there would be as little solace to our dignity as compensation for our suffering, on finding ourselves the victims of combinations we might easily have foreseen, to reflect that we had only made our preparations against more civilized methods of attack.

But, taking the danger as estimated by Lord Derby, who is certainly not given to exaggeration, to afford us adequate security against this—to inspire us, in presence of such a possibility as he contemplates, with that confidence in the stability of our position, without which it is idle to think we shall act in European politics a part worthy of the country and of its traditions—what is the state of our military resources that the case demands? The contingency we have to contemplate is the landing of a hostile army of 100,000 men upon our coasts. Let us suppose we could meet this with a force, not of 40,000 men, but, let us say, of an equal number, and with appointments in all branches not inferior to those of the invading army, he would be a sanguine patriot who could calculate in such circumstances on immediate victory. It is mortifying to think of the generals we should probably have to oppose, at all events in the outset, to the Prince Frederick Charles's and Manteuffels who might be sent against us; and the troops despatched on such an expedition would, we may pay ourselves the compliment of supposing, be the *élite* of our antagonist's forces. Under such circumstances we might surely esteem ourselves fortunate if the early encounters issued in doubtful battles; and we should not be unprepared for even serious reverses. Against the loss of a few battles, against heavy temporary disaster, it is scarcely possible that any military system could quite secure us; but there seems no reason that security might not be attained, such security as is permissible in human affairs, against national collapse, against such a complete break-down of our defensive apparatus as has happened to France—a break-down which should throw us for our defence on an undisciplined population, and place our people at the mercy of the foe. There seems no reason, I say, why we should not be secured against such a catastrophe as this; but, bearing in mind the nature of the force that might be sent against us, it appears also pretty plain, that this is possible on one condition only, namely, that we oppose to it a force of the same kind. What we want is not a large standing army, to crush us with its cost during peace, and then, when the time of trial comes, to fall to pieces at the first shock, leaving us helpless in presence of our adversary, but an organization, entailing small expense in time of peace, but capable, when the need arises, of giving us army after army till the invader is subdued—an organization in which every man should know his place and fall into line with the certainty of disciplined habit. Such an organization might suffer defeat, but it would not succumb with defeat, and, presenting line behind line to the enemy, it would offer to an invader a task of ever-increasing difficulty. We may understand what it would be capable of by considering what would have been the consequence if, in the present war, the French had been successful in the early battles. It is now plain that they would have merely beaten back the first German line, and at the end of every fresh advance would have found a new German force of equal calibre arrayed against them. Nor would it have fared differently with France had she been organized on the German system. The capitulations of Sedan and Metz would have been merely the destruction of the first line of French defence, and the German army would, after these achievements, have found itself in presence of a new force equally strong with that which it had conquered, but nearer its base, instructed by experience, and animated by a spirit as superior to the spirit of its adversary as patriotism is superior to vindictive greed. An organization such as I have described, such as Germany and Switzerland maintain, powerful as we see it can be for aggression, would be virtually invincible for defence—so visibly so, that I cannot but think, were nations in general organized in conformity with this plan, there would be good hope that aggressions might cease.

As to the utter hopelessness of developing anything adequate to the occasion out of our present system, if any proof were needed, it has been abundantly supplied by the experiments of the last autumn. Six months of energetic recruiting has succeeded in drawing to our standards some 20,000 men—not, be it observed, an addition to our army of this number, for a large proportion* of the new recruits have merely gone to supply "the great drain which always requires to be made good," but a gross total of this amount; and this result our present War Minister considers highly satisfactory.† And satisfactory it no doubt is, judged by the standard Mr. Cardwell evidently adopts—the requirements of the past.‡ But this is precisely the fundamental fallacy of all that has been said and written in defence of our present military system. The capital fact of the case is, that the method of warfare has been changed. The struggle has been transferred from standing armies to armed populations; and until we recognize this fact, and adapt our defence to the altered circumstances, our position cannot be other than precarious. In very truth, however, it signifies little whether our present method of recruiting be effectual or not; for were we thus to obtain an army numerous

---

* What proportion Mr. Cardwell does not say.

† Mr. Cardwell's words are: "I do say that recruiting without bounty is going on briskly, and, if not quite without precedent, it is almost so, considering that bounty has been abolished."—*Times*, January 3rd, 1871.

‡ "Well, gentlemen, if we are not to have a much larger force at home than our predecessors thought necessary, it must be manifest that those battalions must have fewer men than before, or else these objects would not have been maintained. . . . And my opinion is, that we have improved the tone of the army, and that while it was not less numerous than before, it never was more efficient."—*Ibid.*

enough for our purposes, the expense of such a force, maintained on the principle of a standing army of the English pattern, would be simply ruinous.* Our entire revenue applied exclusively to military purposes would not suffice for the drain; and we might as well be crushed at once by the enemy, as ruined by the slow torture of the tax-gatherer. And I venture to go further still. Even though the needful force could thus be raised, and the means of supporting it were forthcoming, what just confidence could be placed in an instrument of the quality which alone such a process could give us? The system remaining the same, the character of the men composing our army would continue to be what it now is;† and we should thus, in the last resort, have to stake our national existence on a struggle in which the *prolétaires* and the pariahs of our community would be matched against the average citizens of other states.

---

* I may observe that this is distinctly Sir Charles Trevelyan's opinion. "He came to the conclusion that it would be totally impossible to support a standing army equal to the requirements of England. . . . . If a large army were required, the expenditure would mount up to fifty or sixty millions at once. He considered therefore that the financial argument against a standing army was conclusive." (Report of Meeting held at the Society of Arts, February 17th and 19th, and March 1st, 1869.)

† This is fully admitted by our military authorities :—" Could your Royal Highness suggest any mode of improving that system [recruiting]? —I think that it would be impossible. With the volunteer system you must get the men where you can find them. Of course, if you can get a better class of men, so much the better, but our experience has not proved that we can do so; and, therefore, my fear is that, do what you will, you must take what you can find, whether it is exactly what you wish or not. . . . And even though you wish it, you cannot be very particular as to the place in which you recruit?—No; I do not think that you can help that." (Examination of the Commander-in-Chief before the Royal Commission on Recruiting.)

I come then to the conclusion that a reform of our military system, on the principle of a National army, is a necessity of the case; but this leaves many important questions still open; and, in the first place, the question as to the means by which our popular force is to be raised. Is it possible to raise such an army by voluntary enlistment? If this be feasible, unquestionably it is the course which will be most in keeping, if not with the best traditions of the country, at least with the present taste of its inhabitants; and it must at once be owned, that some of the ablest and most experienced of those who have advocated a popular army in this country believe in its feasibility.* Foremost amongst these is Sir Charles Trevelyan, who is of opinion that, " by rendering the conditions of service more attractive," it is possible to procure an "abundant supply of recruits from all classes of the population, without departing from the voluntary principle, or having recourse to conscription." And this appears also to be Mr. Edwin Chadwick's view.† With the greatest respect for both these gentlemen, whose services in the cause of army reform it is

---

* I just observe that a high authority, General Sir William Mansfield, has declared himself on the other side. "I believe it to be absolutely necessary to revert to that principle of obligation—that is to say, that every man, without respect to his rank or to his position in the world, shall be liable to serve in his own person in the ranks of the militia.... A primary obligation should rest on every man to serve in person, and no pecuniary sum of any amount should enable a man, whatever his rank or whatever his position, to save his person by means of his purse."—*Times*, January 16th, 1871.

† So I inferred from expressions in his paper read at the Royal United Service Institution, 2nd May, 1870. From a note just received from Mr. Chadwick, I learn that he does not object to the principle of compulsion, but would confine its application to the school stage.

impossible to overrate, I am obliged to confess that, after the best consideration I have been able to give to their proposals, I am quite unable to discover any adequate grounds for the expectation they entertain. The inducements on which Sir Charles Trevelyan relies for filling the ranks with an abundant supply of recruits from all classes of the population, while maintaining the present system of voluntary recruiting, are comprised in his scheme of military reform. The fundamental idea of this plan is that which has been already described as the principle of a popular army, namely, a small permanently embodied military force, supported by a numerous militia; the latter serving in the ranks for one year only, after which they pass into the reserve, while the select body of "general service battalions," which are to form *cadres* of instruction, and, according to Sir Charles's illustration, to serve as a mill, in which any amount of soldiers may be ground, are to be engaged for a longer term of seven years. In conjunction with this arrangement, it is proposed to abolish the purchase of commissions, to improve the officers' pay, to promote liberally from the ranks, and, lastly, to reserve for non-commissioned officers and soldiers a considerable range of appointments in the administrative departments of the army. I can quite understand that these arrangements, all obviously in the right direction, should draw to the ranks quite as large numbers, and of the right quality, as would be needed to fill the lines of the small professional section of the force, the general service battalions; but I fail to perceive what inducement they would

offer, of a nature to attract the one year's militiamen. These men, it must be remembered, would
enter the ranks, not with a view to the army as
a profession, but merely as a temporary condition
qualifying them to pass to the reserve, and entailing
the liability of being called to the standards in time
of war. Neither the prospect of promotion from the
ranks, nor of employment in the administrative departments of the army, would apply to them ; * and it

---

* From an article in the current number of *Good Words*, I observe
that Sir Charles Trevelyan proposes to supplement the scheme described
in the text (and which I gathered from some speeches delivered at
a meeting of the Society of Arts in February 1869) by opening to non-
commissioned officers and soldiers the lower grades of the Civil Service.
I am not sure that I quite understand the scope of the proposal. If
it be only that ex-soldiers should be admissible for examination, who
would otherwise be excluded on account of age, the concession would,
at all events, be free from objection ; though the inducement it would
offer to recruits for the army would seem to be small. On the other
hand, if it be meant that service in the army should be substituted for
competitive examination as the qualification for the Civil Service, there
would, I think, be strong reasons against such a change. But, for our
present purpose, the important point is that the proposed privilege, whatever it be, would apply only to the regular army, *i.e.*, as I understand Sir
Charles, to the small permanently embodied force, not to the masses of
militiamen filling the reserves. Thus the difficulty which I have pointed
out would still remain. What Sir Charles would seem to rely upon
mainly for rallying the militiamen to the ranks is the strength and per-
manence of the military spirit in the country. But I venture to think
one of the capital facts of modern civilization, and also one of the most
hopeful, is the decline of the military spirit. The phenomenon is, I
think, apparent enough in this country. In the United States it is too
plain to be questioned. The decreasing taste for military life is not
indeed at all inconsistent with a sudden and even sustained martial
enthusiasm under the stimulus of what the nation regards as a worthy
cause for war. The volunteering in America during the civil war, and
the sudden rise of our own volunteer force, are sufficient proofs of this.
But we must distinguish between what people will do under the excitement of a great emergency and from a sense of duty, and the tastes
which determine them in their ordinary pursuits. Where are now the
great armies of the civil war? What proportion of the American people

is difficult to imagine the prospective benefits which could weigh with any large proportion of our middle and working classes, to draw them to the ranks in disregard of the manifest inconveniences implied in giving up an entire year of their life to military training. It is here that, it seems to me, Sir Charles Trevelyan's plan would, as a practical scheme, be destined to break down. He would no doubt get his *cadres* of instruction, his general service battalions, but where is the bait that is to attract the masses to the reserves? What is to bring the grist to his military mill? I confess I see no escape from the difficulty.

Over and above the reforms recommended by Sir Charles Trevelyan, Mr. Chadwick has advocated with great earnestness and ability the introduction of military exercises into schools; and no one who has read his publications upon this subject can entertain a doubt of the high importance of his suggestions. Indeed, the feeling his arguments produce, is not so much acquiescence in his views, as surprise that a measure, in every point of view of such obvious utility, should not have been long ago adopted as a

now think of entering the army? Nor can much be inferred from the case of the English volunteers. Their number—after all only 150,000 out of a population of 24,000,000—has been barely maintained; and it is yet to be seen if it will be so, when they are submitted to the stricter discipline which must be enforced if they are to become really efficient forces. In Belgium the volunteer element of the army is declining. Between 1850 and 1860 (as I learn from a paper read at the Berne Congress of the International Association), the decline reached 20 per cent. I observe from the article in *Good Words* that Sir Charles does not object to the principle of compulsion; for he adds: "If this should not suffice, then no doubt a limited application of the conscription would be necessary."

national scheme. As Mr. Chadwick points out, the practice would be attended with numerous advantages quite irrespective of its military uses, advantages of a physical, moral, and sanitary kind; but, in connection with the question of a popular army, the important consideration is, that by this means the training of soldiers might be largely transferred from the mature to the juvenile period of life: that is to say, economically speaking, from the productive to the unproductive stage. The plan, fully carried out, would thus, to a large extent, remove one of the most serious objections to a system of universal military service—the interference it would cause with the industrial work of the country. But the proposal may also be regarded in another light. It may reasonably be expected, that a system of universal school drill would have some effect in developing military tastes as well as aptitudes in rising generations. Would the bent thus given to the youthful mind be powerful enough, assisted as it would be by other reforms in our military system, to draw to the ranks, under a voluntary *régime*, that abundant supply of recruits which a popular army needs? I frankly avow that, if I thought so, the fact would with me be an argument against the proposal strong enough to outweigh all that can be said in its favour. A reform which would so turn the mind of the people of the country to military ideas, as to send them thronging to the military schools, not with a view to make the army a profession, for this would be out of the question in the case of the great majority, but simply to gratify a taste for military pursuits, would, in my view, be a most fatal boon, and one which, I think, every friend of civil liberty should repudiate. But, for my part, I utterly disbelieve that the plan would possess any such efficacy. The tide of things, in spite of the present gloomy outlook of Europe, is setting far too strongly towards the predominance of the civil and industrial spirit in human affairs to render such a result in the least degree probable. A European crisis like the present, a threat of invasion such as produced our Volunteers, a great cause like that which in 1861 woke up the people of the United States, may kindle a momentary access of military fervour; but the influences which work in favour of industrial and civil life are abiding, and grow with the growth of civilization. The introduction of military exercises into schools would probably turn into the channel of military enthusiasm some portion of that extravagant zeal for athletic sports which now, to so little purpose (to put the case mildly), engrosses so much of the time and thoughts of our youth; and the elementary parts of a soldier's training having been got over at school, the repugnance which would now be widely felt to spending a year in the ranks of the army, would probably be much diminished. The path towards the goal in view would thus be smoothed. But I believe that the mass of the population would be as far as ever from looking to the army as a career, or from regarding the obligation of military service in the ranks as other than a disagreeable necessity and a rather onerous tax. If so, then the difficulty of recruiting a popular army would still remain. The voluntary system, in a word, can only be effective on the condition of offering to the masses of the people an adequate motive to enter the army; to enter it, not as a profession, but as a temporary condition entailing liabilities of a serious kind. Then where is this motive to be found?

But the principle of compulsory service, I shall be told, will never be accepted by Englishmen. Perhaps not; and in that case Englishmen, as the foregoing considerations lead me to believe, will never enjoy that "cheap defence of nations" furnished by a popular army. But if this principle is to be rejected, let us at least know the reason why. From the phrases current on the subject, the prevalent notion appears to be that, in the claim of the State to the personal services of the citizen in defence of the commonwealth, there is something strangely abnormal in relation to our political system and traditions, violently unsuited to the habits and ideas of a free people. The writer of the political article in the *Edinburgh Review* talks of "the hard law which dooms the capable citizen, will-he nill-he, to a certain period of service." The tone taken, moreover, is that of one conscious of occupying a position of moral vantage, as the *voluntary* character of the English military system is contrasted with the *coercive* systems of Continental countries. But let us look at these assumptions a little more closely; and, in the first place, it must be remembered that the very existence of a nation as an organized community is founded upon the recognition of duties obligatory upon all, and which the State may at need enforce. In the early and simple stages of political union, the discharge of those duties takes mainly the form of personal service; and if with the progress of society the performance of personal service has been commuted for money payment, this has been done solely upon considerations of convenience, and not in the least as the assertion of any political principle whatever. In point of historical fact, the transmutation of the obligation generally accompanied, and was indeed made the instrument of, an abridgment of popular liberties. Military service, as it was the most important public duty in primitive societies, offered the earliest example of the practice of pecuniary commutation; but gradually the same grounds of convenience led to its extension to other spheres of political action, until now the general right of the State to command the services of its citizens finds practical assertion almost exclusively in the single act of taxation—a form in which it for the most part eludes observation. This is the state of things which we have reached in this country, though only within half a century. Even now the permanent law of the country requires that every one (with specified exceptions) shall, if called upon, venture his body in the militia, and only fails of being enforced through the enactment of an annual Act suspending the militia ballot. Nor is this the only example in point. In the civil sphere compulsory attendance on juries and the obligation to give evidence in person in courts of justice still attest and illustrate the original practice. In point of principle, therefore, the right of the State to compel the services of its citizens, "to doom the capable man, will-he nill-he," to defend his country, is implied in the right of taxation; the question of enforcing the primitive obligation in one form or another being merely one of convenience. So little is the prerogative out of harmony with our general institutions, that it is, in fact, the foundation and origin of them all.

But then the public feeling revolts against the practice "in a country where the sentiment of individual freedom and conscience is as highly developed as here."* Now the times are serious; let us purge our souls of cant. What does this system of "voluntary" recruiting, which we are asked to believe is the only system suited to our highly-developed political and moral feelings, mean? Simply this, that people who have sufficient means, instead of being required to pay their just debt to their country in their own persons, are allowed to hire others, who have little choice but to accept the offer, to expose their persons in their behalf. No less lofty principle than this, it seems, can satisfy the highly-developed consciences of the English people. The moral fastidiousness displayed is only surpassed in China, where, it is said, men may procure substitutes for the gallows. The principle would, indeed, need to be high; for it is certainly not redeemed by the practice—by what is known as "our pot-house system of recruiting," in which men are entrapped, to borrow the words of the late Sidney Herbert, "by every kind of cajolery and inducement we can devise—and in our necessity we descend to those means which men do not have recourse to till they think all others are exhausted."

* Lord Derby's speech at Liverpool.

Well, all this may be highly convenient; but, in the name of common decency, let us cease to put it forward as a national distinction to be proud of—a practice entitling the people who employ it to look down, as from a lofty height, on the nations who expect each capable citizen to bear his share in his own and his country's defence.

Nor let it be supposed, because the recognition of general liability to serve in the army implies the power in the last resort to coerce the refractory, that therefore the military service obtained under this principle would necessarily, or as a general rule, be unwillingly rendered. On the contrary, what we should expect is, that the will would go before the law, and that good citizens would perform, spontaneously and cheerfully, what the law declares to be for the good of all. If it be asked, Where then would be the need of compulsion? I reply, to satisfy all that all shall do their part, that the common burden shall not be shirked by any. There are not a few public duties, recognized as such by average citizens, which yet do not get performed, simply because each person feels that the obligation attaches to him only in common with others. What is every man's business is no man's business. But make it plain that all shall take their share in the common burden, and the men who before hung back will now cheerfully do their part. As a matter of fact, alike in Germany and in Switzerland—the only two countries in Europe where the experiment of a national army has been fairly tried—the army is a highly popular institution. It is only where the conscription prevails, with its inequalities and unfair preferences, that such practices as self-mutilation to escape military service are resorted to. In Germany and Switzerland they are unheard of. The public spirit of Swiss and Germans is thus powerful enough to carry them in advance of the law, and to make the principle of compulsion unfelt; and why are we to assume that a level of sentiment easily attained by Swiss and Germans is impossible for Englishmen?

But, in considering the question of compulsory service in the army, one point above all must be clearly understood. The entire virtue of the rule, as a means towards obtaining a national army, lies in its being applied with rigid impartiality. Exceptions there must of course be on grounds of physical and moral disability, as well as in consideration of some few exceptional incidents of the citizen's position. But privileges to the rich—permission to purchase, at whatever price, exemption from personal service—vitiate the principle at its core. For what results? At once to throw the burden of military service exclusively on the poor; to lose, that is to say, the characteristic and capital advantage of a national force. The army thus obtained will not be a national army—an army combining in due proportion all the elements of power existing in the nation, but such an army as that vanquished at Sadowa,* and such an army again as that vanquished at Sedan. The truth made manifest in both these instances—so manifest that those who run may read—is that moral and intellectual

---

* Austria has not scorned to learn from her enemy, and has since remodelled her forces on the German plan.

qualifications are elements in the strength of armies, and elements which can only be obtained when armies derive their materials from the whole range of the community from which they are drawn. To do full justice, however, to this portion of our argument, regard must be had in an especial degree to the present condition of the art of war, and to the bearing of this circumstance upon the need of intelligence in the soldier. At the present moment the most prominent, and, let us freely admit, the most deplorable and shameful fact of the time is the extent to which scientific knowledge has been applied to perfecting the arts of destruction. But of what avail will it be to perfect the organization of our armies if the men comprising them are, from stupidity and ignorance, incapable of carrying into effect any but the simplest manœuvres? To what purpose shall we waste our ingenuity and money in improving our arms of precision, if we cannot put them into hands that can be trusted to use them?* As M. de Laveleye pertinently reminds us, the two nations who have made the most marked advance in military aptitude of late years have been precisely those amongst whom education is most widely diffused—the Germans and

* "Military officers," says Mr. Chadwick, "have objected to putting the arms of precision into the hands of our uneducated rank and file, on the ground that they were incompetent to wield them; they objected to putting into their hands breech-loaders or repeating-guns, on the ground that they would fire wildly and rashly, and soon exhaust their ammunition. This is just what has happened with the like uneducated rank and file of the French army. In their hands, inferior use has been made of the superior weapon—the chassepôt—which has a range one-third longer. In the hands of the better educated German rank and file, according to all testimony, superior use has been made of the inferior weapon. They have been cool and steady, and have fought more intelligently and effectively."

the people of the United States. "Vivacity of mind, foresight, are useful everywhere, even upon the field of battle; better far to command intelligent men who understand what they have to do, than troops the most irreproachable in military exercises. All Prussian officers are in accord upon this point, that it is to the intelligent decision of their soldiers that they owe their success."* I need not say how abundantly the present war has confirmed the truth which the Sadowa campaign had already made clear.

I turn now from the consideration of principles to that of organization; and, assuming the principle of a National army as the only one capable of satisfying the needs of the present time, I proceed to advert to the form, or at least the main outlines of the form, in which, in a community like ours, the idea of a national force may be most conveniently embodied, keeping in view the special circumstances of the country, and the aims, in the main purely defensive, of its foreign policy. The most prominent model in this kind available at the present moment is of course the army of Prussia. But the Prussian military system, however suitable it may have proved itself for the purposes of that country, is not one which any nation will deliberately adopt unless under the pressure of urgent need, least of all a nation so widely separated in many respects from Prussia as is ours. Three consecutive years taken at the most important period of life from the proper vocation of the citizen to be spent in the ranks of the army, followed by four

---

* "La Prusse et l'Autriche depuis Sadowa," vol. i. p. 70.

years more in which from two to three months are abstracted from useful pursuits for the same purpose,— this constitutes beyond question a serious encroachment on the field of productive industry and of civil life. But the Prussian pattern, though it has been the most widely copied, is not the only one that Europe supplies. Another, still more thoroughly popular in its character, is furnished by a State with which, small as it is, England has, both in its civil constitution and in its foreign policy, many more analogies than with Prussia. The popular army of Switzerland has lately elicited occasional notice from the press in this country; but the system is not, I imagine, very distinctly understood here, even in its general outline. A brief description, therefore, of its leading arrangements may not be out of place.*

The widely different results which may flow from the adoption of the popular principle in military organization, according to the views entertained by its promoters, are strikingly shown by a comparison of the Prussian with the Swiss military system. In Prussia, as we know, the permanent army, on a peace footing, amounts to no fewer than 300,000 men. In Switzerland no permanent army of any sort is maintained in time of peace; the entire force exists exclusively in the reserves; yet in Switzerland, equally as in Prussia, every able-bodied citizen is bound by law to serve in person in the ranks, and does actually undergo com-

* The following particulars are taken from several papers read before the Congress of Berne in 1866, and published in the *Annales de l'Association Internationale pour le Progrès des Sciences Sociales*, 5me livraison —a work for the use of which I have been indebted to the kind offices of M. Émile de Laveleye.

plete military training. How does it happen that the same principle, rigorously applied in both instances, issues nevertheless in such strikingly discrepant results? The answer is to be found in two circumstances: in the extensive use made in Switzerland of the school stage of life for military training, which renders possible a corresponding reduction of the training period in the mature years of the citizen; and, secondly, in the different views animating the Swiss and Prussian Governments in framing their military organization: the former aiming exclusively at producing a system effective for defence; while the views of the latter notoriously extended to other contingencies.

The military education of the juvenile Swiss begins in the primary schools at the age of eight years. He there undergoes drill and other elementary exercises suited to his years. On passing into the secondary and the superior schools, he is instructed in the use of light arms as soon as his strength fits him to wield them, and takes part in annual exercises and reviews. With the advantages of this preparation he enters at the age of nineteen the ranks of Recruits, when he passes to a school of military instruction. Here he remains, according as he is destined for the infantry, cavalry, or artillery, for from four to seven weeks. On reaching twenty the recruit undergoes training in the corps of his canton—a process which lasts, again, for from four to five weeks, according to the nature of his future service. After this he is enrolled as a member of the *Élite*, in which category he continues till his twenty-eighth year, presenting himself annually during this time for (according to his service) a week or a fortnight's exercise. At twenty-eight he passes into the Reserve, and from the reserve at the age of thirty-four into the Landwehr. He finally quits the service at the age of forty-four.

Over and above all the exercises just enumerated, the troops of all arms are mustered and exercised in large bodies periodically. The effective results obtained by this organization are as follows :—

Élite	80,000 men
Reserve	45,000 ,,
Landwehr	75,000 ,,
In all	200,000 ,,

armed, equipped, and trained, of which 20 per cent. (or 40,000) constitute special or scientific corps. These were the figures for 1866; and the system had only then been in existence for sixteen years, having been established on its present footing in 1850. As the entire period of liability to service covers twenty-five years, the scheme will not have received its full development till 1875, when it will yield a total force of 250,000 men out of a population of about 2,500,000.

So far as to the organization. The expense of the system is thus stated :—

	frs.
The Confederation pays about	2,800,000
The Cantons	4,700,000
Cost to the soldiers, as estimated by M. Staempfli, "ancien chef du département militaire fédératif"	750,000
Total	8,250,000

or £333,000 sterling.

The amount of interruption given to civil and industrial pursuits by the calls of the army is represented as follows :—

From the age of twenty to forty-five each infantry soldier spends in military exercises and training, in time of peace, from 100 to 110 days.

Each engineer, artilleryman, and carbineer, 160 days.

Each cavalry soldier, 170 days.

Non-commissioned officers spend, in addition, 50 days.

And officers, in addition, 100 per cent.

The entire time, it should be observed, is distributed into portions, never exceeding from four to seven weeks in duration, over the total period of twenty-five years.

As has been already stated, no troops are maintained permanently on foot; the army is composed of contingents from the cantons; the only military elements of which the central authority has direct control being the Staff, which is composed of 180 superior officers and an indeterminate number of subalterns.*

* [Since the above was written a good deal of light has been thrown from various quarters on the organization and present condition of the Swiss army, with the result, I am bound to say, of convincing me that I had very greatly overrated the efficiency of that force. The defects, however, which have been disclosed, are in no way connected with the popular principle on which it rests, but in all cases are plainly traceable to one or other of two causes :—1. The excessive and even absurd parsimony of the Swiss Federal Government, which refuses to incur the outlay indispensable to maintaining the efficiency of the training centres, and the proper equipment of the scientific corps; and, 2. The obstacles offered by the cantonal constitutions to the due organization and training of the force. As some high military authorities in Switzerland as well as others occupying official positions in that country have shown themselves fully alive to the evils of this state of things, it is to be hoped that it will ere long cease to exist.]

Such are the leading facts of the system; and, I think, candid people will admit that the results obtained—an effective army of 200,000 men from a country less populous than Scotland, and at a cost less than we pay for ineffectives alone—are such as, in these times of military reform agitation, deserve attention.

How far, then, is such a system suited to the requirements of a country like England?* And here, I imagine, the objection that will occur to most people, on contemplating the facts just stated, is that the scheme is over-efficient for our purposes. A system which from a population of two millions and a half is capable of giving an army of 250,000 men, would, from our population, yield an army of some 3,000,000; and this result will probably be thought to confirm Lord Derby's observation that "if you apply the principle of compulsory service universally, you are met with the difficulty that you are making ten times the amount of preparation you can possibly require." But a little consideration will show this to be a hasty conclusion.

In the first place, it is to be observed that, in proportion as the population is numerous, there would be room for greater rigour in applying the tests as to qualifications for service. We might, for example, raise the physical standard; nor do I see any reason why, more especially with a view to the qualities

---

* The reader will bear in mind that I am considering only the question of home defences. The garrisoning of India and our military stations abroad—for the colonies proper, it is now understood, will provide for their own defence—is a distinct question, and will, no doubt, have to be dealt with on some such plan as that suggested by Sir Charles Trevelyan.

required for the new arms, we should not enforce an educational test. I have not seen any statement of the requirements of the Swiss system in this respect; but from the large proportion of recruits obtained, it must be supposed that at least the physical standard is low. In Prussia, on the other hand, we know that the standard is very high; and the effect of this, in conjunction with the rule for exemptions, is shown in the elimination of more than one-half the whole class attaining the age of military service from the category of able-bodied available for the army.* On the assumption, therefore, that we adopt the compulsory principle, having regard to our large population and comparatively limited requirements, we could afford to be proportionately strict in applying our test of "able-bodiedness;" by which means we should, while pruning the exuberance, improve the quality, of our force. But a still more effectual resource remains. Those who are overwhelmed at the magnitude of the imaginary consequences they have conjured up as flowing from a system of universal liability to military service, overlook the fact that the results may be brought within almost any limits desired by the simple expedient of reducing the period of liability to service. The results obtained by the Swiss system are enormous in proportion to the population, because, the population of the country being exceedingly small, the principle was applied with the express aim of extracting from it the largest possible results. But supposing the Swiss had been satisfied with a small army, they could just

* See *ante*, Note to pp. 213-14.

as easily have obtained it, without departing from the strictest rigour of the principle of their system. It would have been only necessary to cut down the extravagantly long period of liability to service—a period two-thirds greater than that enforced in Prussia —to, say, a third of the time, making it terminate, for example, with the expiration of service in the *Élite;* and the aggregate army would at once have been reduced to a third of the number now obtainable— namely, to 80,000, the number now existing in the *Élite.* In speaking, moreover, of the great scale of force obtainable from military organization on the popular plan, it should be remembered that we are not speaking of forces actually on foot, and weighing on the resources of the country; we are speaking, not of actual, but of potential armies—armies which have no existence in peace, and only make their appearance in the hour of need, in the dire extremity of war. Even supposing that our possible forces did attain the stupendous figure of 3,000,000, the expense of such a force, constituted on the Swiss plan, would after all be little more than the cost of the requisite subsidiary services. More than twenty-nine thirtieths of the men would be, to all intents and purposes, citizens engaged in the ordinary industrial work of the country. They would, indeed, have undergone military training; but, as has been shown by Mr. Chadwick [*] and others, this, far from impairing, would greatly increase their

---

[*] See "On the Expediency of the General Introduction of the Military Drill and Naval Exercises in the School Stages of the Elementary Schools; and of employing Soldiers on Civil Works in time of Peace," by Edwin Chadwick, C.B., Correspondent of the Institute. Also Mr. Cole's paper read before the Society of Arts.

industrial efficiency, while their liability to be called to the standards in war would be simply unfelt.

The feature of the Swiss system, on which, after the vast scale of its results, the English critic will probably fasten, is the extremely short time allowed under its rules for the training of the soldier. People who are accustomed to regard twelve years as the ordinary period of a soldier's service, and who have been taught to believe that his martial quality improves even up to twenty-one years—for why, otherwise, should distinct inducements be offered to him to re-engage himself for nine years more at the end of his twelve years' term ? —will be startled to find a Swiss recruit pronounced fit for the *Élite* of the force after four or five weeks' training. The question is mainly one of professional experience ; one, therefore, on which the opinion of a civilian can be of no value, unless so far as it is supported by unquestionable facts, or professional authority. But facts and professional authority alike place it now beyond doubt, that, whatever be the precise *minimum* requisite to give complete efficiency to the soldier, it is some period very greatly less than the prevailing ideas in this country assume. In the case of Switzerland, the extremely short time allowed is at once to a large extent explained by reference to the training given during the school stage. Still, even taking account of this, the time assigned for converting the military tyro into a proficient, will appear, even to military reformers in this country, extraordinarily short; and the doubt which will be felt respecting this provision of the system will seem to find confirmation in the much longer training time required by the rules of the Prussian service. It cannot be denied that there would be great force in the Prussian precedent, if we could be sure that the three years required by that service indicated the opinion of Prussian military authorities on the point in question. But this would be a quite gratuitous assumption. On the length of time passed in the ranks depends, *cæteris paribus*, not merely the efficiency of the soldier, but the amount of standing force maintained on foot in time of peace; and it was to this point, doubtless, that the attention of the present king and his advisers was directed when, on the remodelling of the army in 1861, they insisted on the three years' term. Had we any hesitation as to the ground of the Prussian rule, it would be removed by what we now see. From a letter from the Berlin correspondent of the *Daily News* of January 5, we learn that, in the event of further prolongation of the war, it is in contemplation to reduce the standard of height for the army, — a measure which would at once bring under liability to service large numbers of men who have never yet undergone drill of any kind. And what is the time considered sufficient to put these raw forces into a state fit to take the field? Precisely "a three months' drill, for which, in case of need, a six weeks' drill may be substituted." For the rest, we have the testimony of military authorities to the admirable efficiency of the Swiss forces;* and we know that the Swiss themselves, whose remarkable military aptitude has always

* See the papers read before the International Association Congress of Berne, 1866, *passim*; and in particular the paper read by M. Cérésole (*Annales*, 5ᵉ livraison, p. 683).

been famous, have the most unbounded confidence in their system. On one important point, at all events, it is certain that they have not overrated its capacity. "In three days," said M. Staempfli* in 1866, "the whole Swiss infantry and cavalry may be ready to take the field. In four days, all the artillery may be harnessed. And what is more remarkable, at all times the munitions and *matériel* of war are in readiness for this army of 200,000 men, who are themselves always prepared to fall into line on the first signal." The boast was actually made good this summer—so far, that is to say, as the exigency called for performance. Within a week of the French declaration of war, this small State placed 40,000 men— infantry, cavalry, and artillery—in line upon her frontier. *Parvis componere magna*, the fact may well take its place beside the world-famous exploit in the same kind of Count von Moltke.

"But granting," I think I hear some liberal friends interposing, "granting the complete success of your scheme as a military contrivance, what, after all, does the proposal mean but a return upon the past, a recurrence to that military *régime* which we had hoped to have long left behind us? Are military ideas, then, to be again the dominant influences of our social life? Is our country once more to be turned into a camp? Nay, is the accursed thing to be taken even into the haunts of childhood, and the nursery and the playground to resound with eternal drill? What can all this issue in but a resuscitation of that militarism

---

* Ancien Membre du Conseil Fédéral, et Ancien Chef du Département Militaire Suisse.

still rampant in Germany, and the dire source of our present dangers?" I frankly own I have not a little sympathy with this line of reflection, and cannot contemplate the change of prospect, which has suddenly brought military organization into the foreground of political questions, with any other feelings than intense disappointment and sorrow. But what avails it to live in a fool's paradise? Look at the Continent. The day

"When the kindly earth shall slumber, lapt in universal law,"

has quite certainly not yet dawned. Between us and the promised land lie still, it is but too evident, some weary lengths of rugged wilderness, which must even be traversed as best we may. Facts are stubborn things, and are not in this age to be conjured away by acts of faith. The obvious truth is we must for a while longer be prepared to struggle for our national existence, or, as a nation, submit to be trampled under foot. "Militarism," in some form, we must have; and, it seems to me, our wisdom will lie, not in holding up our hands and screaming against the inevitable, but in endeavouring to minimise, as far as may be, the necessary evil, and in extracting from it, while it lasts, whatever accidental element of good it may contain. Now this, I contend, is what the scheme of national armies does accomplish; while the influence of standing armies is distinctly in the opposite direction. Standing armies concentrate, and in the same degree intensify, the military spirit, producing all the evils and dangers of an armed caste, out of sympathy with civil society, which is left unarmed and helpless at its mercy. Our ancestors were surely not unwise in their inextinguishable jealousy of standing armies; and, if their fears have not been realized, we have to thank, it seems to me, certain fortunate accidents of our political and social state, rather than any virtue in the constitutional precautions taken against the danger. What would avail the expiration of the Mutiny Act and the parliamentary refusal of supplies, in presence of an army leavened with the taint of military caste feeling, heedless of civil liberty, and not too scrupulous to help itself? * On the other hand, the popular principle by diffusing attenuates the evil, renders caste impossible, and, making every man potentially a soldier, places the liberties of the country on the only sure foundation, the ability of all in the last resort to defend them. These considerations seem to me, I confess, to determine decisively the question as regards its political aspect; to determine it, that is to say, for all who are in favour of popular government and the supremacy of civil life. But it is supposed that the features now most prominent in the social state of Prussia, I mean the strongly pronounced character of her military aspirations, furnishes an argument too strong on the other side to be shaken by any mere general reasoning.

So much has been made of this phenomenon of Prussian militarism, that it may be worth while to consider for a moment how far the current allegations

---

* According to Macaulay, the power of the House of Commons over the national purse is an absolute security against the danger of military usurpation of our liberties. Does not this argue extraordinary faith in Acts of Parliament?

sustain the inferences built upon them. I concede, for the purpose of argument, the question of fact. Let it be granted that the militarism of Prussia is as intense and all-pervading as the most violent anti-Bismarckist would allege, what, after all, does it prove against the principle of popular armies? Where is the evidence that the militarism of Prussia has been produced by the Prussian military system?

That system dates, as a legal institution, from 1814. Down to 1806 the armies of Prussia were standing armies, recruited on the voluntary plan; yet will any one say that the military tendencies of the Prussian national character only showed themselves after those years? It is surely a fact that the noxious plant flourished with some vigour under Frederick II., not to mention anterior and subsequent manifestations. Why then are we to attribute to the reforms of Scharnhorst a characteristic already in full bloom long before those reforms were thought of? And then, as to the present war, the shooting of Franc-tireurs, the enormous requisitions levied on defenceless towns, the burning of villages, and the other horrors, —all again adduced as the dire fruits of the ruthless propensities engendered by the military training of Prussians,—where is the proof of the connection? One would think people had never heard of prisoners being shot in cold blood before; as if the rule had not been formally promulgated and acted on, only a few years ago, by Marshal Bazaine in Mexico; and as if people had forgotten the massacre of Fort Pillow— atrocities which somehow contrived to get perpetrated without the authors having undergone any special preparation in the form of popular training for military service. Moreover, in judging the present conduct of the Germans in France, and before attributing such excesses as it presents to the peculiar institutions of Germany, it is only fair to remember the aggravated provocation they received, and the naturalness in a people just escaping from so awful a danger as they have surmounted—a life and death struggle with the greatest military power in Europe—to confound the passion of vengeance with the desire of security. I disclaim all sympathy with the present aims of the Germans. They seem to me to have missed a splendid opportunity of placing international morality on a higher level, and European peace on a surer footing, than either has ever yet attained. But there is no need that we should attribute what offends us in their present conduct to a wrong source. The truth is, those who argue against popular armies from the example of Prussia, mistake the effect for the cause. The Prussian military system is the fruit and practical expression of Prussian military aspirations. It had its origin in the national uprising that followed the first Napoleonic conquests; and the latest remodellings of the system in 1861 and 1867 were undertaken with a distinct view to the realization of the military aims which are now being worked out. If we desire to trace the phenomenon further back, and to seek for the source of the military aspirations of Prussia, we shall find it, I apprehend, in the conditions which have made her position in Europe hitherto a militant one—in the historical traditions and geographical situation of the country. After all, the question is not as to the introduction of the Prussian military system into England. The model for us, with whatever modifications it may be adopted, is manifestly the system of Switzerland; and now I beg attention to the language in which a Swiss citizen* sets forth the social and political tendencies of this bugbear of some of our advanced thinkers :—

> "We have confidence in our military organization; but, were it even proved that this institution had but small value as an agency for defending the country, we should even so remain attached to it. We see in it a republican institution of capital importance, a school of equality, a means of union amongst all citizens, and a powerful instrument of national life. It is in the manœuvres, in the life of the barrack and of the camp, that the sons of the rich eat the same bread as the children of the poor; it is there that they are called to forget the pleasures of a luxurious existence; they may make their bed beside men accustomed to severe toil, and whom, were it not for such opportunities, they would never perhaps have encountered. To those for whom such instruction may perchance be needed, the days passed in militia service teach habits of cleanliness conducive to health, and ideas of good order. It is there, moreover, that the Swiss, differing in manners, language, and religion, live in common, form ties of acquaintance and friendship, and feel the sentiments of national unity germinate and grow within them. . . . Such are the causes which make us feel for our system of militia an attachment of which no one can form an idea who is not himself a Swiss." †

And now a word, in conclusion, on what is certainly not the least important aspect of this momentous subject—the bearing of popular armies on the disposition

---

* M. Cérésole, Conseiller d'État du Canton de Vaud, Président du Département Militaire Vaudois.
† *Annales*, &c., p. 689.

of nations towards war. The tendency of standing armies to produce the evil against which they are supposed to be the safeguard, if it were not obvious on the face of the facts, is too well established by reiterated experience to need argument here. The professional soldier, if he have really the instinct of the soldier within him, and be not a mere carpet knight or loafer in taverns or clubs, cannot choose but chafe at the inaction of peace, with its slow promotion, its monotony and enforced idleness, and the waning importance to which it inevitably consigns him; and cannot but welcome every chance which offers him a stage for practice and the *éclat* of active service in the field. When the class is a large one, its influence must work powerfully in exacerbating every international difference into war; and the peril will be at its height when the Government itself is under the influence of military traditions. On the other hand, where, as with us, the Government is in the hands of the civil population, the danger takes another form. The decision of peace and war is now thrown upon persons who, under ordinary circumstances (for actual invasion is too rare an occurrence to be taken into calculation), are but slightly and remotely identified with the event. War, it is true, brings even to the citizen who remains at home an increase of taxation; a friend or relative will now and then be found in the lists of killed and wounded; but, against this, there is the agreeable excitement of reading of battle-fields, and the proud consciousness of belonging to a nation that is winning glory by martial deeds. Where those with whom rests the momentous decision have only this sort of remote and moderate interest in the awful results, what wonder if nations should sometimes rush into war "with a light heart"? But note how all these conditions are reversed, where the military force is the people itself. The army now exists as a profession only for an infinitesimal fraction of the nation; and war for the able-bodied masses means in the first place a vexatious interruption of their proper pursuits, with loss and sore anxiety for their families; and then, for themselves, the fiery ordeal of the actual campaign, almost wholly uncompensated in their case by the *éclat* and the rewards that await the professional soldier. To be sure, while nations were merely hordes of warriors, war would be their natural vocation, and perhaps pastime; but that a nation engaged in industrial pursuits, and in full career of civil life, should turn aside from its fields, its workshops, its desks and books, to gird on its armour, and throw itself into war, for any reason short of the gravest, for any reason not tantamount to self-defence—this is not easily conceivable. It will be said that Prussia has done so, if not in the present, at least in former wars. But, without entering here into the morality of the Danish and Austrian contests, it suffices to remark that Prussia is in truth not a fair example of the influence of a national army. Her army undoubtedly belongs to that type; but, owing to the immense active force kept on foot in time of peace, it possesses also not a few of the attributes of a standing force. And even of the army of Prussia, M. de Laveleye testifies, referring to the war of 1866, that "no warlike enthusiasm animated the Prussian armies. The men, summoned to their flag, set out with regret for a war generally condemned; but, once in the regiment, they desired to sustain the military honour of the corps, and to do their duty bravely." "I have had the opportunity," adds M. de Laveleye, "of reading several letters written by soldiers campaigning in the army of Bohemia before Sadowa. 'We will do our duty,' they wrote; 'the better we fight the sooner we shall have achieved our task, and the sooner we shall return to our homes,'—reasoning characteristic of the labourer who desires to accomplish his work, not of the soldier, for whom war is a career."* Every newspaper teems with evidence that this is at the present moment the prevailing feeling in the rank and file of the German armies.

If anything were wanting to complete the argument for the pacific tendency of the principle of popular armies, it is found in the fact, that the strength of the system lies in defence. This is universally recognized by those who have studied those organizations, and is

* It cannot be denied that the words of M. de Laveleye, while reassuring as regards the influence of the popular principle in the Prussian army, suggest uncomfortable thoughts. This people, so little prone to war, may, it seems, be made the powerful instrument in waging a war of which it does not approve. Here, no doubt, is a real danger. But let us not mistake its character. So far as it is incident to the military system at all, it is not the wide popular basis of the army that favours it —on the contrary, this acts as a hindrance and check—but the aristocratic organization of the higher ranks, which keeps the officers in intimate accord with the aims of the dynasty, and with the classes on whose support the dynasty rests. But in truth, the source of the danger is less in the military system than in the political constitution of Prussia; and the remedy lies, not in abandoning the popular organization of the army, but in bringing the government under parliamentary control—not in curtailing, but in developing the democratic principle.

indeed very obvious. It follows that, were civilized countries generally organized upon this principle, aggressive wars would be unsuccessful wars. Here is surely a weighty plea, thrown by the policy for which I am contending into the scale of peace—one which, we may hope, would have its influence even where better reasons might not prevail.

VI.

THOUGHTS ON UNIVERSITY REFORM

À-PROPOS OF THE IRISH EDUCATIONAL CRISIS OF
1865–6.*

A MOTION, made by an Irish Member at the close of the last Parliamentary session, which received little and rather slighting notice at the time, has raised some issues, both practical and theoretical, in the province of education, of very grave importance. The motion was a demand for a charter for a Roman Catholic College established some twelve years ago in Dublin, and commonly known as "The Catholic University," though hitherto without the power of granting degrees. It was met on the part of the Government by a counter proposal, to the effect, that, instead of constituting a new university in Ireland by the grant of a charter, the Catholic establishment should be affiliated as a distinct college to one of the universities which now exist; to wit, the Queen's. This compromise was eagerly embraced by the mover, and in general by the representatives of the Catholic party in Parliament, Mr. Hennessy being the single dissen-

* *Theological Review*, January 1866.

tient. The precise form which the Government scheme is destined to take is not yet known; but it has been shadowed forth in a series of announcements which purport to be authoritative, and which—as they proceed from the section of Catholics whom the concession is designed to conciliate, and who have certainly through their leaders been in communication with the Government—may be assumed to embody, with more or less exactness, the principal features of the pending arrangement; and the prospect has elicited a discussion which at all events exhibits very clearly the hopes and the fears of the supporters and the opponents of the proposed change. These hopes and fears alike point to the same result — a remodelling of the liberal and "mixed" system of State education hitherto maintained in Ireland in a denominational, which in the present instance means an ultramontane, sense—to a direct reversal therefore of the policy pursued in that country for the last thirty years. When we add that the controversy has brought up, in a practical shape, some of the nicest and most perplexing problems regarding the relations of the State to education, it will be seen that the occurrence is highly deserving of attentive study, whether we regard its bearing on the welfare of Ireland or on the prospects of educational progress.

I shall perhaps best introduce the reader to this controversy by a brief narrative of what has been done in recent years in promoting that department of education in Ireland which is the subject of the present discussion. Down to 1845, Trinity College, with the University which it includes, formed the only provision made for the higher secular learning in Ireland. Founded in the reign of Queen Elizabeth for the purpose of promoting the Protestant religion, its constitution and character were suitable to the circumstances of its origin. I shall perhaps convey a sufficiently precise notion of this establishment for my present purpose, if I say that it belongs, with many differences in detail, to the same order of educational bodies of which Oxford and Cambridge are the type in this country. It was of course inevitable that, as originally constituted, its basis should be rigidly sectarian: every religious denomination, save that established by law, was excluded alike from its degrees and its emoluments. But towards the end of the last century, under the influence of the more liberal ideas which then began to prevail, Trinity College opened its doors to Roman Catholics for admission to degrees; and a succession of measures, introduced at intervals from that period, and conceived in a spirit of consistent liberality, has placed it now in a position very decidedly in advance, in point of comprehensiveness and national character, of either of our ancient universities; Roman Catholics and Dissenters being now freely admitted to all its degrees, except those of divinity, to its senate and parliamentary constituency, and to a large share of its emoluments. In spite, however, of these substantial reforms, it would scarcely, I should imagine, be maintained by any candid Churchman, that Trinity College—retaining, as it did, its essentially Protestant character and traditions, and still excluding all but Protestants from its higher distinctions—formed an adequate provision for the higher education in a country of which three-fourths of the population were Roman Catholics. This was the view taken by a Select Committee of the House of Commons appointed in 1835, of which the late Sir Thomas Wyse was chairman. Among other recommendations of this Committee was one for the establishment of four colleges, one in each of the provinces of Ireland, which should extend to that portion of the people not already provided for in the National Schools the opportunity of an education, to borrow the language of the Report, "of the most improved character," "general, common to all, without distinction of class or creed." The policy advocated in the Report was adopted by the Government of Sir Robert Peel. It was determined to supplement the Elizabethan university by institutions conceived in the spirit of modern times, and directed to promote the interests of all classes of the community. In 1845 two measures were introduced: one for the re-constitution of Maynooth on an independent footing, and with a liberal endowment, as a seminary for the Roman Catholic priesthood; and the other for the establishment, in the interest of the laity, of three provincial colleges in Belfast, Cork, and Galway, constituted on the principle of strict religious equality, and designed to attract the various religious denominations to receive there an education in common: in the words of Sir James Graham, in the speech in which he introduced the measure, "The new Collegiate system was avowedly an extension, and nothing more than an extension, of the present system of National Education* from the children of the humblest to the children of the upper and middle classes."

Such was the origin of the Queen's Colleges: they were opened in 1849; and in 1850, in conformity with the original conception of the scheme, the Charter was granted by which the Queen's University was founded. In the words of the Charter, its object was "to render complete and satisfactory the courses of education to be followed by students in the said Colleges," and, with a view to this, it was invested with the power "of granting all such degrees as are granted by other universities or colleges to students who shall have completed in any one or other of the Colleges the courses of education prescribed and directed for the several degrees:"—the University was thus the natural completion and crown of the collegiate edifice. It needs only further be said, as regards this part of the case, that, while considerable powers were assigned to the local Colleges, the general government of the central institution, including the fixing of the courses of study for degrees and the appointment of university examiners, was placed with the Chancellor and Senate of the Queen's University.

And now I would ask the reader's attention to an important part of this story—the attitude assumed by the Roman Catholic community towards the new institutions. It was the expectation of the Government of that day—surely not an unreasonable one,

---

* Established in 1831 on the basis of "combined secular and separate religious instruction," and which had already, in 1845, achieved a remarkable success.

considering the essential fairness, and, account being taken of the grant to Maynooth, even liberality, of the arrangement, and further that the scheme was but an extension to the higher education of that plan which had already in the primary schools of the National System been received amongst Roman Catholics with all but universal favour — that the Queen's Colleges and their University would have been accepted by priest and people in the spirit in which they were offered. And for a brief moment there was every prospect that this expectation would be realized in the fullest sense. Doctors Murray and Croly occupied then, as Archbishop of Dublin and Primate, the highest places in the Irish Roman Catholic Church; they had both from the first accepted with cordial loyalty the principle of the National System, which they had aided in working, and the success of which was largely due to their enlightened efforts. They were now, with other leading members of the hierarchy, in communication with the Government on the subject of the Queen's Colleges. With such negotiators the Government had no difficulty in coming to an understanding. The statutes were drawn up, submitted to their inspection, and approved. It was admitted that the securities provided for the protection of "faith and morals" were ample. It will probably sound strange to many people now that amongst the names of the original members of the Queen's University Senate the third in order is that of Daniel Murray, Roman Catholic Archbishop of Dublin. The priesthood, indeed, were not unanimous: there was an active dissentient minority; but

looking to the influence then exercised by Doctors
Murray and Croly, one can hardly doubt that a few
more years of their gentle and enlightened rule would
have carried with them in support of the Colleges, as
it had already carried with them in support of the
National Schools, the great body of the priesthood.
Most unfortunately for peace and educational progress
in Ireland, just at this time—the same year in which
the Queen's Colleges were opened—Dr. Croly died;
and he was followed, two years later, by his abler
coadjutor. The successor to each was Dr. Cullen,
who, appointed in the first instance to the See of
Armagh—through a stretch of papal authority exercised in defiance of the immemorial usage of the Irish
Church, according to which the *dignissimus* of those
recommended for the honour by the clergy of the
diocese is selected—was, on the death of Murray,
transferred to Dublin.ABOVE
Dr. Cullen's preparation for
the post he was now called to fill had been a sojourn
of some thirty years in Rome, where, in the capacity
of Director of the Irish Department of the Papal
Government, he had made himself conspicuous as a
zealous supporter of all the extremest pretensions of
the ecclesiastical party. It was indeed avowedly to
advance the aims of ultramontane policy that he was
sent to Ireland, the better to equip him for which
service he was furnished with the further authority and
distinction of Apostolic Delegate. Scarcely had he
entered on his mission, when, it must be owned with
true instinct, he laid his hand upon the State system
of mixed education as presenting the most formidable
obstacle to his aims. He at once denounced it, alike

in the higher and the primary department; and, finding the Queen's Colleges, then just opened, still struggling with the difficulties of a *début* made in the face of much carefully prepared odium, one of his first acts was to summon a Synod to Thurles for the express purpose of condemning them. As all the world knows, the Colleges were condemned; but it is a noteworthy fact—as showing how entirely the course which the Roman Catholic clergy have since followed has been due to the foreign influences imported by Dr. Cullen into the Irish Church—that the condemnation was only carried by a majority of one; not only this, but—what may not be so well-known—even this slender triumph was obtained by questionable means—through an accident improved by an artifice. During the sitting of the Synod, a bishop, known to be favourable to the Colleges, fell sick: his place was at once filled by Dr. Cullen with a delegate of opposite views; the sick bishop recovered; but it was not deemed advisable to restore him to his place till the vote on the Colleges had been taken. The Queen's Colleges were thus condemned;* and the

---

* Condemned; although (as it may surprise the reader to learn) only nine years before the same mixed system of education which the Queen's Colleges represent had been sanctioned by the same infallible authority in the person of Pope Gregory XVI. I find the fact stated in the following terms by M. de Laveleye in the current number of the *Revue des Deux Mondes*, pp. 227, 228: "Après des discussions violentes et prolongées, les Catholiques des deux partis se décidèrent à en appeler à l'autorité infaillible, aux décisions de laquelle tous deux faisaient profession à obéir. Le Pape Gregoire XVI. répondit en 1841 par une lettre que la *propagande* adressa aux évêques d'Irlande. Cette réponse mérite attention, car elle montre que, même dans une question aussi grave que celle d'enseignement primaire, Rome se décide à transiger quand elle croit y trouver son intérêt. Le Pape ne condamne pas l'école laïque, il exige même qu'on n'y enseigne point du tout la religion, de sorte que le prin-

next step was to start a rival in the same field. For this purpose an apostolic brief was obtained, addressed to "the bishops of Ireland," authorizing and directing them to found a "Catholic University." Ere the Synod of Thurles had separated, a Committee was appointed, consisting of eight bishops, eight priests, and eight laymen (all of course Roman Catholics), to whose charge the organization and government of the projected institution was entrusted. Under these auspices appeared in due time in the middle of the nineteenth century "The Catholic University of Ireland," established, in the admiring language of its accomplished advocate, on "the eternal principles which regulated the relations of the Catholic Universities of the Middle Ages." *

From the sitting of the Synod of Thurles dates the systematic opposition of the Roman Catholic priesthood to the plan of mixed education in Ireland; and from this point, or rather from the elevation of Dr. Cullen, dates also a new policy in ecclesiastical patronage in Ireland, under which, within twenty years, a complete change has been effected in the character of the Irish Roman Catholic priesthood. In 1848 the spirit of that organization was, with few exceptions, national: under the rule of Dr. Cullen

cipe moderne de la sécularisation de l'enseignement primaire donné par l'état, que l'église combat ailleurs comme une monstruosité, est accepté par elle en Irlande comme en Hollande, c'est-à-dire là, où le pouvoir étant Protestant, elle ne peut espérer régner en souveraine." There is thus, it seems, an infallible declaration in favour of, as well as against, mixed education. The fact may be commended to Dr. Corrigan in case he contemplates a reply to the author of "Notes" on his pamphlet.

* "Two Articles on Education," by Myles W. O'Reilly, B.A., LL.D., M.P. (reprinted from the *Dublin Review*), p. 53.

it has become, except in the ranks of the lower clergy, an almost purely ultramontane body, absolutely devoted to ideas of which Rome, and not Ireland, is the originating source.*

The Roman Catholic priesthood had condemned the Colleges. We have yet to ascertain how they were regarded by the Roman Catholic people. Now this is manifestly a point of great importance in connection with our present theme. For if the Colleges have failed—or even though they should not have failed utterly, if they have failed as regards the section of the Irish people for whom they were principally intended—the Roman Catholics—then *quæstio cadit;* whatever may have been the benevolent views of the founders, or the abstract excellence of the scheme, there is no reason that they should be a moment longer maintained: by all means let the advice of Major O'Reilly be adopted, that the officials be pensioned off and the buildings sold. But if, on the other hand, the Colleges have in fact succeeded, if provision has by their means been effectually made for training in the higher learning those of the Irish people, not already provided for by Trinity College, for whom (regard being had to their social position) such training is suitable—provision, too, accordant to their wants and feelings—then, whatever the advocates of change may have to say for themselves on grounds of theory, there is at least no substantial grievance to be remedied; and the question for statesmen in this discussion is not of supplying a felt need —of "filling a gap (to borrow Mr. Gladstone's phrase)

* See Note to this Essay.

in university education in Ireland"—but of remodeling, with a view to improvement, a system already practically effective. To the importance of this point ultramontane advocates have shown themselves fully alive, so far as this can be shown by invariably assuming it in their own favour. According to them, "the Queen's Colleges have wholly failed,"* while

---

* Major O'Reilly, from whose pamphlet the above allegation of entire failure has been taken, subjoins in a foot-note what I suppose must be regarded as the grounds of that statement :—"This has been admitted (with regret) by both Mr. Cardwell and Sir Robert Peel, and in fact by the Commission appointed to inquire into them."

I confess this statement, proceeding from a writer of Major O'Reilly's usual accuracy, startled me a good deal. I have looked through the expressions of opinion on the subject in question by the authorities referred to, and I shall now lay before the reader a few specimens I regret that space does not permit me to give more—of the results of my search.

On the 25th of July, 1859, Mr. Cardwell said in Parliament—"he had no hesitation in saying that the Colleges had not met with the success which was originally expected by the founders." This, it must be admitted, is not a favourable opinion; but it is something very far from an admission of entire failure—how far, may be seen by reading it in connection with a passage from a speech made by the same minister a few days previously. On the 22nd of July, 1859, in the debate on Mr. Hennessy's motion, Mr. Cardwell said :—

"He thought they would be of opinion that the result which they had attained to might not indeed be an example of complete success, but was an encouragement and a reason for hope. . . . . The attendance of such a number (493) to obtain an education such as was given in these Colleges, was an immense advantage to a country situated as Ireland was. Moreover, it appeared that the pupils had been drawn pretty equally from the various religious bodies into which the population was divided. . . . . That surely gave great cause for encouragement for the cause not only of advanced but of mixed education in Ireland."

These expressions of opinion, it will be observed, were uttered in 1859, at which time the number of students attending the Colleges was little more than half the amount it has since attained. Recognizing this altered state of facts, Mr. Cardwell, speaking on the 5th of July, 1862, on the University vote, said :—

"The Colleges had had great difficulties to contend with, having met much opposition; but the number of students was now continually

"The Catholic University" is in an eminently suc- increasing, and in the last year the number of pupils was 752. Those 750 pupils were nearly equally divided between Catholics, Protestants, and Presbyterians. . . . . The constant increase of pupils, the numerical equality in the religious opinions of those who entered, and the success of the students in public competition, at which they had to meet students from the older universities, from Trinity College, and from every school and seminary in the kingdom, all showed that the sum granted was accomplishing the object for which it was voted—namely, educating indiscriminately the different classes of the people of Ireland."

So far Mr. Cardwell. The citation of Sir Robert Peel in support of the statement that the Queen's Colleges "had wholly failed," I confess I have some difficulty in dealing with. The simple fact is, that Sir Robert Peel's speeches on the Queen's Colleges (and he rarely lost an opportunity of making one) have flowed in a strain of almost unqualified panegyric, equally full of admiration for the past and hope for the future. His only complaint on the subject has been that their endowments are inadequate; to remedy which defect, as all the world knows, he set on foot a public subscription some years ago, to which he himself munificently contributed. I do injustice to the case by making extracts: still I give the following, which strikes the key-note of the whole :—
"I have watched the institution from its commencement, and am glad to trace its development. It has opened to three-fourths of the youth of Ireland those academic advantages which they were before denied, and it has rendered immense benefits not only to the cause of popular education, but to the good government and to the character of this country. And what is the criterion of the success of this institution? Not mere numbers. They would be very significant if we looked only to that. But the proof of its success is the great political gain which has been derived by the establishment of a system in Ireland which has opened to men of different religious denominations combined secular instruction upon the broad basis of religious equality."

Lastly, the Commission, appointed to inquire into the Colleges, and which Major O'Reilly cites as "in fact" admitting that they "had wholly failed," delivered its opinion in these words :—

"We should be glad to be able to report a larger number of students availing themselves of the great advantages held out to them in the Queen's Colleges; but we think that the Colleges cannot be regarded as otherwise than successful, when, notwithstanding opposing causes, to which we shall presently allude, they have in their halls, attending lectures, nearly 450 students."

This was in 1858. Major O'Reilly's pamphlet was published in 1863, in which year the numbers had increased from 450, which the Commissioners thought not capable of being regarded otherwise than as an indication of success, to 787; and it is under these circumstances that

cessful position."[*] They have not in general offered any reasons for these assertions. But, of course, when a demand was made to Parliament to reverse the policy it had followed for thirty years, it became necessary to sustain the allegation of failure with some show of proof. This task was accordingly undertaken

Major O'Reilly thinks himself justified in quoting the authority of the Commissioners for the utter failure of the Queen's Colleges. The following figures show the progress of the Colleges from the period of the Commissioners' report down to the present time :—

        1858-59 490
        1859-60 546
        1860-61 657
        1861-62   758
        1862-63 787
        1863-64   810
        1864-65 835

To exhibit fully, however, the opinion of the Commissioners on the Colleges, the passage quoted above must be supplemented by the following :—

"We think, however, that the good done by the Queen's Colleges as great public institutions in Ireland, cannot be estimated merely by the number of students in their halls, or by the successful candidates whom they may send to the great public contests of the educated youth of the empire. We believe that, beyond this, they are, by the honourable competition existing between the students and professors of the several Queen's Colleges amongst themselves, and also by the healthy and, we hope, friendly competition with the University of Dublin, materially aiding in advancing learning in Ireland. We believe that the Colleges are calculated, and we trust the association of students of various creeds and opinions within their walls does operate, to soften those feelings of party antagonism and sectarian animosity which have heretofore unhappily had too extended an existence in Ireland; and that they are rapidly generating a feeling of local self-reliance and of self-respect, and exciting an interest in the culture of literature and science throughout the community at large."

The reader is now in a position to judge of the value of assertions as to the failure of the Queen's Colleges made by ultramontane writers, of whom, I am bound to say, the most candid and scrupulous I have encountered is Major O'Reilly.

[*] "Two Articles on Education," pp. 46, 78.

by the O'Donoghue, the mover of the resolution referred to at the opening of these remarks, who produced on the occasion certain statistics from which he drew the desired conclusion. Strange to say, the O'Donoghue's reasons were never traversed by the Government, though directly at variance with the repeated assertions of several of its members who had filled the offices of Lord Lieutenant and Chief Secretary of Ireland. But since the parliamentary debate considerable light has been thrown upon this question from other quarters. Those interested on behalf of the Colleges have supplied the answer which the Government, for whatever reasons, declined to give, and the whole case may now be regarded as pretty fully before the public. I shall endeavour to state briefly how the facts in reference to this important matter stand.*

The case for the failure of the Queen's Colleges as presented by the O'Donoghue was briefly this :—

The total number of students in Trinity College he set down (I know not on what authority) at...... 1,000
The total number at the Queen's Colleges at...... 837

Giving an aggregate receiving education in both of... 1,837

Of the 1,000 students in Trinity College, but 45 were Roman Catholics : of the 837 in the Queen's Colleges, but 223; that is to say, 268 Roman Catholics altogether as against 1,569 Protestants, in an aggregate of 1,837, or 14 per cent. With this state of facts he

* [I leave the statistical argument as I wrote it in 1865. Since that time our information on this head has been considerably extended, chiefly through the inquiries of Dr. Lyon Playfair, to whose pamphlets and speeches I refer the reader who desires a fuller knowledge of this part of the case.]

contrasted certain returns of attendance in intermediate schools, from which it appeared that the Roman Catholics and Protestants receiving education in these were about equal in number. His inference was—an inference adopted by the Government—that the Roman Catholics were deterred from going on to the higher education by conscientious objections to the institutions through which it was provided. On these grounds he demanded a charter for " The Catholic University."

The reply on the part of the Colleges has been as follows : Accepting the facts so far as they are given, they do not sustain the O'Donoghue's conclusion. For why is it to be assumed that the relative numbers of Roman Catholics and Protestants in the intermediate schools furnish a just basis for a comparison of their numbers in the universities ? Are there not in every population large numbers who avail themselves of the education afforded in intermediate schools who never think of prosecuting their studies further ? and is it not possible that this class may be larger among Irish Roman Catholics than among Irish Protestants? Notoriously this is the fact. The discrepancy therefore between the comparative returns of the intermediate schools and the universities finds in part an obvious explanation in the social condition of the two classes. But, secondly, it finds a further explanation in a still graver flaw in the O'Donoghue's argument, a flaw so grave as in fact to vitiate it altogether—the entire omission of the principal element of the returns on the Catholic side. The Protestant students are set down at 1,569 a number which includes, besides students intended for the several lay callings, the great bulk of those designed for holy orders in the several Protestant Churches; but the 268 Roman Catholics who are contrasted with them comprise *lay students only*. For the education of the Roman Catholics intended for the priesthood the State has provided Maynooth with an endowment of £26,000 a year; and besides Maynooth, several other colleges exist in Ireland maintained from private sources for a similar purpose.* The students attending these, and who have their counterpart on the Protestant side in the divinity classes of Dublin and Belfast included in the quoted figures, the O'Donoghue wholly omits! It illustrates curiously the spirit in which this gentleman's argument was encountered by the Government, that in the discussion which ensued this huge and glaring omission was never detected. It has, however, since been both detected and supplied by less complaisant disputants. As corrected, the comparison stands thus :—

Protestant students, lay and clerical, receiving higher education 1,569
Roman Catholic ditto ditto 1,155

---

* "Of seminaries for the education of ecclesiastics in 1800, Maynooth, which had existed just five years, was the only one; in 1864, besides the national seminary of Maynooth, which has now an annual endowment of £26,000, and numbers 500 students, our bishops have also established seventeen diocesan seminaries; and in addition to these institutions for the education of the priesthood, several of the religious orders have houses in Ireland where their members are educated for the priesthood: such are the Calced Carmelites, Dominicans, Augustinians, Cistercians, Jesuits, Vincentians, Passionists, Redemptorists, and oblates of Mary."— *Progress of Catholicity in Ireland in the Nineteenth Century:* a Paper read before the Catholic Congress of Mechlin, Sept. 1864, by Myles O'Reilly, LL.D., M.P., pp. 15, 16.

I think it must be allowed that this considerably alters the aspect of the case. But the consideration remains : does the number of Roman Catholic students, thus enlarged, fairly represent the proportion of the body who would in the present social condition of Ireland naturally aspire to an academic status ? Now on this point an accurate criterion is plainly not attainable ; but such facts as the following will serve to give the reader an approximately correct idea as to how the matter stands. It appears * that in an aggregate of 6,483 members composing the learned professions in Ireland, the Roman Catholic proportion is 2,219, or 33 per cent. : in the aggregate magistracy Roman Catholics stand for 24 per cent. ; amongst those returned in the Census as " ladies and gentlemen," for 27 per cent. These facts do not, indeed, afford an accurate measure of the comparative need amongst Roman Catholics for university education ; but they furnish an approximate standard, which, taken in connection with the statistics of the higher education just given, justifies the assertion that, as regards this department of instruction, Roman Catholics in Ireland are already not badly provided for.

Such, substantially, has been the reply on the part of the Colleges. It is, in my opinion, as conclusive as a reply founded on mere statistical data can be. I will now add a consideration which, if I am not mistaken, renders the argument complete, and converts strong presumption into something very like positive

* See the table of the Census setting forth the " occupations " of the population.

demonstration. A common objection urged against the Queen's Colleges, and, it must be owned, with some plausibility, is, that they foster among the people a habit of looking to the State for a career. Major O'Reilly has adopted this amongst other charges. In a footnote to page 31 of his pamphlet he thus states the point in somewhat triumphant style:—

"We will stake our reputation for accuracy on a very simple test: let any one of our readers go into a national school, and after a little conversation with the cleverest lad in it, find out what his highest aspirations are: we will answer for it they will be found to be a Government clerkship or an appointment in the Post Office. Let him also try a Queen's College, and ten to one, the goal of the student's ambition will be found to be a cadetship in the constabulary, a clerkship in one of the public offices, or a Government appointment in India."

Now, passing by the case of the National Schools, with which we are not at present concerned, I have little doubt that, as regards the Queen's Colleges, the gallant author's accuracy would be sustained by the experiment. Beyond all question, a considerable proportion of the Queen's College students look for their future career to such openings as are offered by the constabulary, the public offices, and India; but what does this prove? That the Queen's Colleges foster a habit of dependence upon State employment? I am paradoxical enough to think that the tendency to look to the State for employment follows rather the amount of patronage at the disposal of the State, than the means which exist for qualifying for the effective discharge of such State work as is to be done: I venture even to believe that if the Queen's Colleges ceased to exist to-morrow, there would not be an Irish candidate the less for the public offices. The effect would be felt, as it seems to me, not in the number of candidates, but in their qualification; nor can I conceive anything better calculated to correct the evils of the bureaucratic spirit than the liberalizing effects of an university education. But, not to dwell on this point, what does the fact—for fact no doubt it is—to which Major O'Reilly calls attention prove? That there is a gap in university education in Ireland still to be filled up? Rather does it not conclusively establish the very point which Major O'Reilly and his allies are never weary of denying—the practical success of the Queen's Colleges; since it shows that the number of the Irish population to whom university studies are through their means accessible, is largely in excess of that which the private demand for intellectual services furnished by the learned professions will absorb? No student in the Queen's Colleges who saw a prospect of success in one of the learned professions would think of offering himself as a candidate for the constabulary or the public offices; but the professions being, like most other industrial walks in Ireland, much overcrowded, students, not conscious of more than average ability, but who have received some tincture of university culture, will naturally prefer the constabulary or the public offices to a mere mechanical or a purely rural calling. This is the true explanation of the fact—an explanation so obvious that I venture to say no one could have missed it who had not a theory to support. Had it been Major O'Reilly's object to prove that the Queen's Colleges had overdone their work, the test which he proposes of his accuracy would have been also much to his general purpose; his object being to prove that their work has been left undone, the verification of his accuracy necessarily results in the defeat of his argument.

To the argument, in the position to which it has now been brought, there is but one objection which we can imagine a candid opponent of the Queen's Colleges to advance—the suggestion that, though the Queen's Colleges have in fact succeeded, they have succeeded only as a *dernier ressort;* that the Roman Catholics have gone to them because they desired university education, and had no other means of obtaining it. But unfortunately for the case of the ultramontanes, they have, by the establishment of their model institution, effectually estopped themselves from this reply. It can scarcely be said that the Queen's Colleges are a *dernier ressort*, while there is the alternative for students which this institution offers. If the Roman Catholics entertain conscientious objections to the Queen's Colleges, is there not abundant room for them in " The Catholic University " ? We shall be told " The Catholic University " has not a charter; which is true; but if " The Catholic University " cannot confer degrees on its *alumni*, London University can, and does.*

---

* And it would seem by methods entirely in accordance with the views of the extreme Catholic party, at least if Major O'Reilly may be taken as an exponent of those views. In reference to this point he writes: " The London University does not undertake to teach, or to regulate the teaching of the different institutions whose pupils present themselves at its examination; nay, it carefully avoids, even in laying down the

It may not be generally known that, according to a recent admirable arrangement entirely in keeping with its true character, that body now holds its examinations in all parts of the United Kingdom; indeed in all parts of the British Empire. This year one matriculation examination was held in the Mauritius, another in the Irish town of Carlow. It is a central institution with its centre everywhere. Practically, therefore, as regards facilities for obtaining degrees, the students of the Queen's Colleges enjoy no advantage which is not shared by those of the rival institution. Nor can it be said that the former are successful through the superior attractions which, as State institutions, they hold out; for it seems—a fact creditable to the zeal of its promoters—that, even in the matter of endowments, "The Catholic University" stands in a position little, if at all, inferior to that occupied by a Queen's College;* and if we admit that there is something in State *prestige*, it must be admitted, on the other hand, that there is also something in spiritual *prestige*.

subject of examinations, anything like a dictation as to the opinions to be taught: and for this reason a general statement of the subjects of examination in moral philosophy has been substituted by the Senate for an enumeration of certain works of Butler and Paley; as the latter might, it was thought, be looked upon as requiring an assent to the teachings of those writers. . . . Thus education is left absolutely free and voluntary; and the State only interferes to ascertain results, and that only through the medium of bodies wholly independent of Government control."

* According to Major O'Reilly ("Progress of Catholicity," p. 15), the sum raised (partly by subscriptions from abroad) for the first foundation of "The Catholic University" was £40,000, which has since been sustained by an annual collection of £8,000, about the income of one of the Queen's Colleges.

So far the rival institutions stand, in regard to the prospects which they open to students, pretty nearly on a par; but, over and above the considerations which have been adverted to, there is one more which must be taken account of, if we would fairly appreciate the value of the experiment made by the Queen's Colleges' system on the intellectual tastes of the Irish people. The Queen's Colleges have succeeded not merely against the legitimate rivalry of an institution founded on different principles, but—a cardinal fact in this controversy—against the illegitimate and tyrannical opposition of a priesthood, who have refused to leave the decision to the unbiassed judgment of those whom the question concerned,—against an opposition availing itself of all the arts at its command for inspiring superstitious terror, of denunciation from the altar, exclusion from sacraments, in a word, of expedients resembling rather the spiritual appliances of Jesuit despots dictating to Paraguayan savages than remonstrances fitted to be addressed to reasonable and civilized men. For example, every Roman Catholic entering a Queen's College does so under a fire of this kind :—

"The Holy Father sees the conspiracy that has been organized to withdraw the education of youth from the influence of the Catholic Church; and in the anguish of his paternal heart he declares that the result will be moral and intellectual corruption. He invites us all, clergy and laity, to join with him in deploring that Satanic scheme for the ruin of faith in the rising generation. . . . Parents and guardians of young men are to understand that by accepting education in them [the Queen's Colleges] for those under their charge, they despise the warnings, entreaties, and decisions of the Head of the Church. . . . Adhering to the discipline in force in this diocese, we once for all declare that they who are guilty of it shall not be admitted to receive the holy sacrament of the Eucharist, or of Penance, whilst they continue in their disobedience." *

Am I unreasonable in concluding that popular success, achieved against opposition such as this, proves something more than simple preference for the denounced system on the part of those who accept it? It seems to me that nothing short of singular adaptation to the wants and aspirations of the Irish people would account for so striking a phenomenon.

It would seem, then, that "the gap" in university education in Ireland has yet to be discovered: in plain terms, there is not a tittle of evidence to show that any appreciable proportion of Irish Roman Catholics are by conscientious objections, or by any other cause than their social position and circumstances, excluded from the existing Irish universities. Let us now add to the presumptive proof, arising from the absence of any apparent want, the positive evidence of what has been performed. Omitting details, then, the general results accomplished by the Queen's University and its Colleges in a career of fifteen years are these: they have in that time educated 3,330 Irishmen, that is to say, 957 members of the Established Church, 938 Roman Catholics, 1,197 Presbyterians, and 238 of other denominations. They are at the present moment educating more than at any previous time; their students now being within one-fifth as numerous as

* Pastoral of Dr. Derry, Bishop of Clonfert, addressed last March to the faithful of his diocese.

those of Trinity College, Dublin, and within one-third as numerous as those of thé University of Oxford. In a period of fourteen years the Queen's University has conferred 886 degrees (exclusive of diplomas and *ad eundems*); the number conferred by the London University during the corresponding period of its career being 841, or about five per cent. less.* The Colleges have since their establishment trebled the number of Roman Catholic laymen receiving university education.† The quality of their education, as shown by every available test, is not inferior to that obtainable in any of the older universities. Lastly, they have eminently succeeded in what was a leading object of their establishment—the bringing together in the same class-rooms of students from all the various religious bodies in the country.

I have been anxious to dispose of the questions of failure and practical grievance before engaging in the discussion of the projects of university reform,

---

* I borrow these figures from a "Statement adopted by the Graduates of the Queen's University in Ireland, assembled in Public Meeting in Belfast on Wednesday, 6th December, 1865,"—a paper which gives with admirable clearness and precision all the important facts of the question.

† At p. 47 of Major O'Reilly's pamphlet, the following passage occurs: "On the other hand, the recognized authorities of the Catholic Church would decide, with judgment and prudence, what changes were necessary to remove the objections *which prevent Catholics attending Cork College*." Considering that, when this was written, there were 123 Catholics on the rolls as attending Cork College—a fact with which Major O'Reilly would surely not have failed to acquaint himself—one is driven to suppose that that gentleman refuses the name of "Catholics" to those who attend a Queen's College. In this he may or may not be justified; but it seems to me that it would have been only fair, before adopting this course, to have apprised his readers of this habit. I call attention to the circumstance, because it may furnish a clue to his meaning, and possibly to the meaning of others who share his opinions, when they assure us that "the Queen's Colleges have wholly failed.'

which the announcement by the Government that they were prepared to concede some modification of the existing system has naturally brought upon the carpet. The course of the controversy has already disclosed the fact, that the ideas of those who criticise the present arrangements do not run in a single channel. Under the assumed banner of " freedom of education," two distinct, and to some extent conflicting, policies are advocated; one of these, that of the ultramontane party proper, aims avowedly (its liberal watchword notwithstanding) at the erection of " The Catholic University "—an institution, it will be remembered, established at the instigation of the Pope, and now worked through a committee of which two-thirds are Roman Catholic ecclesiastics—into a position of paramount and pervading authority over the whole higher education of Roman Catholics in Ireland; the other— whatever may be our judgment on its general merits— would seem at least to be conceived with a *bonâ-fide* desire to promote educational freedom according to the ideas of those who support it. One might even be disposed to suspect that its advocates (who, I may observe, are Roman Catholics, but laymen) have, consciously or unconsciously, not been uninfluenced by a desire to counteract the aims of the *parti prêtre;* though, I own, I have been led to this conclusion, more from the violence with which the policy in question has been assailed by that party, than from anything that can be discovered in the proposals put forward calculated to offer an effectual obstruction to its designs. However this may be, my object now is to place before the reader each of these schemes of educational reform, so far as I have been able to collect them from the manifestoes of the two sections, and, without reference to a possible *arrière pensée*, to endeavour to estimate, as correctly as I am able, their real character and tendency.

Taking, first, what for distinction I may describe as the *lay* proposal, its leading idea would seem to be to remodel the existing institutions for the higher education in Ireland on the pattern presented by the London University and the various seminaries which prepare candidates for its degrees. The adoption of the principle in its integrity would require the abolition of both the present Irish universities: on their ruins would be raised a new university, to be called the University of Dublin or of Ireland, which would be in fact simply an examining Board, under which would be ranged as strictly co-ordinate institutions the various teaching bodies of the country, including amongst these as equal members Trinity College, the Queen's Colleges, St. Patrick's College, Maynooth, "The Catholic University," &c. These would send up candidates for matriculation and degrees to the central institution, where, without reference to the antecedents of their training, they would be received, examined, and certificated. But this scheme, though "comprehensive, well-founded in theory, and national in aspect,"* it is thought advisable, from considerations of practical

* "University Education in Ireland," p. 3. This pamphlet, by a distinguished member of the Queen's University Senate, which I take as the best exposition of the views I am now considering, has not been published; but as it has enjoyed a very large circulation, probably much larger than if it made its appearance in the ordinary way, I do not think that, in treating it as public, I am violating any rule of literary etiquette which deserves to be held sacred.

expediency, suggested by the opposition which it would be in the power of Trinity College to offer, to relinquish, in favour of another less perfect but more feasible. It is accordingly proposed to leave Dublin University with its College aside as refractory elements, but to throw the remaining educational institutions of the country into the crucible. The connection between the Queen's University and its Colleges would be dissolved; the University in its present character would cease to exist; and the outcome would be an examining Board, to be named the Queen's University, and a group of co-ordinate institutions, amongst which the Queen's Colleges and "The Catholic University" would rank with a host of preparatory schools now little conscious of the dignity which is intended for them. These would work together on an equal footing, engaged in the common task of preparing candidates for the matriculation and degree examinations to be held by the Central Board.

Such in outline is the scheme which has been propounded, and which enjoys, I understand, in Ireland, a certain amount of favour. It is also a part of the proposal that the Senate of the University should be increased from sixteen (the present number) to thirty members,—twenty of these to be nominated by the Crown and to consist in equal numbers of Protestants and Catholics, the remaining ten to be elected by Convocation. Further, it is proposed that the appointment of Professors in the Queen's Colleges should be transferred from the Crown to a local Board, constituted on a plan, as it seems to me, equally complicated and unpromising. For the present, however, I purpose confining myself to the more fundamental and characteristic features of the scheme.

And in the first place, it occurs to me to ask, why, supposing it is proper to abolish one or both of the existing Irish universities, erect another in their room? According to the theory propounded, the proper function of a university is to test actual acquirement, without reference to the place or mode of acquisition. A university is thus conceived as a sort of intellectual mint to which all the pure metal of knowledge in the country is to be brought to receive the stamp which is to make it current. Well, adopting this view, is there not already the London University to perform the required office? It is not denied that it performs its office well: on what principle, then, are we required to establish a second mint for knowledge, and thus to introduce into the economy of letters double standards and measures? The writer who has advocated this plan takes the "*Jury Central*" of Belgium (the exact position of which in the Belgian scheme of education, by the way, he seems to misconceive) as the model of a national university; and he tells us that the London University is in this country the analogue of that institution. Then why not act upon this analogy, and re-organize the "unharnessed" Irish seminaries under the London "Central"? It cannot be said that local convenience would require a second Irish university; for, as has been already pointed out, under the arrangement which now exists the staff of the metropolitan establishment is brought to the doors, it may be to the halls, of the Irish Colleges. Nor can it be supposed—at a time* when the mischief of keeping alive a distinct national sentiment is just receiving such painful illustration, when even to the Irish Lord Lieutenancy everything which looks in this direction is carefully discountenanced—that an Irish "Central" will be demanded on *national* grounds. It seems to me, therefore, that the leading feature of the scheme stands condemned upon its author's own principles. The present universities of Ireland, *constituted as they now are*, may have something to ·say for themselves: how far this is so I shall presently examine: an Irish university constituted on the plan proposed, as a second "Central Jury," would be absolutely without a reason for its existence. Nay, there would be abundance of reasons for its non-existence; for what other effect could the creation of such a body have but to introduce between it and the university already in possession of the field a vicious competition for candidates, such as this writer himself, in the case of the medical schools, has shown almost necessarily results in a degradation of the standard knowledge?

But the policy of the scheme just described is open to objections more fundamental far than this. What is the conception of education which it presents to us? Simply that of a preparatory process for a uniform examination. For culture properly so called, for the process by which the mind is opened, liberated and rendered productive, for any

* [1865.]

results which may not be tested by categorical question and answer, the scheme I have described makes no provision: nay, there are abundant indications that these objects lie absolutely outside its author's mental horizon. It is laid down, for example, that universities should "test the man for what he knows, not where he learned it," apparently under the impression that the object of restricting University degrees to those trained in particular institutions, is to create a "monopoly" in favour of the institutions, or the localities where they happen to exist. The same view is almost grotesquely brought out in another passage :—

"The student of St. Patrick's College, Carlow, passes through Dublin, where the Queen's University ignores him, on his way to the London University, which admits him —surely such an absurdity cannot be permitted to continue."

I do not know whether the fact that the student of St. Patrick's College, Carlow, can now obtain his degree from London University *without* passing the site of the Queen's University, will diminish in our author's eyes the absurdity which he here discovers; but to my mind the only absurdity in the case—and it is a very great absurdity—is the application of such tests to such subjects.

In presence of arguments of this order, it may perhaps be well to state that the end of a university system—the purpose by success or failure in which it must be justified or condemned—is not to bring aspirants to academic degrees by the shortest route before the nearest examining Board, much as criminals are hurried before the nearest justice, but to furnish the means for the largest, freest, and most varied development of the human faculties. Now this is not to be accomplished by a system which proposes no other aim, and provides for no other result, than success at an examination, a system which converts the entire educational machinery of a country into an apparatus for encouraging and facilitating "cram." I am not one of those who regard with anything but unmixed satisfaction the application in recent years of the method of competitive examination to the public service. Employed within certain limits, and applied with discretion, it is, I believe, an invaluable expedient in working the machinery of administration. But the method obviously, admittedly, has a tendency to engender certain well-known intellectual defects, of which the chief is the habit of loading the memory with the mere results of knowledge rapidly accumulated, and, when the pressure is passed, almost as rapidly forgotten. Nor will it be denied that the evil is one which many other modern influences powerfully contribute to foster. This being so, it would seem to be the part of wisdom so to frame our educational arrangements as to neutralize as far as possible this besetting tendency. One obvious means—I own, so far as I can see, the only effectual means—of accomplishing this object is to supplement the examination test by others; for example, by the condition that the student before presenting himself for examination, shall have gone through certain prescribed courses of study under the guidance of the best minds which the teaching body of the time can furnish. This is what the academic or collegiate system* seeks to do, and what, with more or less success, it accomplishes; and this is the condition which the plan we are considering proposes altogether to annul. Under the notion that it is placing all localities on a par, that it is excluding the element "where" from the conditions of the acquisition of knowledge, it in fact places all methods of instruction on a par, and excludes from the conditions required as evidence of knowledge that one which forms the chief and almost the only security for its thoroughness. Far from providing checks against the prevailing intellectual vice of the time, it makes a clean sweep of such inadequate securities as now exist, and even invites the advances of the enemy by opening to his ambition a new and boundless field.

But perhaps I shall be told that these consequences are not involved in the proposed scheme. The plan —so we can imagine an advocate might put the argument—far from favouring any scheme of instruction in particular, is essentially neutral as regards all, and neither seeks, on the one hand, to discourage the system of collegiate training, nor, on the other, to promote private teaching. People under the new *régime*, it may be said, might continue, if they thought proper, to send their sons to colleges as now; and no doubt (such a reasoner might add), if the advantages of this course are as great as is pretended, this is

* I may explain here, to avoid misapprehension, that by the "collegiate system" I merely mean instruction carried out through regular attendance on courses of lectures delivered in institutions established for the purpose of general mental cultivation. This necessarily implies residence near a college, but not necessarily mensal residence.

what would happen. The essence of the scheme, in short, it might be urged, is not protection or favour, but freedom—the extension into the field of knowledge of that stimulus to effort and improvement which healthy competition supplies—in a word, "free trade in education."

But this, however plausible, is, in reality, wholly irrelevant to the issue which I have raised. My objection to the proposed scheme is, not that it applies the examination test unfairly, but that *it applies no other test.* If the condition of passing an examination be the only one required by a university for obtaining its degrees, it is plain that the qualities of education which an examination is competent to elicit are the only ones which such a university will tend to develop. The Central Board of Examination would, no doubt, be perfectly impartial as between the various systems of which the results would be submitted to it; but if its tests are only fitted for the discovery of merit of a certain kind, it could not but favour the systems which were most efficacious in producing that sort of merit. But we need not on this point rely altogether on speculative considerations. We have already had tolerably large experience of the working of such a system in the examinations for the Indian Civil Service. These examinations are probably conducted in a manner as well fitted to defeat "cram" as in the nature of the case is possible; and what is the lesson which the experiment teaches? I believe it is this, that in such a contest the places of education in which collegiate training is enforced are not competent to hold their ground against the competition of the professional "coach." Unfortunately it is not possible to exhibit the results of the experiment in statistical form, as it is the custom of the Civil Service Commissioners to ignore in their returns the places of special instruction, in which the majority of the candidates spend two or three years before presenting themselves for examination. The effect of this is that the work of the professional trainers is concealed; the universities and schools obtaining credit largely for successes which are in fact due to other means of instruction. The working of the system, therefore, as regards the point in hand, cannot be exhibited statistically. I will, however, quote the opinion of a friend who, with the advantage of some experience as an examiner, has watched the experiment. "My own opinion," he writes, "is that university candidates are declining and must decline in numbers; the Indian Civil Service examinations are making a sort of university themselves. A lad of 16 or 17 goes to a 'coach,' and at the end of a year goes in to the examination to see what it is like; he thus feels his way, ascertains his weak points, and has some means of judging whether he may be successful in a second or third venture; and it constantly happens that a selected candidate has been up once, if not twice, before. The Civil Service Halls, Institutes, and what not, are thus in the same relation to the Indian Civil Service examination that the affiliated Colleges of London University are to it. It is quite impossible that the older Universities can compete with this system." Such, in the opinion of careful observers, is the tendency of competitive examination in relation to collegiate training in the most important instance in which it has yet been tried; and this may enable us to form an idea of what would be the result of remodelling our entire university system on the plan of the Civil Service Commission, which is in effect the reform now proposed. It could only, as it seems to me, discourage, and ultimately lead to the abandonment altogether in the higher education of systematic training in colleges,— the one effectual safeguard which we possess against the gravest intellectual danger of the time. The older universities might, under such a *régime*, for a time hold their ground : their *prestige* would not at once perish. But for places like the Irish Queen's Colleges, — institutions of yesterday — institutions which, far from being aided by *prestige*, have had to struggle against a weight of disingenuous misrepresentation and carefully fostered odium,—the result of such a policy could only be quick destruction.*

Nor would the mischief of this movement be confined to its intellectual consequences. With the collegiate system would also be lost advantages of a moral and social kind, scarcely, if at all, less important than its more direct and palpable benefits, —those manifold helps to the formation of character which arise from bringing young men together at

* I am inclined, on consideration, to think that it would prove even more certainly the destruction of "The Catholic University." Over and above the causes indicated, which would affect this institution (as it also enforces the collegiate principle) equally with the Queen's Colleges, there would be the desire to escape ecclesiastical dictation. To the plea of poverty, with which the recommendation of the priesthood to parents to send their sons to "The Catholic University" could easily be met, there would be no effective reply. Hence, no doubt, the strenuous repudiation by the clerical party of this lay scheme.

the most impressionable period of life, and placing them under the influence of minds not unsympathetic with theirs, while instructed and mature. In the friendly intimacies and honourable rivalries of those three or four years, what opportunities occur for lessons in the practical ethics of life!—lessons at once in modesty and self-respect, laid silently to heart as the student measures himself against his fellows, and ascertains his true mental stature—lessons in candour and toleration as he discovers how most questions have two sides, on either of which good and earnest men are found to range themselves—lessons in the practical value and skilful handling of the truths learned in the lecture-room, afforded by conversation with his companions and by the opportunities of the debating club;—lastly, lessons in self-reliance, simplicity, and manliness of character, inhaled with the moral atmosphere of a place in which the only distinctions known are those which in the actual arena have made their pretensions good.

These are advantages incidental to the Collegiate system wherever it is established; but for a country like Ireland, long torn with religious dissensions, where for centuries Protestants and Catholics educated in opposite camps have learned to regard each other almost as natural enemies, the system, carried out as it is in the Queen's Colleges, has manifestly a special adaptation. What can be better fitted to qualify the virus of bigotry and engender feelings of mutual consideration and respect, what better preparation for the duties of citizenship in a country of mixed religious faith can be imagined, than a system of education which furnishes to the youths of all religious denominations neutral ground on which they may meet and cultivate in common, without reference to the causes which divide them, those pursuits in which they have a common interest? It is a noteworthy fact, and one for which, let us observe in passing, the authorities in those institutions deserve some little credit, that throughout the fifteen years of their existence, with one single and transient exception,* not an instance in any of the colleges has occurred of dissension due to religious differences. And this result has been attained, while religious controversy has been raging with the utmost fury all around, and while propagandist societies—in the case of one of the colleges at least, and that one in which Catholics and Protestants meet in almost exactly equal numbers—have been pushing their operations almost at the college doors. Yet, in spite of these provocatives to discord, Catholics and Protestants have left those institutions, and are leaving them year by year, having there formed friendships which will last their lives.† These are

* On one occasion some students, at a visitation of Belfast College, raised "the Kentish fire." The incident has, I believe, been much exaggerated; at all events, it was unique. There was a fine illustration of the habitual spirit of the place at a recent very numerous meeting of the graduates to protest against the proposed changes in the University. Each of the speakers referred to the advantage he had derived from mixing with men of different creeds, but the tone of the remarks, and the patient attention with which the assembly listened to a solitary dissentient, were better evidence of their tolerance than any direct testimony.

† It will be instructive to contrast these results with the theory of education inculcated in the following passage from a pamphlet which has just appeared expressing the views of the clerical party:—

"You say young men of different religions mixed together, refrain,

achievements to which the academic system, as carried out in Ireland through the Queen's Colleges, may point with pride; and they are such as, it seems to me, no wise government would lightly imperil or willingly let die.*

The writer, indeed, whose scheme of university reform we have been criticising is, as one would

even from a motive of pride for their own religion, from discourses against religion or morality: that is to say, Catholic youths—for it is chiefly with regard to them that we are discussing what educational system is the best—Catholic youths find the society of Protestant, of irreligious—am I to add, of immoral?—youths, provided they are not Catholics, less likely to lead to irreligious or corrupt conversation, than the society of young men who have the happiness of professing the true faith. I suppose, you admit, that 'as there is but one God and one baptism, there is but one true faith,' and that they who profess it are, *cæteris paribus*, better Christians and better men than they who do not. Well, then, association with those who, *cæteris paribus*, are better Christians and better men, is more corrupting than association with others, who, through God's inscrutable judgment, are in the darkness of error! In other words, good companions are no longer good companions; evil company is no longer the occasion of evil, but of greater virtues. This is not the lesson which the experience of all time teaches. From it we learn that of all the agencies for the corruption of youth, evil company is perhaps the worst," &c.—*Notes on "University Education in Ireland,"* by U. R.

What hopeful promise for future peace and progress in Ireland when the principle maintained in this passage is taken as the basis of its educational system, and the youths of each religious denomination are warned to shun those of the others as they would shun "evil company"!

* One objection to the enforcement of residence in the Queen's Colleges might be, and indeed has been, urged with much apparent force —that it is unsuited to a poor population. So serious did this consideration seem to the Commissioners who reported on the state of Trinity College in 1852, that, while expressing in the strongest terms the value they attached to academic residence, they yet declined to recommend that it should be made indispensable. Fortunately, the advocates of the collegiate system are now enabled to meet this reasonable apprehension with the most satisfactory of answers—the fact of success. In spite of the rule of residence, the Queen's Colleges, as has been seen, have attracted to their halls quite as large a proportion of the several classes as the social circumstances of the country give warrant for expecting.

expect, sceptical of these advantages. He tells us: "It is held that the intimacies and associations thus formed may be, and indeed often are, as much for evil as for good, when young men or boys are sent for three years away from guardians and parents. Studious and well-disposed young men do not obtrude their advice or example on their companions; the idle and ill-disposed are always obtrusive, and their persuasions and example often exercise a most injurious influence over their companions." Now I have no hesitation in repudiating this representation, which one can scarcely believe to be the reflex of an actual experience, as a fair account of the influences evolved amid the intercourse of undergraduate life. At least, speaking from my own experience, self-distrust and morbid reserve are not the characteristics which I remember to have observed in the men who took the highest places in the honour lists and the foremost parts in the debating club. Of course, where many youths congregate, there will be "studious and well-disposed young men" whose virtue will seek the shade, and "idle and ill-disposed" who will thrust themselves into the foreground; but these, I submit, are not the prevailing types. Self-assertion, rather than morbid shyness, is the side on which I venture to think youthful merit, intellectual and moral, is apt to err; and it would speak little indeed for the administrative adroitness of those who bear rule in collegiate circles, if this natural proneness of the best minds under their authority to impress themselves on all who come within their range, were not turned to account in generating a public opinion favourable to virtue and honourable distinction. As a matter of fact, I believe that this result is generally attained. In the great academic bodies of the country, undergraduate opinion is, I make bold to say, in the main healthy and sound. If it is not invariably so, the exceptional result is, doubtless, due to an exceptional cause; to something, I should conjecture, radically wrong in the constitution of the bodies which yield the noxious fruits. The fact, if it be one, ought not to be blinked; but its proper moral is, not the abolition of the academic system in education, but the reformation of the peccant institutions.

As I have ventured to impugn the theory of university reform advanced in the proposal just considered, it may perhaps be expected that I should indicate, in lieu of the principle I have combated, what in my opinion is the sound ideal of a university system. Reverting, then, to what was said a few pages back, that the true end of universities is to provide means for the largest and freest development in all directions of the national mind, and remembering that culture implies systematic training, and that distinct forms of culture imply distinct and independent institutions, a perfect system for the higher education would, in my opinion, be one in which university degrees should represent, not a mere quantum of uniform attainment, but, along with knowledge, types of culture; and in which the number of distinct universities should correspond with the number of distinct types of culture which mental movement in a country may assume. Of course it would be necessary in practice to restrict the application of this principle to those forms of mental movement which are sufficiently characteristic, and at the same time the expression of the intellectual condition of a sufficiently large number of persons, to make the establishment of independent institutions for their promotion worth the labour. And it would also be necessary, in order to the complete freedom of education,—inasmuch as there are in all communities persons who, whether from narrowness of means, mental idiosyncrasy, or from other causes, decline to take part in the collegiate system through which alone types of culture can be generated and maintained,—that the universities, constituted on the plan indicated of representing culture, should be supplemented by a university constituted upon that of representing attainment merely; or, to state our meaning in concrete language, that, in addition to universities of the Oxford, Cambridge, and Dublin type, there should be a university also of the London type. There is no reason that persons, unable or unwilling to take part in the collegiate system, on giving proof that they have acquired a due amount of knowledge, should not be admitted to the intellectual rank of university-educated men; and the natural and obvious means of effecting this object would be through a university in which collegiate training was not imperative. Such a system, it seems to me, would realize the conditions requisite at once for the freedom and the solidity of mental progress; and, in fact, it is a system of this kind at which in the natural course of things—practice in this instance as in others preceding theory—we have arrived in this country. Under the impulse of particular motives, with slight regard to general views, the founders of our universities, whether private individuals or governments, have traced out an organization of the higher learning which, in its actual condition, does not differ materially from that which would have been realized if the principles I have indicated had been deliberately followed. We have not one, but many universities, which in the main represent specific and distinct intellectual results. The culture of Oxford is not the culture of Cambridge; and both are distinct, on the one hand, from the culture of Scotland, on the other, from that represented by Trinity College, Dublin. To these types of culture we can now add that imparted in the Queen's University and its Colleges, which I venture to assert is not less specific and distinct than any of the better-known forms. It is true it is not possible, in the case of colleges fifteen years old, to justify this language by an appeal to experience. But if the time and the object of the establishment of the Queen's Colleges be considered—the time, when the modern languages and the physical sciences had just begun to attract that attention as instruments of education which has of late been so liberally accorded them; the object, to educate the youths of different religious denominations on equal terms in common—the candid will, I think, acknowledge that a system of education conducted on a plan so different from any which has been tried elsewhere, and which draws its adherents from classes of society not hitherto reached by the higher education, is not unlikely to yield intellectual fruits equally characteristic and distinct. The system provides for wants not hitherto supplied, and provides for them in a way fitted to generate and preserve a type of culture suited to the circumstances of the country and to the character of the people; and herein consists its justification on the principles which have been set forth. But to return to our immediate point—in the main, according to my view, the several universities of Great Britain and Ireland justify their separate existence by representing distinct forms of culture; while over and above the universities representing culture, there is the University of London representing attainment merely, wherever or however acquired, adapted, therefore, to meet the wants of all who are unable to find a place in the more normal institutions. Now, if these views be sound, it follows that the principle and entire scope of the scheme of centralization now advocated for the higher education in Ireland are essentially a mistake. The scheme starts with a false ideal; it moves in a wrong direction; and, if carried into practice, it must inevitably issue in pernicious results. What is wanted in our university system is not revolution and re-organization, but remedial legislation, directed to the correction of inequalities and minor abuses which have come down to us from ages of bigotry, and embracing no doubt also the adaptation of its courses and methods to the advancing conditions of human knowledge.

And from the principles just laid down we may

deduce one or two more conclusions not irrelevant to the question in hand. We may perceive in them, for example, a new reason, in addition to that already adduced, in favour of maintaining the collegiate system in university education. The connection of universities with particular colleges, far from being the factitious and obstructive incident which it has been represented—a hindrance to be got rid of by all means—is, we may now see, in truth an essential condition to their fulfilment of the main purpose for which they exist; since it is manifestly only by maintaining this connection that degrees can be what they mainly ought to be—the representatives or emblems of culture. And again those principles furnish the reply to another question, of which, so far as I know, no intelligible solution has yet been given—the question under what circumstances and within what limits the competition between universities or other bodies granting degrees is productive of good. Everyone recognizes the fact that in some instances such competition is beneficial, in others injurious; but I am not aware that anyone has furnished an explanation of these apparently conflicting phenomena. We are now, however, in a position to do so. Competition will be useful among such bodies, so long as their number is confined within the limits indicated by the principles laid down; that is to say, so long as they represent distinct types of culture, or, as we may otherwise state it, so long as they render distinct services to the community; and it becomes mischievous the moment this line is passed. It will not be difficult to sustain this position by examples.

Thus a notable instance of the mischief caused by competition among bodies granting degrees is furnished by the medical schools of the United Kingdom. There are, we believe, altogether in the country some nineteen independent schools and colleges granting degrees in medicine and surgery. Of these the greater number perform identical functions, and as a consequence address themselves to the same classes of the population; their constituency being one and the same, their competition inevitably takes a commercial turn, and they seek to recommend themselves to their "customers" by cheapening the commodity in which they deal. The result is that which is deplored by every eminent member of the profession[*] —a general deterioration of the standard of medical knowledge. And such inevitably would be the tendency of the proposal which has been advanced of establishing in Dublin a second university on the London University plan. Such a university could only render services already adequately rendered by the University of London. The two bodies would stand to each other in precisely the same relation as the competing medical schools, and, we cannot doubt, with the same result. Now take an example of competition of another kind amongst degree-granting bodies—the competition of Oxford with Cambridge, and of both with the University of London, and an instance more pertinent to our purpose still—the competition between Trinity College, Dublin, and the

[*] Amongst others I may cite the author of the scheme just considered. In reference to the evils in question, he observes: "They have arisen from the competition among the nineteen licensing Universities and Colleges for the profits arising from candidates and pupils."—P. 21.

Queen's University and its Colleges. With regard to the former, it will not, I imagine, be denied that the effects of the competition, so far as it is felt, are altogether salutary; and as regards the Irish universities, I can from personal knowledge affirm that this has been eminently the case. Not only has their mutual rivalry heightened the *esprit de corps* of each, and stimulated the ardour of scientific and literary pursuit, but it has also borne fruit in substantial measures of great practical utility. And why is this? Manifestly because in all these cases the degrees of the universities represent something specific and distinct, and because in virtue of this fact they address themselves in the main to distinct classes in the community. The competition under these circumstances has no tendency to degenerate into a process of underbidding, but rather becomes a race for distinction. The graduates of the several universities meet in the lists of life—in the professions, in politics, in literature, in society: they are known as Oxford, as Cambridge, as Dublin, and as Queen's University men: the world takes note of the connection between the achievement and the preparation; and the university from which each has issued gains or loses *prestige*. Such has been the working of competition in this country under legitimate conditions. We borrow the following account of the operation of the same principle in Germany from Major O'Reilly's able and instructive, though one-sided and prejudiced, essay:—

"The existing government of Prussia retains the entire direction of education—of the village school, the college, and the university. . . . But with regard to their internal organization and the regulation of their studies, the Prussian Universities differ wholly from the French: instead of one University organized by fixed and uniform rules, there exist six, subject indeed to the Minister of Public Instruction, but having each their own independence, their own organization and administration, and, so to speak, their separate life. Each is a corporation; has jurisdiction over its own students; has its own senate, and its own faculties; determines its own courses of study, its own examinations, and grants its own degrees. . . . Such is the Prussian system; of which the chief characteristics are the great freedom left to the Universities under the nominal control of the Government, and the freedom of emulation in teaching.* . . . . As Mr. Loomans says, 'The foundation of the Prussian organization is the *esprit de corps* which keeps up the emulation between the different Universities; and the competition which keeps up the standard in each. To form an idea of the emulation, we should rather call it the rivalry, which exists between the German Universities, one must be in the midst of that German society so occupied with the interests of science. The Universities have acquired a consideration and an

* I may point out in passing the essential similarity in several fundamental points between the Prussian University system, highly applauded by Major O'Reilly, and that of the Queen's Colleges, for which he has only terms of reprobation. A more apt characterization could not be given of the organization of the latter institutions than in the words quoted above—"Great freedom, under the nominal control of the Government." Thus the governing bodies in the Colleges are Councils consisting of the Presidents and Professors representing the several Faculties; and these are vested with very considerable powers, having full authority to prescribe the courses, arrange the lectures of the Professors, settle all questions connected with the internal management of the Colleges, and in general, in the words of the Charter, "not being in any way under the jurisdiction or control of the University Senate further than as regards the regulations for qualification for the several degrees." I desire especially to call attention to the following point. "The Professors" [in the Prussian Universities], says Major O'Reilly, "are named by the King on the proposition by the Faculties of a list of three." The plan adopted in the Queen's Colleges does not in effect differ from this. The President reports to the Government—it is presumed after consultation with those most qualified to judge—upon the merits of the candidates.

influence which are surprising. Not only are they at the head of education, but they rule all scientific and literary movement. This situation is the principal cause of their prosperity; placed, as it were, under the eyes of the entire nation, they naturally seek to conciliate the sympathies of all.'"

This is healthy, invigorating, elevating rivalry, rivalry, too, identical in principle with that which is now in this country actually yielding similar fruits, similar in kind if still inferior in amount and quality; and it is rivalry of this kind which it is now proposed to abolish in Ireland in favour of a rivalry between two central institutions "open to all comers," performing precisely the same functions, and addressing themselves necessarily to precisely the same classes of the population; in favour of a rivalry which, judging from experience, could only issue in the double evil of encouraging "cram" and degrading the standard of knowledge.

So far as to the lay scheme of Irish university reform. Turning now to the demand of the clerical party, it will be remembered that originally this was for a charter for "The Catholic University." Let me here frankly express my opinion that I see nothing in such a demand on the face of it inadmissible. On the contrary I freely concede that it is for those who resist such a claim to make out grounds for their resistance. It signifies in my view nothing that the ideas of those who founded "The Catholic University" on "the eternal principles" first evolved in the dark ages may have little in common with prevailing modes of thought in this country; if those ideas are in fact the ideas of a section of the Irish people, there seems no reason that every facility should not be afforded—a charter of incorporation if that be desired—in order that such separatists from the thought and feeling of the age should, *so far as they are themselves concerned*, carry into effect their educational designs. On the assumption, therefore, that the demand for a charter for " The Catholic University" means simply a demand, on the part of persons holding certain peculiar views, to be placed on an equality, as regards State recognition, with the rest of the community, my principles would certainly lead me to the conclusion, that such a claim ought to be conceded.

But, in truth, to discuss the question now before the public as if it were confined within such dimensions as these, would be to ignore all the most important elements of the case, and in fact to beat the air. The leaders of the ultramontane party have never disguised the fact that their object in this movement has been to supplant, not to supplement—to carry over the Roman Catholic population as a whole from the institutions which they now frequent to others which it is their purpose to establish, not merely to provide an exceptional institution for some exceptionally constituted persons. That this is their aim is implied in the whole course of their procedure, from the sitting of the Synod of Thurles down to the publication of Dr. Cullen's latest pastoral; in the name and pretensions of their university, and in all the circumstances of its origin; above all, in the system of spiritual terrorism put in force against those who have dared to avail themselves of the mixed schools and colleges of the country. The necessity of resorting to such courses—of resorting to them, not occasionally, but incessantly and on system, of year after year raising the pitch of denunciation, till it has culminated in threats of exclusion from the sacraments and other ordinances of the Church—a measure, be it remembered, equivalent in Roman Catholic estimation to exclusion from salvation—shows more conclusively even than the statistics which in a former part of this article were adduced, that the system of education against which such expedients are employed is as agreeable to the people of the country as it is obnoxious to those who have recourse to such measures of attack. No doubt those who have brought forward this cause in Parliament have taken care not to present it in this form. Parliament hears only of "the Irish people" as chafing against the grievance of liberal institutions and hungering for a mediæval university; the bishops, if they are brought upon the scene, only appearing as intercessors in behalf of their much-enduring flocks. But, even as thus stated, the argument at least implies that those who urge this demand contemplate nothing less than the overthrow of the institutions to which the "Irish people" now resort. To be sure, it is denied by these advocates that the Irish people *do* resort to them, but I have already furnished the reader with the means of judging of the value of such denials.

Such, then, and not a mere demand for freedom of educational development for a dissentient section, is the real scope and aim of the question now before the public. Started, indeed, and still upheld by a mere section, its purpose is to deal with the intellectual interests of the whole Irish people. A fraction of the community—the ultramontane bishops of Ireland—seek a place for their exotic institution in the national system of the country, not for the legitimate purpose of offering its services to those who have need of and desire them, but, if not avowedly, at all events by necessary implication from their acts, in order that they may thus obtain a vantage-ground from which with more effect to coerce* into the adoption of their scheme the entire Roman Catholic

---

* I use the term "coerce" advisedly. The following specimen—it occurred quite recently, and has been pretty generally commented on by the press—of the mode of conduct pursued will enable the reader to say whether I do so justifiably. The transaction in question was not connected with the particular subject of this essay; but the principles of conduct laid down and acted on are obviously applicable to that and all like cases.

Some time ago some Roman Catholic gentlemen in Belfast formed themselves into a Society for the cultivation of science and literature, under the title of "The Belfast Catholic Institute." From causes which I need not enter into here, the Society flourished financially, and in course of time a question arose as to the disposition of some surplus funds. The majority of the directory had certain views upon this subject; Doctor Dorrian, the Coadjutor Bishop of the diocese, had others. The Bishop, in fact, desired to apply the disposable funds to ecclesiastical purposes, and moved a resolution to this effect, which the majority of the directory negatived. The Bishop remonstrated, at first with the directory, afterwards with the shareholders individually; but the Society stood firm. Whereupon the Bishop addressed to each member of the Society a circular letter, in which he made the following announcement :—

"The following, as conditions of recommendation and approval, I cannot forego. They are essential to my sanction being given to this or any new company into which the Institute may be transformed, as the above condemned propositions prove :—

"1—*The approval by the Bishop of such articles of association as he shall judge satisfactory, and their adoption as the basis of any new company to be formed.*

"2—*The same right on the part of the Bishop, of approving the rules of management of Lecture-hall, Library, and News-room.*

"3—*A veto by the Bishop on any member acting on the Directory, whose morals, religious principles, and habits of life the Bishop may object to.*

community; in order that their fulminations and threats having fallen short of their object—they may reinforce terror by attraction, and bring such honour and emolument as the State can confer to second their ineffectual anathemas.

I confess I am wholly unable to see that this country is called upon by any principle of freedom to yield to a demand of this sort. Tyranny is not the less tyranny when its seat is in the human soul, and when it seeks its ends by threats of torture to be inflicted hereafter instead of now; and though it may be true that in this form it eludes the grasp of human legislation, though it may not be possible to bind the subtle essence of spiritual terrorism without at the same time endangering the play of legitimate moral influence—though, therefore, intolerance itself when it assumes this garb must needs be tolerated—at least there seems no reason that a liberal State should play into its hands, and make itself

"4—*The approval by the Bishop, or one appointed by him, of all books and newspapers to be admitted for reading into News-room or Library; and the like approval of any lecturer to be invited to lecture for the members.*

"If these conditions be not made the basis of the Institute, I wish to give fair notice that, by whatsoever name the new association be called —and to change the name, if such be in contemplation, is not a very hopeful sign—I SHALL CONSIDER IT MY DUTY, FOR THE PROTECTION OF MY PEOPLE, TO DEBAR FROM SACRAMENTS ALL AND EVERY ONE WHO MAY BECOME A MEMBER, OR AID IN ITS CONSTRUCTION—these securities for its proper management not being first provided."

It seems to me that this is "coercion" as truly as if the menace had been of direct physical chastisement; and this, it will be observed, is not an isolated instance, but a specimen of a system of conduct. Another example, to which I have already referred, occurred within the present year in the Bishop of Clonfert's pastoral denouncing the Queen's Colleges, and, were there any need, it would be easy to fill these pages with similar brutal episodes.

by deliberate action the accomplice of its designs. Many unworthy acts have been committed in the name of Liberty; but we question if the sacred word was ever more audaciously prostituted than when invoked by ultramontane bishops against the system of education established by Sir Robert Peel.

The question, however, is no longer respecting a distinct charter, but of affiliation to the Queen's University: it remains to consider how this modification affects the considerations just urged. Affiliation may, of course, mean very little or a great deal, according to the terms by which the relation is determined. As has been already said, the Government has not yet made public its plan; but the *parti prêtre*, though they have on the whole kept their counsel well, have not been altogether silent. I have just had the advantage of reading a pamphlet which, though appearing anonymously, I have reason to believe, proceeds from a source than which none is more likely to be well informed on the subject in hand.* It is in the form of a reply to the lay proposal to which I have devoted so large a portion of this paper. That proposal the writer of the pamphlet repudiates with unmeasured scorn, and, in doing so, takes occasion to lay down certain negative conditions as well as certain prin-

* This production, entitled "Notes on 'University Education in Ireland,'" is announced as "printed for *private* circulation *only*;" but as it is unquestionably intended to influence *public* opinion on a matter of the gravest *public* importance, I do not feel myself bound to acquiesce in what I must regard as an unfair artifice for evading the ordinary liability to legitimate criticism, which is the proper condition attaching to such attempts in a free country.

ciples of a positive kind, which, in his view, must govern the arrangement. Amongst other significant passages, I find the following :—

"Permit me to say" (the writer is addressing himself to the author of the lay scheme) "that I think you have fallen into two or three mistakes: first, in supposing that the bishops would for an instant entertain the thought of affiliating their University to the Queen's University as at present constituted; secondly, in thinking that the Catholic University would ever be changed by them into a 'Queen's College,' or into an institution at all like a Queen's College; thirdly, in taking for granted that the Catholic University and its founders and guardians, the bishops, would surrender all 'pretensions' to its present title and to its University privileges derived from the Pope and admitted by all Catholics, although not recognized by the State. Nay, more, I believe you are wrong in thinking that any Government which deserves the name of 'Liberal,' would offer the Catholic Bishops of Ireland the insult of asking them to do any one of the three things I have mentioned. Solely with respect to the third, the bishops might waive the question of the recognition by the State of the style, title, and University privileges of the Catholic University.... But now to answer your question: Where is the line to be drawn in a system of affiliation?—I answer: *It is to be drawn so as to secure for the Catholic University the position she is entitled to, at the head of Catholic Education in Ireland.* (The italics are the author's.) Less than this the Sovereign Pontiff will not sanction; and it was at his suggestion the University was first established. With less than this the bishops of Ireland will not be satisfied, and it was they who founded the University, and who by their continued and determined opposition to dangerous systems of education have brought this question to its present stage; less than this our Catholic people will not accept, and they have shown themselves able and determined to discriminate between godless and Catholic education."

The writer does not state what constitution of the Queen's University would lead the bishops to "entertain the thought" of affiliation; but I infer from the whole passage that they would not accept the modification suggested by the lay reformer. That suggestion, it will be remembered, is that the Senate should consist of thirty members, of which twenty (equally divided between Protestants and Catholics) should be nominated by the Crown, and the remaining ten elected by Convocation; and this suggestion, it seems, is inadmissible. Here then, at least, we have a negative *datum*. A further clue to their requirements on this point may be found in the composition of another body in which the bishops *do* place confidence. The governing committee of "The Catholic University"—I mean the present body—is composed, as has been already stated, of twenty-four members, of which eight are bishops, eight priests, and eight laymen, the last, I believe, the nominees of the Episcopate. Keeping this in view, and remembering that this institution has been put forward as in all things a model, it will argue singular moderation if, in the constitution of the Senate of the new University, the same party is satisfied with simple preponderance, symbolized, say, by the presence on the Board of some leading members of the Episcopate. And this is the body that is to preside over and regulate the only university education to be permitted to Catholics in Ireland.

Then "The Catholic University" College is to be "at the head of Catholic education in Ireland," or, as the condition is more clearly expounded in another passage, "although there may be many halls, that is to say, colleges or schools, where Catholic youth can study, still there should be but one University College, and it should have the right to mould all according to its own idea." On this principle, it seems, "the line is to be drawn" in the system of affiliation, and such is to be the first practical exemplification of "freedom of university education" for Catholics.

I must call attention to one passage more:—

"Again, in the system you [the lay reformer] propose, why, I ask, are the colleges to be still maintained? If the University does not need its special colleges, why is this great expense to be annually incurred? The answer is obvious. Some endowed colleges would be an anomaly, unless our rulers wish to maintain the system of State education apart from religion, on whose principle these colleges were founded, and to give no countenance to the Catholic University, which was established for the maintenance of the contrary principle. But I would beg you to remember, that such an arrangement will not meet the views of the bishops, priests, and Catholic people of Ireland; and it was precisely in order to meet their views, that the present educational movement was set on foot."

I cannot say what reply the lay reformer would give to these questions; but my answer would be, that the Queen's Colleges are to be maintained because they are based on equality and justice; because they represent the ideas of the nineteenth century, not those of the thirteenth; because they have proved themselves by success suited to the requirements and tastes of the people for whom they were designed—in a word, because they are *national* colleges ; and, on the other hand, that " The Catholic University" is undeserving of support, because, in spite of its pretensions, it is sectarian and not "Catholic;" because it is out of relation with the ideas and wants of the time, and has given no evidence of being acceptable to any considerable section of Roman Catholics outside the episcopal order ; because, in short, such a step would be retrograde and fatal to the best interests of Ireland ; and for the rest, I would remind the writer of what he and others who advance claims of this kind seem to have become wholly oblivious, that there is now a College at Maynooth in possession of the handsome endowment of £26,000 annually, established for the special and exclusive benefit of the Roman Catholic priesthood; this sum, I may observe in passing, being larger than that assigned to the Queen's University and its Colleges — institutions performing, to borrow the language of the *Times*, " truly national service."

But it is idle to criticise further. If there be any value in the foregoing remarks on the proposition for a distinct charter, they are obviously applicable with augmented force to this scheme. This is not a plan for affiliating the " Catholic University " College to the Queen's University : rather it is a plan for reconstructing the system of the Queen's University on the pattern of the " Catholic University " College. The " compromise " when examined turns out to be *the* original demand so shaped as to comprise an ulterior, over and above the original, object. *This* contemplated the establishment of a " Catholic University," but left the Queen's University in its present position. *That* would equally establish a "Catholic University;" but would do so on the ruins of its rival.

To conclude. I know not how far the Government may have committed itself in concession to this party; but it seems unquestionable that to some extent it has done so. A pledge given on the eve of a general election can scarcely, after the price has been paid, be recalled with honour. But the pledge was given by the Government, not by the Liberal party or the English people; and we have yet to see how far the country is prepared to sacrifice a great and successful policy to the exigencies of a party struggle. But should it prove that the intellectual interests of the Irish people are only thought deserving of regard as they may be turned to account in weighting the scales of an English party, at least let us hope that a greater sacrifice will not be made than the due adjustment of the political balance imperatively requires. If "something must be done," let us hope that it will be done in a manner as little mischievous as possible. If "mixed education" as a principle must be given up, let us at least save the collegiate system, and with it, as far as possible, accomplished results. If a mediæval university must be recognized, let us at least maintain in its integrity the single university in Ireland which represents the ideas of the nineteenth century. The concession of the original demand of the Episcopate would at least leave a rival in the field; and it is not absolutely certain, in spite of the thunders of the Vatican, and the more incessant and more telling cannonade maintained from Irish altars, that this rival might not yet hold its own.

NOTE TO p. 265.

[The statements in the paragraph to which this note is appended and the preceding one were challenged by Professor Sullivan of the Catholic University, in a pamphlet which appeared shortly after the publication of my essay. The following, which I have extracted from a pamphlet published the same year in the form of a letter to Mr. Mill, was my reply to Professor Sullivan's strictures. The issues raised have in truth but slight bearing on the general argument; but I have thought the transactions connected with the condemnation of the Queen's Colleges by the Synod of Thurles of sufficient general interest to warrant me in preserving a record of the facts brought out in the discussion.]

The drift of the passage, it will be seen, was to establish the origin and character of the opposition to the Queen's Colleges, and more particularly to show that not even amongst the clergy was the movement a national one, being distinctly traceable to that section of the body, formerly of small weight, but since the elevation of Dr. Cullen rapidly increasing in numbers and power, which represents the extremest pretensions of the Holy See, and is commonly designated by the term "Ultramontane." Well, how does Professor Sullivan meet this argument? In the first place, by suggesting doubts as to the existence of Ultramontanism as anything more than a maggot in the brain of certain weak and credulous enthusiasts, or a convenient bugbear for others who seek to practise on the ignorance and prejudices of the English public. He admits, indeed, that the word has a certain historical import as the antithesis of Gallicanism in the Church; but, as bearing upon modern controversies, and more particularly with regard to such questions as have been raised by the new educational policy of the Government—the pretensions of the clergy in reference to human knowledge and the modes of cultivating and imparting it,—" Ultramontanism," Professor Sullivan tells his readers, is a "phantom,"—"one of those handy words which float about in society in search of an idea to which to attach itself;" so much so, that in using the word, lest he should be thought to acknowledge any fact corresponding to it, he is careful invariably to insert it in quotation marks. I do not think that I need spend words in dealing with this suggestion, more especially while Mr. Whittle's able sketch of the modern developments of Ultramontanism is in everybody's hands. I beg, therefore, to refer such of my readers as may desire information on this point to Mr. Whittle's pamphlet, though I should imagine there are few persons who take an interest in controversy, whose acquaintance with modern history will not enable them, even without Mr. Whittle's assistance, to appreciate the candour and ingenuousness of this portion of Professor Sullivan's reply. That a *collaborateur* of the *Home and Foreign Review*, addressing Sir John Acton, should pronounce Ultramontanism visionary, may perhaps be thought just a little audacious.

Passing from this, Professor Sullivan takes exception to my account of Dr. Cullen's appointment, contending through three pages of letter-press, that the disregard by the Pope on that occasion of the recommendation of the diocesan clergy was not in defiance of "immemorial usage." Now, on this I may observe that the establishment of the literal accuracy of the words placed in inverted commas is by no means necessary, I will not say to the general scope of my argument—for it does not even touch that—but to the special and subordinate point in support of which Dr. Cullen's appointment is referred to. Suppose, for example, the fact were that the proceedings of the Papal Court on the occasion in question were at variance, not with "immemorial usage," but with the ordinary routine observed in the appointment of Irish Roman Catholic bishops, would my statement, on being modified in conformity with this state of things, lose appreciably in force? Now I think Professor Sullivan will not deny that the facts are in accordance with this supposition. He tells us, indeed, that the power exercised by the Pope in setting aside the recommendation of the diocesan clergy was in conformity with a decree of the Propaganda issued in 1829. That may be so, and yet the exercise of the power may have been a very rare one, so rare as to be not unfairly characterized as "a stretch of papal authority." Will Professor Sullivan deny this? Will he mention a single instance from the time the voting system came into use down to the appointment of Dr. Cullen in which *the three names returned by the clergy were all passed over?* I venture to say that he cannot do so, though doubtless some instances might be given of this having occurred *since* Dr. Cullen's appointment, in pursuance, too, of the same Ultramontane policy.* Yet, while the fact stands thus, it is surely rather idle to enter into a lengthy discussion respecting the mode of appointing Catholic bishops in Ireland in the middle of the eighteenth century, when, owing to the penal laws, the entire economy of the Roman Catholic Church was in a state of disorganization. Professor Sullivan may thus, indeed, succeed in convicting me of using an inaccurate expression; and if he thinks the game worth the candle, I cannot grudge him the fruits of his diligence. But does he thereby deprive Dr. Cullen's appointment of the significance which I attached to it, as indicating the anxiety of the Ultramontane party at that juncture to place a man of Dr. Cullen's known character and views at the head of the Roman Catholic Church in Ireland?

* In one instance even the form of taking votes was dispensed with. The person named on this occasion—when it was thought desirable *not* to consult the clergy of the diocese—was the Dean of the Catholic University.

But, secondly, I am "equally incorrect" in what I have said about Dr. Cullen's office of "apostolic delegate." Indeed, I could hardly have been otherwise, seeing that, as Professor Sullivan informs me, I do not even know what the term "delegate" means. On this point, however, he is good enough to enlighten me, as well as, with much condescension, to explain how, in a certain sense, every bishop in Ireland is an "apostolic delegate," and to set forth, besides, other subtle and abstruse distinctions in ecclesiastical technology, which, lest I should again betray my ignorance, I shall not venture further to describe. But, while thanking him for his recondite information, I must honestly confess that, after much and painful pondering of what he has said, I am quite unable to discover wherein my error consists. What I said was that "it was avowedly to advance the aims of the Ultramontane policy that he (Dr. Cullen) was sent to Ireland, the better to equip him for which service he was furnished with the further authority and distinction of apostolic delegate." This was my version, and the orthodox version as rendered by Professor Sullivan is as follows :—"Nor has he ever been appointed apostolic delegate simply. He was appointed on the 6th of April, 1850, in order that he might canonically convoke the Synod of Thurles, and for the causes which might arise out of the special legislation of that Synod ; and he was so appointed because he was Archbishop of Armagh and Primate of all Ireland." It seems to me that this is only saying somewhat more circumstantially than I did that he was appointed apostolic delegate, "the better to equip him for advancing the aims of Ultramontane policy."

So much for Dr. Cullen's appointment. Coming next to what I have said respecting the occurrences at the Synod of Thurles, I am told that on this subject I have displayed, "if possible, still greater ignorance." Professor Sullivan, in the first place, controverts my statement as to the source from which the original suggestion of a National Synod to pronounce upon the Queen's Colleges came. My statement implied that it came from the Roman Court. Professor Sullivan asserts that it proceeded from a meeting of Roman Catholic bishops, held in Dublin in 1849, and presided over by Archbishop Murray. But on this point his informants have misled him. No doubt the resolution which he quotes was passed at the meeting of 1849, but this resolution was taken in conformity with a suggestion contained in a papal rescript of the previous year—that dated 11th October, 1848, and addressed by Cardinal Fransoni to Dr. Slattery, then Archbishop of Cashel, as will be seen by the extract I subjoin in a note.* As regards this point, then, it would seem that my ignorance was

---

* "Inter cætera, SSmo. Domno. nostro probante, illud commemorandum vobis censuit Sacra Congregatio, *ut Sacerdotales conventus ex ordine, et ad SS. Canonum et librorum liturgicorum tramitem in posterum fiant ;* alioquin sententiarum varietas indies augebitur, nihilque boni ex hujusmodi conventibus, qui potius sæcularem quam religiosam speciem præ se ferant, exurget ad Ecclesiasticam disciplinam, cui solummodo inservire debent, rite dirigendam : proindeque utillimum [sic] erit acta conventuum ad Apostolicam Sedem transmittere, sicuti etiam statis temporibus litteras dare de statu vestrarum Ecclesiarum prout sancitum est, ut opportuna hinc responsa excipiatis."

It was in obedience to the words I have italicised that the determination was taken to transfer

nearer the mark than Professor Sullivan's knowledge. The Holy See *did* " originate the idea of the Synod," and " Ultramontanism had [something] to do with the matter."

Nevertheless, I think it is extremely probable that Professor Sullivan may be correct in what he says of the " alarm " created at Rome, on the news arriving there of what had taken place at the meeting in Dublin. That meeting was presided over by Dr. Murray, and Dr. Murray was then the strenuous advocate of the cause of the Queen's Colleges. Considering the position which Murray then occupied in the Irish Church, it would have been only natural that he should have been selected for the dignity of presiding at the forthcoming Synod, and, had this happened, we now know, beyond controversy, what would have been the result. In short, it is plain that Dr. Murray, while accepting the suggestion of the Sacred College, that " meetings of the clergy should in future be held in due order, and agreeably to the course of the sacred canons and rituals," was by his prompt action—availing himself of his great and deserved influence in the Irish Church—on the point of taking the game out of the hands of the Roman Court. We can, therefore, have no difficulty in understanding the " alarm " with which the intelligence of the proceedings at the meeting of 1849 was received in that quarter. The moment was evidently critical, and the Roman authorities met the danger with their accustomed address. The death of Dr. Croly occurring just at the time, Dr. Cullen was appointed to succeed him, and was at once invested with the authority of " apostolic delegate," " in order," says Professor Sullivan, " that he might canonically convoke the Synod of Thurles, and for the

the consideration of the question of the Colleges from the informal Dublin meeting of 1849 to a regularly constituted Synod, as expressed in the resolution quoted by Professor Sullivan. That this was the relation in which the two incidents stood to each other, is placed beyond doubt by the following passage from a letter, addressed by Dr. Murray a few months subsequent to the Dublin meeting (22d Dec. 1849), to the Cardinal Prefect of the Sacred Congregation. Having referred to the Dublin meeting, he continues :—" His peractis, decretum est, ut quæ in hujusmodi conventibus agi solebant, ad aliud tempus opportunum rejicerentur, cum nempe, *ut sanctissimus Pater Noster monere dignatus est, synodice conveniremus.*" And in the letter of instructions to Dr. Cullen from the Sacred Congregation (18th April, 1850), the same words are thus referred to :—" Eoque præsertim hortationes in Apostolicis Litteris contentas dirigi significes oportet." As I am referring to this letter, I may take the opportunity of reciprocating Professor Sullivan's good offices by a word or two of "useful" information. In more than one passage, he scoffs at my statement that the main reason for summoning the Synod was to obtain a decision on the Colleges, adding—" Of the sixty-nine pages containing the printed decrees of the Synod, two only are occupied with the Queen's Colleges," which proportion he would apparently have his readers believe represented their proportional importance amongst the subjects discussed. But what says Cardinal Fransoni? " Licet Hiberniæ Episcopi *ea potissimum de causa* plenariam Synodum celebraturi videantur *ut quoad Collegia uniformis disciplina per Hiberniam retinenda communi deliberatione statuatur,*" &c.

In another place, for having said that the Synod was summoned for the purpose of condemning the Colleges, I am lectured in the following fashion :—"A Synod is a deliberative body, and its acts, like those of Parliament, are passed by the votes of the majority. .... How then could the Synod have been summoned for the purpose of doing an act the nature of which could not have been predicted when the Synod was summoned?" How indeed? But illogical as the idea is, the Sacred Congregation, I am afraid, entertained it. Cardinal Fransoni, in his letter of instruction, writes as follows :—" Quod vero alias controversias spectat eorumdem Collegiorum causa excitatas, *Episcoporum erit, præfatis Rescriptis sedulo perpensis, ut fideles ab iis Collegiis frequentandis retrahantur,*" &c.

causes which might arise out of the special legislation of that Synod." Just so; and by this means the policy of the national party in the Irish Church, and with it the hope of gaining the priesthood to the support of the Colleges, was effectually frustrated. I do not know whether Professor Sullivan will think that the case as thus presented loses in force with a view to the purpose of my argument; but, if he does, he is welcome to the benefit of the fuller statement. To me it seems that the more we go into details, the more conspicuous the essentially foreign character of the ecclesiastical opposition to the Queen's Colleges becomes.

The next point on which, according to Professor Sullivan, I have misrepresented the proceedings at Thurles, is in my statement as to the number of votes by which the condemnation of the Queen's Colleges was carried. I said that they were condemned by a majority of one; whereas, says Professor Sullivan, "the simple condemnation of the principles on which the Colleges were established was carried unanimously." No doubt Professor Sullivan has certain technical grounds for this statement; but I beg you to observe the value of his contradiction as regards the question in dispute between him and me. The proposition which was carried unanimously was that contained in the first of the nine decrees passed respecting the Colleges. As will be seen, by reference to the words which I give below,* it contained merely a formal recognition of the authority of the Pope, coupled with an acceptance of what had been said respecting the Queen's Colleges in the rescripts of the two previous years. These rescripts, it is true, condemned what they described as the principle of the Colleges; but it is well known that Archbishop Murray and the bishops who agreed with him held that the condemnation did not apply to the facts of the case,—that, in fact, it was founded on a misunderstanding:† consequently, the acceptance of the rescripts implied nothing as to the practical issues in debate. The passing of the first decree was thus a purely formal proceeding; and it was this which was carried unanimously. On the other hand, the practical issues were contained in the resolutions which followed,—those, namely, which prohibit ecclesiastics from "taking or retaining" any office in the Colleges under pain of suspension *ipso facto*, and which declare the Colleges to be "*talia quæ omni ratione . . . . rejicienda et evitanda.*" These, I say, were the decrees on which the practical question as to the attitude which the Roman Catholic clergy were to assume towards the Queen's Colleges depended; and *these were carried by a majority of one.* Such is the

* "Cum in Romano Pontifice, Christi in terris vicarium, et Sancti Petri successorem agnoscamus et veneremur, cui divinitus munus optimis doctrinis fideles instituendi, et a pestiferis et veneno infectis pascuis arcendi, commissum; libenti animo, et eo quo par est obsequio monitis et rescriptis assentimur, quæ respiciunt quæstionem de Collegiis Reginæ apud nos nuper erectis, quæque, ipsius Christi vicarii auctoritate munita, a S. Congregatione de Prop. Fide nobis sunt communicata."

† Accordingly Dr. Ennis (Dr. Murray's envoy at Rome), in urging the petition in favour of the Queen's Colleges, pleads:—"The consenting to such a demand cannot offend any party; *it will not contradict or revoke the letter which has been transmitted.*"

state of facts in view of which Professor Sullivan thinks himself justified in charging me with a grave misrepresentation of the proceedings of the Synod. When a writer aims at giving in a few words the gist of a complicated transaction, he is fortunate if, in doing so, he does not leave himself open to contradiction on incidental and irrelevant points. My statement, I acknowledge, is not free from vulnerability of this sort; and Professor Sullivan is entitled to whatever credit belongs to a victory achieved by taking advantage of such flaws.

But his greatest triumph in this line has yet to be recorded. On my story of the sick bishop and the *rôle* taken by his representative in the proceedings of the Synod he is particularly severe. He finds it "difficult to conceive" how "any man of intelligence, however ill-informed, could have penned this passage." "Dr. Cullen," he asserts, "did not secure the 'majority of one' 'through an accident improved by an artifice.' Dr. Cullen did not appoint a delegate of opposite views to 'fill the place' of a 'sick bishop.' No 'sick bishop' was 'upon recovery not restored to his place till the vote upon the Colleges had been taken.' No bishop 'fell sick,' and 'recovered;'" and so the volley of contradictions is prolonged through all the modes of negation. Having, however, ascertained the facts to the best of my means of information, I make bold to affirm that my statement as to the "sick bishop," and the effect of the occurrence on the decision of the Synod, was, for all the intents and purposes of the discussion, substantially correct.

The facts of the transaction, as nearly as I have been able to ascertain them, were as follows:—Dr. French, Roman Catholic Bishop of Kilmacduagh and Kilfenora, was, at the time of the meeting of the Synod of Thurles, in a delicate state of health. The business of his diocese was administered by his Vicar-General, the Rev. Michael Nagle, and the views both of Dr. French and of Mr. Nagle were known to be favourable to the Queen's Colleges. It was generally expected that the Vicar-General would have represented his Bishop in the Synod, in which case the vote of the diocese of Kilmacduagh and Kilfenora would have been given in favour of the Colleges. What happened, however, was this:—Dr. McHale, Archbishop of Tuam, from the first amongst the most violent of the opponents of united education in every form, was Metropolitan of Dr. French, and, I suppose, in virtue of this character, claimed the right of nominating his proxy in the Synod. He accordingly named Dr. McEvilly, then principal of his college at Tuam, now Bishop of Galway. Dr. McEvilly's views on the question of the Colleges are pretty well known. It is he who has commenced in Galway the practice of refusing the sacraments of the Church to the poor people who send their children to the Galway Model school, and his position during the period in question, at the head of Dr. McHale's college, leaves no room for doubt that his views on the subject of education then were not different from what we now know them to be. Amongst the names appended to the decrees of Thurles, Dr. McEvilly's appears as procurator for Dr. French—*Procurator* Rev^{mi.} Ep^{i.} *Duacensis et Fenaborensis* [Kilmacduagh and Kilfenora].* Such, I believe, are the facts of the transaction,—if I have misstated them, I shall be glad to be corrected by Professor Sullivan from his better sources of information,—and I think they justify me in making the following assertions :—That during the sitting of the Synod, a bishop known to be favourable to the Colleges was sick [in my former statement I said, " fell sick"]; that his place was filled with a procurator [in my former statement I said, "delegate"] of opposite views ; † and that this procurator actually voted on the decrees involving the essential issues in a sense adverse to the Queen's Colleges, adverse, also, to the opinions known to be entertained on the subject by the bishop he was supposed to represent : in a word, I think the facts I have stated justify me in adopting my former language, and asserting that " the condemnation of the Colleges (in the only sense in which the public are concerned with the act) was carried by a majority of one," and that "this slender triumph was obtained by questionable means —through an accident improved by an artifice." In truth, had I, when writing my former paper, informed myself as fully respecting the details of these transactions as I have since done—had I known then as much about them as I have no doubt Professor Sullivan knew when he undertook to refute me—I might have very materially strengthened the ground of the charge ; for I might have stated, that, of *three* bishops who were absent from the Synod through illness, *two* were represented by procurators, who voted on the question of the Colleges in opposition to the views which the bishops they were supposed to represent were known to entertain. One of the bishops thus " represented " was Dr. French, whose case we have just examined. The other was Dr. Egan, of Kerry, who was also favourable to the Colleges,‡ but whose procurator, Mr. O'Sullivan, P.P. of Kenmare, following the example of Dr. McEvilly,

---

* " There is something painfully grotesque," says Professor Sullivan, p. 53, "in the ignorance which could imagine it possible that Dr. Cullen would dare to exclude from the Synod one of the bishops summoned to attend it, or that he would venture to appoint a ' *delegate*' of another bishop ;" and he asks triumphantly, "Of whom would the person so appointed be the *delegate*? Certainly not of the bishop who did *not* delegate him as *his* representative." Will Professor Sullivan kindly inform us of whom Dr. McEvilly was the delegate?

† It is true he was appointed by Dr. McHale, not by Dr. Cullen ; but Dr. Cullen presided at the Synod of Thurles, and no opposition was offered to the appointment, which was entirely favourable to the objects Dr. Cullen had in view. Is it uncharitable to assume that the occurrence took place with Dr. Cullen's cordial sanction and approval ?

‡ Dr. Egan's name stands second in a list of seven Irish bishops, appended to a document published in 1850, entitled " Breves Vindiciæ contra calumnias in Duobus Libellis, anno 1848 Romæ typis excusis, contentas," and addressed to the Cardinal Prefect of the Sacred Congregation. The "calumniators" were Archbishop McHale and Bishop O'Higgins. That the bishops who signed the " vindication" were favourable to the Colleges appears from the whole document—it was indeed their course upon this question which had been the ground of the attack. If there be any doubt upon this point, it will be removed by the following extract appended to the "vindication":—" Quamvis ab initio, novis instituendis Collegiis nullum præstiteram favorem, attamen, quia firmiter mihi persuasum est, Episcopos, qui eorum institutioni non resistebant, solâ conscientiâ fuisse actos, nomen etiam meum huic eorum defensioni subscribere decrevi.—EDVARDUS WALSH, Ossoriensis." The date of the document is 8 Jan., 1850, six months before the Synod was held.

voted against them. By what "artifice" the "accident" in Dr. Egan's case was "improved" for the benefit of Ultramontanism and the edification of the faithful, Professor Sullivan will perhaps, out of the fulness of his knowledge, inform the public. These things I might have stated; and I might also have referred to the introduction into the Synod of the Abbot of Mount Mellary. Lest I should bring down upon myself another lecture on the ecclesiastical antiquities of Ireland, I shall not venture to say what may have been the usages of the Irish Church in regard to the right of abbots to take part in synodical assemblies: but I think I may venture to assert that Dr. Fitzpatrick, the abbot in question, was at this time a very young man; that he had not long been appointed to his post, which, if not created for the occasion, had a little time before been resuscitated after a prolonged period of abeyance; that his appearance in the Synod, to which he was summoned by Dr. Cullen, caused considerable surprise; and, lastly, that in the proceedings of the assembly he proved eminently serviceable to his patron. It is very possible that Professor Sullivan's information respecting Dr. Fitzpatrick, and the part he took in securing the majority of one, may be fuller than mine; and, if so, I hope he will supply the deficiencies in my account. But, however this may be, he will not, I think, deny that the introduction of this personage into the Synod by Dr. Cullen was at least a questionable proceeding, and one which at the time was in fact questioned by many of the clergy of Ireland, and that on it the indispensable unit of majority depended. In short, I think he must admit that, had it not been for the tactics which I have exposed —the nomination of Dr. McEvilly, an opponent of the Colleges, to represent the "sick bishop," Dr. French, who was known to be favourable to them; the similar manœuvre executed in the case of the Bishop of Kerry; and, lastly, the introduction into the Synod of this youthful Abbot of Mount Mellary—the result, in spite of all the influence of the Apostolic Delegate, would have been, instead of a majority of one in condemnation of the Colleges, a majority of four in favour of supporting them.

But, says Professor Sullivan, to what purpose is this argument, since "the fact still remains," that the "sick bishop signed the condemnation of the Colleges"? This, he says, "is indeed a fact," which "may not be so well known" to me, but which he commends to my attention; and he intimates his opinion that I have never read the Acts of the Synod. I confess I should have thought from the confidence with which he makes this statement that he had not read them; for, with the decrees of the Synod now before me, I assert that the name of the "sick bishop," that is to say, of Dr. French, does not appear amongst the signatures. The place which it would occupy is filled by that of his procurator, Dr. McEvilly. Professor Sullivan is thus mistaken on the matter of fact; and, surely, he is not less mistaken in point of logic. Does he really mean to contend that the presence of Dr. French's name amongst the signatures to the decrees—supposing the fact to be as he assumes—would be conclusive proof that he would have voted in favour of each of them, if called upon to do so before they were carried? With the fact before him that all the dissentient bishops signed the decrees, it is difficult to conceive that this could be his meaning; yet if this be not his meaning, how have I "laboured in vain" in proving that the "sick bishop" would, if present, have supported the Colleges?

VII.

THE PRESENT POSITION OF THE IRISH UNIVERSITY QUESTION—1873.

THE foregoing was written in 1866, *à-propos* of the attempt of the Government of that time to meet the requirements of the Catholic priesthood of Ireland and their supporters respecting the organization of the higher education in that country. As all the world knows, that attempt consisted in the granting of a new charter to the Queen's University (known as the "Supplemental Charter"), the effect of which, had it come into operation, would have been to change the character of the University from that which it then bore and still bears, to a university of the London type, confining its functions to examination, and admitting to its examinations all candidates, without reference to previous academic training. And this measure was accompanied by another —the creation of a new batch of senators, six in number, to be added to the Senate of the Queen's University, all partisans of the new policy. The circumstances under which it was attempted to carry this plan into effect, and the means resorted to for this purpose, are now tolerably well known; but they set in so striking a light the sort of influences which were then operative in Irish politics, and which perhaps are not yet extinct, that it may be well here to recall them. Early in the Session of 1866, it became known that the Government intended to effect modifications in the Irish educational system in a sense favourable to the views of the party who opposed mixed education, and a suspicion arose that, by having recourse to the powers of the Crown, they might practically commit the country to the contemplated change before Parliament should have an opportunity of expressing an opinion on the subject. Under these circumstances notice was given by Sir Robert Peel of a motion for an address to the Crown, praying Her Majesty not to put her seal to any charter affecting the system of education in Ireland until its terms had first been submitted to Parliament. On this Mr. Gladstone came forward in his place in the House of Commons, and disclaiming, on the part of the Government, all intention of acting as the motion implied, proceeded to assure the House that ample opportunity would be afforded for discussing the educational policy of the Government "before the Crown should be committed to any formal act." This took place in February. On the 19th of June the Government, in consequence of an adverse vote on Mr. Gladstone's Reform Bill, resigned. On the 20th, authority to affix the Great Seal to the Supplemental Charter arrived in Dublin. On the 27th, when, in the words of Mr. Bouverie, "the Government was really no longer in existence, although the seals of office had not been transferred to their successors," the appointment took place of the six additional senators. This last step was plainly indispensable to the success of the scheme, both because without it a majority could not be obtained in the Senate for the acceptance of the Supplemental Charter, and because a modification of the Senate was needed to bring the governing body of the University into harmony with the new policy of the Government. The proceedings took Parliament and the country absolutely by surprise. A solemn pledge had been given to the House of Commons, that "before the Crown should be committed to any formal act," an opportunity should be afforded for discussion; and now, while the House was still in entire ignorance of the matter, the formal act was done, and a step taken which, if unreversed, would alter radically the educational system of Ireland. Challenged to explain their conduct, Mr. Fortescue, on the part of the Government, replied that the promised opportunity for discussion had been afforded on two occasions—first, when Sir George Grey's letter to the Lord Lieutenant was laid before Parliament, and again, when, on introducing the Irish Reform Bill, he referred to the plans of the Government with reference to the Queen's University. It is unnecessary to criticise these explanations. As a matter of fact the House of Commons did not understand the announcements in the sense ascribed to them. Everyone was deceived. The Great Seal was set to the Charter, while the House of Commons was still in ignorance that any charter had been granted. Without effectual notice, without discussion, a course was taken which, had it been successful, would have overturned the settled educational policy of the country; and these things were done by a Government *in extremis*, not properly a Government at all, but merely *locum tenentes* for their successors. The Charter was accepted in the packed Senate by a vote of 11 to 9, the six new Senators al voting in the majority. But, though accepted by the Senate, it was challenged by the Convocation. The case was brought into the Court of Chancery, and finally a decree was obtained from the Irish Master of the Rolls declaring the Charter invalid. The Government scheme of 1866 thus fell through; and Irish University education has remained from that year to the present in the first rank of unsettled Irish questions. Once more an attempt has been made to effect a settlement. In fulfilment of pledges given at the general election of 1868, Mr. Gladstone has introduced his Irish University Bill. The fate of that proposal has been sealed by the recent vote of the House of Commons; but the problem of Irish University Education is still unsolved. In 1866, as we have seen, the solution was sought through a reconstruction of the Queen's University. Since that time the question has grown in complexity. The Irish Church has been disestablished, and its downfall has entailed, as an inevitable corollary, the re-organization in a liberal sense of Trinity College and the University of Dublin. So much the authorities of the College and the University have themselves had the wisdom to perceive, and they have accordingly for some years supported Mr. Fawcett in his efforts to accomplish this object. Those efforts have hitherto been unsuccessful. Mr. Fawcett's plan has been year after year opposed by Mr. Gladstone and the present Government, as inadequate to meet the requirements of the case. It was under these circumstances that the Irish University Bill of this year was brought forward. As I have said, that Bill is dead, but in politics as in medicine, a *post-mortem* examination may occasionally have its use; and I do not think the true nature of the situation will better reveal itself, and the difficulties with which it is beset come more clearly into view, than in a study of the aim and general scope of this now celebrated scheme. I shall therefore make no apology for devoting a brief space to its consideration.

The Irish University Bill announces itself in its preamble as having for its object the "advancement of learning;" but Mr. Gladstone's language in introducing the measure was more specific. Though for the advancement of learning, it aims at promoting this object in such a way as to remove a grievance under which, according to the Prime Minister, the Catholics of Ireland are labouring. That the Catholics of Ireland are the victims of a grievance in being excluded, along with various other religionists, from the highest rewards and offices of Trinity College, is what all Liberals have long recognized; and it was to remove this wrong that Mr. Fawcett, at first single-handed, and latterly with the assistance of the College and University, has for five years been steadily striving. But it is very important to observe that this is not the grievance—or at any rate it is not the principal grievance—which it was the purpose of Mr. Gladstone's Irish University Bill to remove. The following words, which occur in his speech on introducing the Bill, deserve careful consideration :—

"It appears to us" (said Mr. Gladstone), "that we have one course and one course only to take, one decision and one only to arrive at, with respect to our Roman Catholic fellow-subjects. Do we intend, or do we not intend, to extend to them the full benefit of civil equality on a footing exactly the same as that on which it is granted to members of other religious persuasions? If we do not, the conclusion is a most grave one; but if the House be of opinion, as the Government are, that it is neither generous nor politic, whatever we may think of ecclesiastical influences within the Roman Church, to draw distinctions in matters purely civil adverse to our Roman Catholic fellow-countrymen—if we hold that opinion, let us hold it frankly and boldly; and, having determined to grant measures of equality as far as it may be in our power to do so, do not let us attempt to stint our action when we come to the execution of that which we have announced to be our intention."

And again, in concluding his speech he recurs to the same point :—

"We have sought to provide a complete remedy for what we thought, and for what we have long marked and held up to public attention, as a palpable grievance—a grievance of conscience."

Now what is the inequality of which Mr. Gladstone here speaks? As the provisions of the Bill and the whole tenour of his argument show, it is not the inequality which Mr. Fawcett's Bill proposes to remedy, and which consists in the exclusion of Catholics from the higher posts of Trinity College—though it is true Mr. Gladstone's Bill does include a remedy for this wrong *—but that arising from the circumstance that a portion of the Catholics of Ireland refuse to avail themselves of the opportunities of education afforded by the mixed institutions of the country. Declining to avail themselves of these institutions, they lie under a disadvantage in respect to university education, as compared with the members of other denominations, or with other Catholics who accept them. It is this inequality which Mr. Gladstone and his Government have distinctly recognized as a grievance, and which his Irish University Bill was introduced to redress. Let us now observe how it accomplished this object.

The main provisions of Mr. Gladstone's Bill are now pretty well known; but it will be convenient to summarize them briefly here. And, in the first place, it provided for the abolition of the two existing universities of Ireland, and for the creation in their stead, and on their ruins, of a new university, to be called the University of Dublin. This new body was to be governed by a Council composed of "ordinary" and of "collegiate" members; the former, twenty-eight in number, being nominated in the first instance by the Crown, and the latter elected by colleges affiliated to the University. After a period of ten years this arrangement was to give place to another, under which the Crown would only nominate one-fourth of the "ordinary members," it being pro-

* So subordinate a place did this provision occupy, in Mr. Gladstone's view of the case, that he forgot to mention it in his speech introducing the Bill, till reminded of it by Mr. Cardwell.

vided that the remaining three-fourths should be elected in turn by the Council, the Professoriate, and the Senate of the University. The affiliated colleges would, of course, comprise Trinity College and the Queen's Colleges, or such of them as were not extinguished by the Bill, as well as the Catholic University, Maynooth, and Magee, Colleges. But an absolute discretion was vested in the Council with respect to the affiliation of colleges; and it could only be a matter of conjecture to what extent this would be exercised.* It might be exercised with a moderation which would leave the "ordinary" members of Council predominant; but it would also be quite possible for the Council to affiliate colleges in such numbers that their representatives might command a majority, and carry matters at their discretion. Such was the constitution of the Council, to which was assigned the control and general management of the University under the conditions prescribed in the Bill. The degrees and prizes were to be open to all candidates irrespective of religious faith, and the principle was adopted, in accordance with the precedent of the London University, of admitting to degrees on examination simply, and without reference to previous academic training. The new University, however, was not to be simply an examining Board. A staff of Professors was provided, to be appointed by the Council, who were to lecture, but attendance on whose lectures was not to be obligatory. Besides professor-

* Mr. Gladstone, on opening the debate on the second reading, announced his intention of transferring the power of affiliating colleges from the Council to the Crown, acting on the recommendation of the Council.

ships, the University was to have at its disposal a liberal allowance of fellowships, scholarships, and bursaries. Lastly, to meet the expenses attendant upon all these arrangements, funds were provided to the amount of £50,000 a year; of which £12,000 was to be paid by Trinity College, £10,000 from the Consolidated Fund, and the remainder from the surplus property of the disestablished Church.

Such are the leading outlines of the scheme; and now to what extent would it have redressed the specific grievance, to remove which was the chief end of its introduction? How far did it succeed in placing Catholics who declined to take advantage of the mixed institutions of the country on a footing of equality in respect to university education with the members of other denominations, or with Catholics who frankly accepted them? What concessions, in short, did the Bill make to the denominational principle in university education? It made the following:—it admitted denominational colleges into what was to be a great national scheme of university organization; it co-ordinated them with colleges of the mixed type, and gave them representation on the governing Board, opening at the same time to the competition of their students all the prizes and emoluments of the University. So much the Bill undoubtedly did in favour of denominational aims; but, it must be observed, that these advantages were offered *on the condition that those accepting them should waive their objections to mixed education.* For the new University was, in theory at least, to be a *mixed* University. Its governing body, it was understood, was to consist of the representatives of different religious denominations, and of different educational schools : its professorships, so far as appeared from the Bill, were to be filled without reference to religious creed ; its fellowships, scholarships, and bursaries would be open to Catholics, but only on the same terms as to Protestants. In short, it was evident that the opponents of existing institutions could obtain no advantage under the Bill, except by abandoning those very objections in deference to which the Bill had been introduced. For consistent supporters, therefore, of the denominational and separate system, the Bill would necessarily be a nullity. Further, even though the Bill were accepted, the inequality which it undertook to redress was as far as ever from being removed. The Catholic University, as well as the various Catholic seminaries through the country, would still remain unendowed, while Trinity College and the Queen's Colleges enjoyed large endowments. So long as this continued, it could not be said that those who accepted the conditions of mixed education and those who rejected those conditions stood on an equal footing with regard to university education.

This was the view taken of the measure by the Catholic Hierarchy, who, accordingly, as we know, rejected with scorn, real or affected, the proffered boon. It cannot be denied that their course, in thus acting, was at least logical and consistent. Nevertheless, the apprehensions aroused against the Bill in the minds of the supporters of mixed education were assuredly not without solid grounds in the facts of the case. The new University, they argued, is to be in theory a mixed institution; but what guarantee is given that it will be so in its practical working? All would depend on the constitution of the Council, and this would be composed of the nominees of a Government who recognized the complaints of the opponents of mixed education as expressing a legitimate grievance, and of the representatives of affiliated colleges of which the large majority would probably be denominational and under the control of the priesthood. The ultramontanes once predominant in the Council, the game would be absolutely in their hands. The curriculum for degrees — the only degrees which would under the new scheme be open to Irishmen — would be shaped to the requirements of ecclesiasticism. The professoriate would be filled by persons having the confidence of Cardinal Cullen; and the entire system would be worked in the interest of the section of Catholics he represents. Assuredly these fears could not be considered chimerical. Without referring to Continental experience, we have seen quite enough of ultramontane action in Ireland to justify the belief that, the system once established, every effort would be strained to turn it to ultramontane purposes; nor were the transactions connected with the Supplemental Charter forgotten, which only too painfully showed to what lengths certain members of the present Liberal administration were prepared to go in seconding such designs. Indeed Mr. Fortescue, in his speech in the debate on the second reading, made no secret of what might be accomplished in this direction. "What I would venture," he urged, "to point out to the Roman Catholics of Ireland is this—that the Bill gives them an opportunity which, if vigorously made use of, will in a few years' time permit them to do almost all that they want to do."

Thus the Bill, while exciting, not without good reason, the apprehensions of the supporters of united education, failed absolutely to fulfil its specific purpose —the redress of what the Government had recognized as the educational grievance of Catholics. Had it been carried, so far from settling the question of university education in Ireland, its enactment would only have been the signal for renewing the agitation, which would now be pushed with all the more energy from the increased sense of power acquired by its promoters, and the distinct recognition by the Prime Minister of the justice of their cause.*

But besides the specific purpose of redressing a civil grievance, Mr. Gladstone's Bill also aimed at "the advancement of learning." Let us now endeavour to appreciate some of the principal bearings of the measure, regarded from this point of view. And taking first the proposal to abolish the two existing universities of the country, and to centralize educational institutions under a single university in Dublin largely controlled by the Government, it must be observed that, apart from the advantages of central-

* Unfortunately this mischief will remain notwithstanding the defeat of the Bill — an example of the truth, of which Mr. Fawcett, in his speech on the second reading, gave other illustrations, that 'the evil which men do lives after them."

ization, absolutely no reason was alleged for disturbing the present universities. It was admitted on all hands that both are doing sound and honest work. Mr. Gladstone indeed complained of the insufficiency of the results, and endeavoured to sustain his complaints by statistics. I will not here enter into his figures, which have elsewhere been amply, and, in my opinion, conclusively, answered; but, conceding all he claims for them, to what do they amount? At the most to reasons for reforming, certainly not to reasons for annihilating, two useful institutions, of which one has long entwined itself with the best traditions of Irishmen, and the other, not yet a quarter of a century old, has already given ample proof of its adaptation to the wants of the country. If the present Dublin University and the Queen's University are to be overthrown in order that a single university of a wholly different character be established on their ruins, the justification of this policy must be looked for, not in the shortcomings of those institutions, but in the still greater results to be expected from the system which is to take their place. Now what are the grounds of this expectation?

As we all know, the present Chancellor of the Exchequer has a theory that universities cannot be too few in number. A plurality of such bodies, he contends, necessarily leads to a vicious competition for students which results in a lowering of the standard for degrees. I have already in the foregoing essay examined this doctrine, and have endeavoured to show under what circumstances competition amongst degree-granting bodies operates injuriously, and when it is productive of beneficial effects. In pursuance of that argument, I shall now only refer to the support and illustration the view there contended for has lately received from the disastrous failure of the principle of centralization as exhibited in the university system of France, in contrast with the distinguished success of the opposite system of independent and competing universities in Germany. Previous to the first French Revolution, France was the seat of numerous independent universities. These were one after another abolished by the Governments which during that convulsion, or in the period which immediately followed, ruled in France, and were finally replaced under the first Napoleon by what in current phrase is called "a great National University"—the present "University of France." The system then introduced has now been in full operation for a period of more than sixty years;—what have been its fruits? Why, such that the most eminent and learned men in the country are now with one voice calling aloud for its overthrow. "The unanimity," says Professor Playfair, "is surprising with which eminent men ascribe the intellectual paralysis of the nation to the centralization of administration and examination by the University of France;" and the statement is sustained by an array of quotations from which I will take the liberty to cull a few specimens. "If the causes of our marasmus," writes M. Dumas, "appear complex and manifold, they are still reducible to one principle, administrative centralization, which, applied to the

University, has enervated superior instruction." "We demand," says Professor Lorain, "the destruction of the University of France, and the creation of separate universities. That is our programme." "The paltry faculties," writes M. Renan, "created by the First Empire in no way replace the great and beautiful system of rival universities with their separate autonomies—a system which all Europe borrowed from France, and which all countries but France have preserved. We must create in the provinces five or six universities, each independent of the other."* And so on through some pages of equally striking and emphatic testimony.

Such has been the experience of France, and such the lesson drawn from it by those most competent to interpret that experience. And this lesson has been enforced and illustrated by the not less striking results of an opposite experience in Germany, where, under a system of rival universities, science and learning have attained a pre-eminence in all that relates to originality and depth of research, now scarcely disputed amongst the nations of Europe. With these facts before us,—facts entirely in accordance with our own experience in England and Scotland,—we may venture, I think, to disregard pet theories, even though proceeding from such high authorities as Mr. Lowe and Sir Dominic Corrigan, and to ask for some better reasons for overthrowing institutions that are doing good work than the virtues inherent in a centralized university system under the control of the State.

The plan of centralization under a single university

* On Teaching Universities and Examining Boards," pp. 9—11.

is the most prominent feature in the measure we are considering; but it is not that which gives it its fundamental character, and constitutes what may be fairly called the vital essence of the scheme. That essence is to be found in the attempt to fuse into a single composite whole two mutually repugnant and incongruous elements. Mr. Gladstone proposes to bring together in the same system, and to compel to work in harmony towards a common object, two schools of educationists who have no common object, whose ideals of education are not merely different, but essentially antagonistic and incompatible. We are familiar in this country with many varieties of view on educational questions. Similar varieties no doubt may be found in Ireland, but these all sink into insignificance in presence of the one great difference which separates the supporters of united education in open colleges from the Catholic priesthood and their adherents. The difference here is radical and profound: it turns, not on means, but on ends. The supporters of united education desire to pursue knowledge in the spirit in which it is pursued in this and other civilized countries where priestly influence is not predominant—with singleness of purpose, with a disposition free alike from *arrière pensée* and foregone conclusion, ever ready to accept with frankness the results of sound investigation and reasoned truth, whatever these may be found to be. On the other hand, the aim of the Catholic priesthood and of those Catholics who place themselves unreservedly under their guidance, is something altogether different from this. Truth, according to their conception of it, is not what facts rightly interpreted and reason stringently applied shall prove it to be, but, over a large domain of human speculation, something which was made known to the world some thousand years ago, and which has since been from time to time supplemented by an infallible authority; and, over the rest, such conclusions as shall best harmonize with the knowledge thus imparted. The aims of the two schools being thus radically different, the methods of cultivating and imparting knowledge approved by each will necessarily exhibit a corresponding difference. The one will naturally desire to give to the human mind the utmost scope and freedom, and will encourage it to roam unchecked over the whole field of human speculation; the other will quite as naturally endeavour to surround the mental movements with limitations and barriers. Finger-posts must be set up pointing the investigator towards the conclusions at which he is expected to arrive; notices warning the ambitious student from straying ever so little upon any pretext from the well-defined paddock of orthodoxy. Astronomy and Geology may be cultivated, but only on condition that their conclusions shall be made to harmonize with the ideas of the writers of the Old Testament, and the *ex cathedra* deliverances of mediæval Popes. As for Political Economy—"the pretended science" of Political Economy, as Dr. Manning calls it—if allowed to speak at all, it must be with 'bated breath and whispering humbleness, taking constant heed of the Sermon on the Mount, and careful not to wound the susceptibilities of monasticism. Such are the two educational ideals which

Mr. Gladstone proposes to incorporate in a single scheme, and to make work together towards a common purpose. Surely we need not go further in order to understand the incongruities, extravagances, and degrading compromises with which the measure abounds. People have been scandalized at what have been well called "the gagging clauses" of the Bill; but that they should have been so, and yet have proposed—as those who voted for the second reading proposed—to retain the measure in its principle, is only a striking proof how inadequately they had conceived the problem which the Bill undertook to solve.* The "gagging clauses" were of the very essence of the scheme: without these it was impossible that the system, if it was to do that which it was ostensibly meant to do—to bring together in the same lecture rooms and examination halls ultramontane Catholics and the cultivators of knowledge in the spirit of modern science—could be made to work for a single day. How are those who pursue knowledge with singleness of aim to be kept within the bounds of ultramontane orthodoxy without gags? Even gags, it was felt, and with good reason, would not suffice in

---

* Far more logical, as it seems to me, is the view taken by Dr. Manning. "If there was one thing," he says, "which struck me with shame, it was the way in which some speakers in the House of Commons treated that most wise and most just provision of the Bill, as if it was a thing not to be defended. ... I will ask you whether there was not a most just reason to exempt all Catholic youth from being forced to undergo examination in a philosophy which is fundamentally false. The study of a false philosophy perverts the form and shape of the intelligence; I may say it alters the structure of the brain." To keep our brain right, therefore, we must only listen to the reasons in favour of our own side. "To force a young Catholic to be examined in heretical matters would be tyranny." (Dr. Manning at the Liverpool Catholic Club, *Times*, 22nd March, 1873.)

the case of mental philosophy and modern history, and so these subjects were lopped off altogether; while no place was provided for Political Economy or Jurisprudence. In truth, one can have little doubt that, had the experiment been fairly tried, it would have soon been found necessary to carry the process of amputation very much farther. Geology, Physiology, and Natural History could scarcely fail before long to share the fate of mental philosophy and modern history; and even such branches of knowledge as were retained would be cultivated under restrictions and limitations incompatible with fruitful study, till an Irish degree came to represent not knowledge, but limitations on knowledge, a mere *caput mortuum*, from which life, energy, and character had departed. Something like this has in fact happened in Belgium, where the plan has been adopted, not indeed of teaching from the same chair, but of examining under a common Board, the pupils of "State" and of "Catholic" universities. Candidates for degrees from Liège, for example, and candidates for degrees from Louvain are required to submit themselves to a common examination, conducted by Professors taken in equal numbers from the two Colleges. M. Laveleye thus describes the result :—

"The rivalry of these four institutions" [Liège, Louvain, Ghent, and Brussels] "ought to have produced an intellectual life and activity of a kind most profitable to the progress of knowledge. That happy result has not been attained, because they adopted a detestable system of examination for conferring degrees. Diplomas are granted by mixed juries composed, in equal proportions, of Professors of one state and one free University. The candidates are questioned by these Professors, under the control of Professors from a rival University. Hence it results, to begin with, that the students content themselves with learning their note-books off by heart; next, that the Professors, thus controlled by their colleagues, have to conform to a uniform programme, and thus by degrees routine stifles initiative and the genuine spirit of research." *

In truth, the problem undertaken by Mr. Gladstone, when once its conditions are clearly understood, cannot but be seen to be in the strictest sense insoluble. It is quite impossible that those who accept the intellectual guidance of Cardinal Cullen and his priesthood should cultivate knowledge in common with those who pursue it in the spirit of modern scientific research. The attempt to effect such a combination, as it began with the mutilation of knowledge, so, if persisted in, could only have ended in the extinction of intellectual life.

And now what is our position with reference to this question, as the result of the defeat of Mr. Gladstone's Bill, and the discussion it has provoked? Two or three points at least have been cleared up which cannot fail to conduce to the simplification of the problem. And, in the first place, it has been made clear that the so-called grievance of the ultramontane Catholics, whatever we may think of it, is not to be remedied by any contrivance for embracing in a single system denominational and mixed colleges. It may or may not be expedient to combine under a single

* Quoted by Dr. Lyon Playfair.

university Trinity College and the Queen's Colleges. For reasons stated in the preceding essay, I believe the interests of knowledge would be best served by each institution retaining its present character of independence. This, however, is a question on which no doubt a good deal may be said on both sides. But a proposal for coupling either with the Catholic University or with any institution framed on that model, stands condemned in the light of what has now taken place. It could not remove the "grievance," while, by introducing a foreign and hostile element into the organization of our national universities, it would effectually impair their working, converting what ought to be a field for the peaceful rivalries of academic life into an arena for the struggle of angry and excited religious parties.

Secondly, the recent discussions have brought very clearly into view the real nature of the Catholic grievance. That grievance, as I have already pointed out, is twofold. As the law now stands, Roman Catholics, in common with Dissenters generally, are excluded from competition for fellowships, and some other prizes in the chief national College and University of the country, and are, as a consequence, excluded also from all share in its government. This is undoubtedly a very substantial grievance—one which, I think, may be properly described as amounting to a civil disability. The reality and the gravity of this wrong, however, are now universally admitted, and the redress of it has even been pressed upon Parliament by the University of Dublin itself. But, over and beyond this, there is the grievance recognized by Mr. Gladstone and the present Government. A portion of the Catholics object to mixed education. They entertain conscientious scruples against cultivating knowledge in common classes with Protestants, or in colleges not under the supervision and control of their priests ; and, as the nation has deliberately determined to confine its support to institutions of the character to which they object, it results that they are under a disadvantage with regard to university education, as compared with other members of the community. Here is an inequality of an entirely different kind, and needing, if it is to be redressed, an entirely different remedy.

For as regards what I have called the real or substantial Catholic grievance,—the exclusion of Catholics from the higher posts in Trinity College,—it is evident at once that a complete and effectual remedy for this may be found in an Act simply abolishing tests, such as Mr. Fawcett has for several years been endeavouring to pass; while it is not less plain that a measure of this kind would wholly fail to touch the grievance urged by the priests and recognized by Mr. Gladstone. Nor can there now be any doubt as to the one and only remedy which would be adequate to meet the latter ground of complaint. One and only one remedy can satisfy the exigency—can place those who object to united education in open colleges on an equal footing with those who accept the assistance of the State on these conditions—the chartering and endowment, on a scale commensurate with the endowments of the National Universities, of a Catholic University, established on principles satisfactory to the priesthood. Nothing short of this can place ultramontane Catholics on an equal footing, as regards the higher education, with other members of the community; and the simple question now for statesmen is—are they, or are they not, prepared to make this concession?

To state my own view of this matter—while I admit the fact of inequality, I am disposed to deny the existence of a grievance in the sense of a disability which the State ought to redress. The State is undoubtedly bound to frame its laws impartially as between the several classes of citizens; but, as I understand the case, it is no part of the duty of the State to provide that all citizens shall derive equal benefit from the laws. This must depend, in part at least, on the character and conduct, and even on the idiosyncrasies of those who are affected by them; and if it happen that, in certain cases, these are such as to exclude some people from the benefit of laws, framed in good faith and with an enlightened regard to the interests of the community as a whole, the unfortunate result is not to be attributed to unfairness in the law, but rather to the peculiarities of temperament or taste of the persons concerned—peculiarities which, so far as they go, unfit those who are the subjects of them for sharing in the general advantages of national union.

In the matter of education the line taken by this country—the ideal towards which it has long been steadily and consciously working, notwithstanding the retention in some of our more ancient institutions of not a few relics of a former scheme of policy—is perfectly clear and unmistakable. The State absolutely refuses to confer endowment or other favour upon any class or religious denomination, as such. Whatever may have been the case in the past, it now grants its endowments only on the condition that all members of the community shall be equally free to share in the advantages arising from them. This is the definitive policy on which Parliament and the country, after a long series of essays and experiments in other directions, have at length deliberately taken their stand, as that at once most consonant to the dictates of justice as between individuals and classes, and most conducive to the well-being of the nation as a whole. Now what the Irish priesthood demand is that this policy should be abandoned in favour of a policy which the nation has already weighed in the balance and found wanting—the policy of concurrent endowment. Manifestly it would be impossible to grant a separate endowment to Roman Catholics, and refuse the same favour to other religious denominations. So flagrant a violation of the rules of equality and justice, committed in the name of equality and justice, could scarcely be endured. The endowment of a Catholic University would thus involve concurrent endowment: in other words, the State would be required to reverse a policy on which it had deliberately entered—a policy conceived in the interests of the entire community, adopted upon national grounds, and supported by the great majority of its citizens—in deference to the scruples of a small minority—of a section which, but for the power which the priesthood from their peculiar position are enabled to wield, would, I venture to assert, be an insignificant minority. I wish to insist upon this point; for let me here say, that I have no desire to press this argument in a pedantic or *doctrinaire* spirit. I quite admit that, if any large section of the people of the United Kingdom, even though a minority of the whole, such as the people of Ireland, should deliberately and persistently reject the national policy, the fact might be a reason for adopting in respect of that section a different policy. It is, no doubt, the position of the priesthood that this *is* the case in the present instance. They put themselves forward as representing the Catholics of Ireland, who are assumed to be the people of Ireland ; and unfortunately the immense influence exercised by them in parliamentary elections gives a colour to this extravagant pretension. In point of fact, nothing is more certain than that the people of Ireland, as a whole, have not rejected the imperial policy of open colleges and united education. The Protestants now almost to a man have accepted it ; and though the Protestants are a minority of the people of Ireland, they are a majority of that portion of the people which aspires to university education. But it is equally untrue that the Catholics, as a body, have rejected the imperial policy. I need not here enter into evidence adduced both by myself on former occasions, and more recently by other writers. It is sufficient to point to the large number of Catholics who persist in attending Trinity College and the Queen's Colleges in the teeth of the most violent denunciations of the priesthood, and, on the other hand, to the scanty band which is all that the utmost efforts of the same priesthood can compel into the Catholic University, to convince those who are open to conviction how very small the party of lay Catholics is, who, being in a position to avail themselves of university education, support the demands of the priesthood. True, indeed, the majority of Irish members in the House of Commons support those demands. But surely we are entitled to go behind this fact, and to inquire as to its real significance. Is it not notorious that the votes which send these gentlemen to Parliament are, in the main part, the votes of men, who do not themselves aspire to university education, and who cannot, from their position in life, be supposed to have formed any independent judgment on the question? What is the value of the opinion of a small farmer or grocer in Munster or Connaught on the question of concurrent endowment *versus* the policy of united education? The small farmers and small shopkeepers in the towns, so far as it is possible for them to show a preference for either principle, have done so by sending their children to the mixed schools of the country, and even to the model schools (when one happened to be within reach), whenever they have not been stopped by the fulminations of the Church. As to university education, probably few of them know what it means, and they therefore almost necessarily take their cue on this subject from their priests. In this way a parliamentary majority is sent from Ireland favourable to the endowment of a Catholic university, and probably prepared to support concurrent endowment. But surely it would be the veriest pedantry of constitutionalism to regard this as decisive of the opinion of Irishmen upon those questions, and as a ground for reversing in Ireland the well-considered and deliberately adopted policy of the country.

Our reasoning, then, leads us to the following conclusions:—There is no valid reason for abolishing either of the present universities. On the contrary, with a view to giving greater freedom and variety to intellectual life in Ireland, as well as to supplying the higher education with the stimulus of a healthy rivalry, it is desirable that both should be retained. This, however, must be added:—if the Queen's University and Colleges are to become permanent institutions of the country, it is essential to their usefulness that they should be put upon a footing—I will not say of equality with the University of Dublin and Trinity College, but at least on a footing less widely removed from equality than that on which they now stand. It is a simple truth that the endowments of the Queen's Colleges are at present miserably inadequate. Their libraries and museums are starved for want of funds to support them. Their Professors are most insufficiently paid. The highest income, for example, that a Professor, holding one of the best chairs in Belfast College, can attain to is little over £400 annually—surely a wretched pittance as the ultimate and crowning reward of a laborious life spent in the service of learning. If things are to remain thus, it is scarcely possible that the provincial colleges should continue to command the services of competent men, or perform those functions, the performance of which constitutes the reason for maintaining them. The permanent maintenance, therefore, of the system of competing universities clearly requires a rectification of this state of things; and Mr. Gladstone, in his University Bill, has indicated the source from which, without touching the revenues of Trinity College, the funds for such rectification might properly be drawn. The abolition of tests in Trinity College, and the internal reform of that institution and of the University of Dublin, are measures now on all hands admitted to be necessary; and they will probably be at once either accomplished or put in train for accomplishment by the passing of Mr. Fawcett's Bill. Catholics will then in university education, at least so far as the law is concerned, be placed upon a footing of absolute equality with all other subjects of the Queen. They may, of course, decline the proffered boon, and so place themselves at a disadvantage. But this, it seems to me, for the reasons I have stated, cannot be charged as an injustice against the State. At all events, if anyone so regards it, his proper course must now be clear. The grievance, if we are to call it so, admits of but one remedy—a charter and endowment for the Catholic University on conditions acceptable to the priesthood.

* This Bill, retaining the clauses for the abolition of tests and excluding those which provided for the reform of its internal constitution, has become law as these sheets pass through the press.

THE END.

www.ingramcontent.com/pod-product-compliance
Lightning Source LLC
Chambersburg PA
CBHW031428230426
43668CB00007B/480